# The FouNDation

## From Success to Significance

A Proven Blueprint for Entrepreneurs,
Coaches, and Small Business Owners
to Scale, Market, and Make Millions
Online While Making a Difference

## BY NEO DAVIS

**DISCLAIMER**

The advice contained in this material might not be suitable for everyone. The author designed the information to present his opinion about the subject matter. The reader must carefully investigate all aspects of any business decision before committing to him or herself. The author obtained the information contained herein from sources he believes to be reliable and from his own personal experience, but he neither implies nor intends any guarantee of accuracy. The author is not in the business of giving legal, accounting, or any other type of professional advice. Should the reader need such advice, he or she must seek services from a competent professional. The author particularly disclaims any liability, loss, or risk taken by individuals who directly or indirectly act on the information contained herein. The author believes the advice presented here is sound, but readers cannot hold him responsible for either the actions they take, or the risk taken by individuals who directly or indirectly act on the information contained herein.

Published by 1BrickPublishing
Printed in the United States
Copyright © 2025 by Nehemiah Davis
ISBN 978-1949303421

# DEDICATION

This book is dedicated to the dreamers and doers who understand that true success isn't measured by what you accumulate, but by what you contribute. To every entrepreneur who lies awake at night wondering if their work matters beyond the bottom line—it does, and this is your roadmap.

To my family, who supported me when success seemed impossible and reminded me why it mattered when it finally came.

To the community of West Philadelphia that raised me, challenged me, and now inspires the work that gives my success its deepest meaning.

To the mentors who showed me what was possible and the mentees who remind me why it's necessary.

And especially to you, the reader, who picked up this book not just seeking success, but significance. May you find both in abundance, and may your journey transform not only your life but countless others.

Your success matters. Make it count.

With purpose and gratitude,

**Neo Davis**

# DEDICATION REQUEST

Please share this book with anyone who you believe is ready to transform their success into significance. Pass it along to the entrepreneur seeking to create impact beyond income, the leader looking to leave a legacy greater than their achievements, or anyone standing at the intersection of prosperity and purpose. This journey from digital mastery to meaningful contribution isn't meant to be traveled alone—share these strategies with those who will join you in building businesses that don't just make money, but make a difference. Together, we can create a community of entrepreneurs who measure success not just by what we achieve, but by how many lives we touch along the way.

# TABLE OF CONTENTS

# INTRODUCTION

# PURPOSE BEYOND PROFIT

## My Journey from Struggle to Success

I remember the exact moment everything changed.

I was sitting in my small apartment in West Philadelphia, looking at yet another job rejection email. This was my tenth job in two years—I'd been fired from all of them. My bank account was nearly empty, and my mother's worried voice still echoed in my head from our phone call earlier: "Baby, maybe it's time to go back to school."

School hadn't worked for me either. I'd been kicked out of high school, then later college. Traditional paths to success weren't my path.

That night, I made a decision that would alter the course of my life. I wrote in my journal: "It has to work, or it has to work." There was no Plan B. I was going all in on entrepreneurship. Not because I had some grand vision, but because I was out of options.

What I didn't realize then was that this decision—this commitment to success by any means necessary—would not only transform my financial situation but would eventually impact thousands of lives across Philadelphia and beyond.

The early years weren't glamorous. I started a moving company with nothing but a rented truck and determination. I took any job I could get, working 16-hour days, pushing my body to its limits. On days when there were no moving jobs, I'd knock on doors offering junk removal services. When winter came and moving jobs dried up, I shoveled snow until my hands were numb.

Each dollar I earned, I split three ways: living expenses, business reinvestment, and education. That third category confused everyone around me. Why would someone barely making ends meet spend money on books, courses, and seminars?

But I understood something fundamental: my income would never exceed my personal growth. I needed to get in rooms with people operating at higher levels than me. I needed to learn strategies I couldn't figure out on my own.

The turning point came when I invested $2,000—nearly everything I had at the time—to attend a marketing seminar. My mother thought I was crazy. My friends laughed. But at that event, I learned about digital marketing and the concept of creating products once and selling them repeatedly.

I went home and created my first digital product—a simple guide on how to start a moving company—and sold it for $47. The first week, I made

$235. It wasn't much, but something profound shifted in my mind. For the first time, I'd made money while I slept.

Over the next few years, I went all in on digital entrepreneurship. I studied relentlessly, invested heavily in my education, and implemented everything I learned with obsessive focus. I created more digital products, built sales funnels, mastered webinars, and developed high-ticket coaching programs.

As my businesses grew, so did my income. I went from struggling to pay rent to making my first six figures, then seven figures, and eventually eight figures across multiple ventures. I bought my mother a house, built a beautiful home for my family, acquired real estate, and enjoyed the material trappings of success.

But something was missing.

## The Birth of The Nehemiah Davis Foundation

I was back in my old neighborhood in West Philadelphia, driving my new car, when a group of kids stopped me to ask about it. They were excited, curious, full of dreams—just like I had been. But as we talked, I realized they had no roadmap for achieving their aspirations. The same lack of guidance and opportunity that had nearly derailed my life was still prevalent in my community.

That conversation sparked something in me. What good was all this success if it didn't create change where I came from?

That week, I used my marketing skills to organize a back-to-school drive. We gave away 100 backpacks filled with supplies. The joy on those children's faces touched something deep within me. This wasn't just charity—it was investment in potential.

The Nehemiah Davis Foundation was born from that simple event. We started with small community initiatives: turkey drives at Thanksgiving, toy drives during the holidays, mentorship programs for local youth. Each event grew larger than the last as more people joined our mission.

One of our proudest moments came when we opened our community center in the heart of West Philadelphia. This wasn't just a building; it was a beacon of possibility—a place where kids could get homework help, where teens could learn entrepreneurship, where families could access resources.

When the city of Philadelphia renamed a street "Nehemiah Davis Way," it was a profound honor. But standing at that street unveiling, watching my mother's tears of pride, I realized something important: the street sign mattered less than what it represented—a commitment to creating pathways for others.

That's when I truly understood that success without significance is empty. Making money is only meaningful when it enables you to make a difference.

Today, the foundation serves thousands annually through our programs. We've built basketball courts in neighborhoods that had none. We've provided meals to families struggling with food insecurity. We've awarded scholarships to promising students. We've created entrepreneurship programs for those who, like me, might not thrive in traditional educational settings.

And here's what I've discovered: giving back hasn't diminished my business success—it's amplified it. The skills that build profitable companies also build effective nonprofits. The network you develop through philanthropy opens doors to new business opportunities. The reputation you establish through genuine community service becomes your most valuable marketing asset.

## How This Book Will Transform Your Life

This book contains everything I've learned about building successful digital businesses—strategies that have generated millions for me and my clients. You'll learn practical, actionable techniques for:

- Creating and selling digital products
- Building high-converting sales funnels
- Mastering social media marketing
- Running profitable challenges and events
- Developing powerful speaking and selling skills
- Scaling your business to seven figures and beyond

But this isn't just another "get rich" book. The strategies I'm sharing aren't simply about filling your bank account—they're about creating the financial freedom that allows you to make a meaningful impact.

My goal is to help you create a business that not only generates wealth but also gives you the time, resources, and platform to give back in ways that matter to you. Whether that means supporting existing foundations, starting your own charitable initiatives, creating jobs in underserved communities, or mentoring the next generation of entrepreneurs.

As you read this book and implement these strategies, I have one request: when you succeed (and you will), find a way to give back. Support the Nehemiah Davis Foundation if our mission resonates with you, or identify causes that matter to your heart. Use your prosperity to create positive change.

Because at the end of our lives, we won't be measured by the money we made, but by the difference we made. Success without significance is hollow. True fulfillment comes from building a foundation—not just of wealth, but of impact.

Let's begin this journey together.

*Nehemiah "Neo" Davis*

# CHAPTER 1

---

# THE DECISION
# THAT CHANGES
# EVERYTHING

" *This is not another day.*"

I want you to write those words down on the first page of a notebook right now. Go ahead—I'll wait.

The fact that you're reading this book means you're searching for something more. Maybe you're tired of the 9-to-5 grind. Maybe you've started a business but hit a plateau. Maybe you're making decent money but feel trapped by your own success, trading all your time for dollars.

Whatever brought you here, I want you to understand something profound: Reading this book won't change your life—but making a decision will.

# The Day Everything Changed

Let me tell you about a moment that transformed my life.

I was sitting in my car outside a job interview, my ninth in two years. I'd been fired from every previous position. My bank account was nearly empty. My self-confidence was lower. I'd been told all my life that I wasn't cut out for success—that my energy was too much, that I didn't fit the system, that I needed to "get realistic."

In that moment, I had two choices: believe what everyone was saying about me, or make a different decision.

I closed my eyes and whispered to myself: "It has to work, or it has to work." There was no Plan B, no safety net, no fallback option. I was choosing entrepreneurship as my only path forward.

That decision—that total commitment to success by any means necessary—changed everything.

Within two years, I'd built a six-figure business. Within five years, I'd crossed the seven-figure mark. Today, I run multiple eight-figure enterprises and have helped hundreds of entrepreneurs create life-changing success through digital products.

The difference wasn't some secret strategy or lucky break. It was my decision to succeed, no matter what.

# Why Most People Never Succeed

Take a moment and look around at the people in your life. How many are truly living their dreams? How many talk about what they want but never actually achieve it?

The harsh truth is that most people fail before they even begin. They never make the uncompromising decision to succeed. Instead, they:

- **Dabble:** They try something for a few weeks or months, then abandon it when it gets difficult.
- **Retreat:** They pull back at the first sign of failure or criticism.
- **Hedge:** They always keep a backup plan, which becomes their primary plan when challenges arise.
- **Wait:** They constantly prepare but never launch, waiting for the "perfect moment" that never arrives.
- **Blame:** They find external reasons why they can't succeed, absolving themselves of responsibility.

Does any of this sound familiar? I'm not asking to make you feel bad—I'm asking because I've been there too. We all have. The difference between those who break through and those who stay stuck isn't talent, education, or connections. It's the quality of their decisions.

The most successful people I know—the ones who've built empires, who've transformed industries, who've created lasting change—all share one trait: they decided to succeed and eliminated all other possibilities from their minds.

# The Commitment Statement

I want to introduce you to a powerful tool I use with all my coaching clients: the Commitment Statement.

This isn't just a goal or an affirmation. It's a binding contract with yourself that, once made, changes how you operate in the world. Here's what I want you to write in your notebook right now:

*"I, [YOUR NAME], am committed and devoted to making an extra [YOUR FINANCIAL GOAL] with my digital business. I am willing to do whatever it takes to make it happen. I sign this on [TODAY'S DATE] as my declaration of financial independence."*

Now sign it.

This may seem simple, even trivial. But there's profound psychology at work here. When you put your commitment in writing and sign it, several things happen:

1. You move from vague intention to concrete declaration
2. You activate the psychological principle of consistency
3. You create a tangible reminder you can return to when motivation wavers
4. You begin to see yourself as someone who honors their word

My client Jasmine was a hairstylist working 60+ hours a week when she came to me. She was talented but exhausted, trading all her time for money. When I had her write and sign her commitment statement to build a digital education business teaching her styling techniques, she cried. "I've never actually committed to anything this big before," she told me.

Within six months, she'd created an online course that generated $87,000 in its first launch. Today, two years later, her digital business does $1.2 million annually while she works just 20 hours a week. The product was important, but the decision came first.

## Finding Your "Why"

Making a decision is powerful. Making a decision with purpose behind it is unstoppable.

Below your commitment statement, I want you to write down who you're doing this for. Is it:

- Your children, so they can have opportunities you didn't have?
- Your parents, so you can repay their sacrifices?
- Your community, so you can create jobs and opportunity?
- Your future self, so you can live with freedom and purpose?
- A cause that matters deeply to you, which you could support with resources?

Your "why" is personal. There's no right or wrong answer. But it needs to be powerful enough to get you through the inevitable challenges ahead.

For me, my initial "why" was simple: I wanted to prove everyone wrong who said I couldn't succeed. That motivation got me started, but it wouldn't have sustained me. As I grew, my "why" evolved to include my family, my community in Philadelphia, and the thousands of aspiring entrepreneurs I now serve.

Today, much of what drives me is the work we do through the Nehemiah Davis Foundation. Every dollar I make in my businesses fuels our ability to create opportunities for underprivileged youth, provide resources to families in need, and revitalize communities.

When your "why" extends beyond yourself, you tap into motivation that no setback can diminish.

## Overcoming the Voice of Doubt

The moment you make your decision and identify your "why," something predictable will happen: the voice of doubt will speak up.

"Who do you think you are?" "What makes you think you can succeed when so many others fail?" "You don't have the right background/connections/resources/skills." "This is just another thing you'll start and not finish."

This voice may sound like your own thoughts. It may echo things people have told you throughout your life. It may disguise itself as "practical thinking" or "being realistic."

I want you to recognize this voice for what it is: resistance. It's the guardian of your comfort zone, trying to keep you safe by keeping you small.

Everyone faces this resistance. Even now, after all my success, that voice still appears when I set new, bigger goals. The difference is that I've learned to recognize it and move forward anyway.

Here's a powerful technique: Name your doubt. I call mine "The Critic." When those thoughts arise, I acknowledge them: "Thank you for your input, Critic. I hear your concerns, but I've made my decision."

By separating yourself from the doubt, you can observe it without being controlled by it.

## From Decision to Action

A decision without action is just a wish. Now that you've made your commitment, identified your "why," and prepared for doubt, it's time to take your first step.

One of my mentors taught me a principle that transformed my business: success loves speed. The faster you move from decision to action, the more likely you are to succeed.

Right now, before you move on to the next chapter, I want you to take one concrete action toward your goal. It doesn't have to be big. It could be:

- Researching domain names for your new digital business
- Making a list of 10 potential digital product ideas
- Reaching out to one person who might be interested in your expertise
- Setting up a social media account dedicated to your business
- Blocking out two hours on your calendar this week for product creation

Whatever you choose, do it now. Not after you finish the book. Not tomorrow. Now.

This immediate action does two things: it creates momentum, and it reinforces your identity as someone who follows through on commitments.

## The Power of "This Is Not Another Day"

I began this chapter with a phrase I want you to remember: "This is not another day."

Every time you pick up this book, every time you work on your business, every time you face a challenge or setback, I want you to say those words to yourself.

This is not just another book you'll read and forget. This is not just another business idea you'll dabble in. This is not just another goal you'll abandon when it gets hard.

This is the day you decide to transform your life and the lives of those around you through the power of digital entrepreneurship.

This is the day you begin creating wealth that will enable you to make a difference. This is the day everything changes.

Because a true decision—a commitment to succeed by any means necessary—is the foundational element that makes everything else possible.

In the next chapter, we'll dive into eliminating excuses and creating the mindset of unstoppable success. But first, take a moment to appreciate what you've just done. You've made a decision that most people never make. You've taken the first step toward building a business that will create both prosperity and purpose in your life.

# Chapter Summary: Key Takeaways

- Success begins with an uncompromising decision to succeed by any means necessary
- Most people fail because they never fully commit to their goals
- Creating and signing a Commitment Statement transforms vague intentions into concrete declarations
- Your "why" provides sustainable motivation when challenges arise
- The voice of doubt will appear—recognize it as resistance and move forward anyway
- Take immediate action to create momentum and reinforce your new identity
- Remember: "This is not another day"

# Action Steps:

1. Write and sign your Commitment Statement
2. Identify and document your "why"
3. Name your doubt voice and practice acknowledging it without being controlled by it
4. Take one concrete action toward your goal before moving to the next chapter
5. Create a daily reminder that "This is not another day"

If you're passionate about **impact, purpose, and real results,** we want to hear from you. **Partner with Neo**. Visit PartnerWithNeo.com/apply to explore how we can collaborate.

# CHAPTER 2

# ELIMINATE ALL EXCUSES

There's a moment of truth that comes in every entrepreneur's journey. It's not when you make your first sale or hit your first million. It's when you find yourself face-to-face with your favorite excuse and have to decide: Will I let this stop me again, or will I push through?

In the previous chapter, you made a powerful decision to succeed. You signed your commitment statement. You identified your "why." You took your first action. That's a strong foundation—but even the strongest foundation can be undermined by the habit of making excuses.

## The Excuse Epidemic

Let's be honest with each other. We live in a society that celebrates victimhood and normalizes excuses. Social media is filled with people explaining why they couldn't do something rather than showing what they accomplished.

I want you to understand something fundamental: *Excuses are seductive because they protect your ego while keeping you exactly where you are.*

Think about the comfort an excuse provides. When you say, "I would have started my business, but I don't have enough time," you get to keep your dream intact ("I could be successful") while not risking failure. It's a perfect system for staying stuck while preserving your self-image.

The problem? Excuses are costing you everything you say you want.

## The Common Excuses

Let's identify the usual suspects—the excuses that keep showing up in your life. Which of these sound familiar?

**1. I don't have enough time.** This is the universal favorite. But here's the truth: You have exactly the same 24 hours as every successful person on the planet. What you're really saying is: "This isn't a priority for me right now."

**2. I don't have enough money.** Money is a resource, not a requirement. Some of the most successful businesses started with minimal investment. What you're really saying is: "I'm not creative enough to find a workaround."

**3. I don't have the right knowledge/skills/experience.** In the age of the internet, this excuse has expired. What you're really saying is: "I'm not willing to learn what I need to know."

**4. The market is too saturated.** There are nearly 8 billion people on the planet. What you're really saying is: "I'm not confident I can stand out."

**5. I'm too old/young.** Age is irrelevant to success. What you're really saying is: "I'm afraid people will judge me."

**6. I'm waiting for the perfect time.** There is no perfect time. What you're really saying is: "I'm afraid to start."

**7. My situation is different/special.** Everyone's situation has unique challenges. What you're really saying is: "I want a reason why the rules don't apply to me."

**8. I don't have the right connections.** Connections can be built. What you're really saying is: "I'm not willing to put myself out there and build relationships."

**9. I tried once and it didn't work.** Failure is part of the process, not the end of it. What you're really saying is: "I'm not resilient enough to try again."

**10. My family/friends don't support me.** Support is wonderful but optional. What you're really saying is: "I need external permission to pursue my dreams."

I want you to circle the excuses that resonate with you. Be ruthlessly honest with yourself. Which of these have been holding you back?

## My Personal Battle with Excuses

I wasn't born excuse-free. In fact, I was the king of justifications and rationalizations.

When I first started my moving company, I had every reason why it would be difficult. I didn't have a truck. I didn't have employees. I didn't have business experience. I didn't have a website. I didn't come from a family of entrepreneurs.

But my biggest excuse was my background. I grew up in a neighborhood where success stories were rare. I was kicked out of high school and college. I had been fired from nine jobs. I had a record. Who was I to think I could build a successful business?

One day, I was complaining to a mentor about all the obstacles in my way. He listened patiently, then asked me a question that changed everything: "Are any of those things going to change by tomorrow?"

When I said no, he replied: "Then they're not obstacles. They're circumstances. Obstacles can be removed. Circumstances have to be worked with or worked around."

That distinction hit me like a thunderbolt. I had been treating my circumstances as if they were immovable obstacles, when in reality, they were just the playing field I had been given.

I made a decision that day: No more excuses. Whatever hand I'd been dealt, I would play it to the best of my ability.

## The Cost of Excuses

Before we dive into how to eliminate excuses, I want you to really understand what they're costing you.

Take a moment and calculate this: If you had started your digital business one year ago and made just $1,000 per month, you would have an additional $12,000 right now.

If you had started five years ago and grown that business by just 20% annually, you would have made over $74,000 by now.

Excuses aren't just abstract concepts—they have a precise dollar value attached to them.

But the cost goes beyond money. Excuses are costing you:

- **Freedom**: The ability to control your own time and make your own decisions
- **Impact**: The people who won't be helped by your product or service
- **Growth**: The person you would become through overcoming challenges
- **Legacy**: The example you could set for others in your life
- **Fulfillment**: The deep satisfaction that comes from living on purpose

When I look at the work we do through the Nehemiah Davis Foundation, I often think about what would have happened if I had let my excuses win. Every child we help, every family we support, every community we impact—none of it would exist if I had continued to justify why my dreams weren't possible.

The cost of excuses isn't just personal. It's paid by everyone who would have benefited from your success.

## The Excuse Elimination System

Now that you understand what excuses are costing you, let's implement a system to eliminate them from your life. This isn't about positive thinking or motivation—it's about creating a practical framework that makes excuse-making impossible.

## Step 1: Identify Your Top Three Excuses

On a new page in your notebook, write down the three excuses that have held you back the most. Be specific. Instead of "I don't have enough time," write "I tell myself I don't have enough time because I work 50 hours a week and have family responsibilities."

## Step 2: Find the Fear Behind Each Excuse

Excuses are almost always fear in disguise. For each excuse, ask yourself: "What am I actually afraid of?" Common fears include:

- Fear of failure
- Fear of success
- Fear of judgment
- Fear of rejection
- Fear of the unknown
- Fear of not being good enough

For example, if your excuse is "The market is too saturated," the fear might be "I'm afraid no one will choose my product over established competitors."

Identifying the fear takes away much of its power. You can't address what you don't acknowledge.

## Step 3: Create an Excuse-Busting Plan

For each excuse, create a specific plan to neutralize it. This plan should include:

1. A perspective shift: How can you view this situation differently?
2. A practical solution: What specific action steps would overcome this obstacle?
3. An accountability measure: How will you ensure you follow through?

Let me give you an example from one of my clients:

**The Excuse**: "I don't have enough time to create a digital product because I work 60 hours a week as a real estate agent."

**The Fear Behind It**: "I'm afraid that if I reduce my client hours to work on my digital product, my income will drop and I'll fail at both."

**The Excuse-Busting Plan**:

*Perspective Shift*: "Creating this digital product isn't separate from my real estate career—it's an extension of it that will eventually give me more freedom and higher income."

*Practical Solution*: "I will dedicate the first hour of each morning (5-6 AM) to product creation before my regular workday. I will also batch-record content on Sundays when I don't have showings. This gives me 10 hours per week without reducing my client availability."

*Accountability Measure*: "I've booked a launch date for my product and announced it to my email list. I've also paid a designer a non-refundable deposit for my course materials that must be completed by a specific date."

This plan neutralizes the excuse by finding time that wasn't being utilized, reframing the project as part of his current business rather than competing with it, and creating external commitments that would be painful to break.

## Step 4: Create a No-Excuse Environment

Your environment either supports your goals or sabotages them. Here's how to create surroundings that make excuses difficult to maintain:

1. **Physical Environment**: Organize your workspace for productivity. Remove distractions. Create visual reminders of your goals and commitments.
2. **Digital Environment**: Unfollow accounts that normalize excuse-making. Install website blockers during your work hours. Set up automated reminders of your goals.
3. **Social Environment**: Inform your close circle about your commitments. Find an accountability partner who will call you out on excuses. Join communities of action-takers.
4. **Mental Environment**: Curate what you consume—books, podcasts, videos—to reinforce your commitment to action over excuses.

One of the most powerful environment changes I made was starting each day by reading my commitment statement and reviewing my goals before looking at any messages or notifications. This simple habit primes my mind for action rather than reaction.

# Step 5: Implement the "Do It Anyway" Philosophy

The ultimate excuse eliminator is a simple mantra: "Do it anyway."

- Too tired? Do it anyway.
- Don't feel ready? Do it anyway.
- Uncertain of the outcome? Do it anyway.
- Had a setback? Do it anyway.
- No one supporting you? Do it anyway.

This mantra cuts through the noise of justifications and brings you back to the fundamental truth: your success depends on your actions, not your circumstances.

I have this phrase written on a card in my wallet. During difficult times, when excuses are flowing freely in my mind, I pull out this card and remind myself of the commitment I've made.

# The Power of Constraint

One of the most effective strategies for eliminating excuses is to create constraints that force action. This might seem counterintuitive—don't we want more freedom, not less?

But constraints actually enable creativity and eliminate the decision fatigue that leads to inaction.

Here are some powerful constraints you can implement:

1. **Time Constraints**: Set a non-negotiable 90-minute block each day for working on your digital business. No matter what, this time is sacred.
2. **Financial Constraints**: Put money on the line. Pay for something related to your business that you can't get refunded, creating a financial incentive to follow through.
3. **Public Constraints**: Announce your intentions publicly. Tell your audience when your product will launch. The social pressure will push you through excuse-making moments.
4. **Resource Constraints**: Limit yourself to the tools you already have. This prevents the "I need to buy X before I can start" excuse.

My client Tasha was a consultant who had been talking about creating an online course for three years. Every few months, she would get excited about it, then find reasons why the timing wasn't right.

I challenged her to create a non-refundable constraint. She prepaid a videographer for three recording sessions scheduled over a three-week period. She also announced to her email list that her course would be open for enrollment on a specific date.

With $2,500 on the line and her reputation at stake, suddenly her excuses evaporated. She completed her course, launched on schedule, and made $38,000 in her first week of sales.

The constraints eliminated her ability to procrastinate.

# When Legitimate Obstacles Arise

Let me be clear: I'm not suggesting that real obstacles don't exist. Life happens. Health issues arise. Financial emergencies occur. Family needs emerge.

The difference between an excuse and a legitimate obstacle is your response to it.

When faced with a real challenge, excuse-makers use it as a reason to abandon their goals. Action-takers find a way to work with or around it.

When I was building my moving business, my only truck broke down. This was a legitimate obstacle—I couldn't move furniture without a truck. I had two options:

1. Use this as a reason to cancel jobs and lose momentum
2. Find a creative solution

I chose the second option. I called a competitor and negotiated a profit-sharing arrangement to use their truck on days they weren't using it. This not only solved my immediate problem but led to a valuable business relationship that eventually resulted in acquiring that company when the owner wanted to retire.

The obstacle wasn't eliminated—it was transformed into an opportunity.

Whatever legitimate obstacles you face, ask yourself:

- Is this truly a roadblock, or just a detour?
- What's the creative solution I'm not seeing?

- Who could help me overcome this?
- What's the smallest step I can still take despite this obstacle?

## The Daily Excuse Audit

To maintain your excuse-free lifestyle, implement a daily excuse audit. At the end of each day, ask yourself:

1. Did I make any excuses today?
2. What were the circumstances surrounding those excuses?
3. What was the real fear or discomfort I was avoiding?
4. How will I respond differently next time?

This practice develops your self-awareness and helps you catch patterns before they become habits. It's not about beating yourself up—it's about training your mind to recognize and reject excuse-making in real-time.

I keep a small notebook specifically for this purpose. The simple act of writing down my excuses forces me to confront them objectively rather than letting them run unchecked in my mind.

## From Excuses to Execution

When you eliminate excuses, you create space for execution. And execution—not ideas, not intentions, but consistent, persistent action—is what builds successful businesses.

I've worked with thousands of entrepreneurs over the years. The ones who succeed aren't necessarily the most talented, the most connected, or the most privileged. They're the ones who refuse to let circumstances determine their outcomes.

They're the ones who, when faced with a choice between an excuse and an action, consistently choose action.

By implementing the Excuse Elimination System, creating a no-excuse environment, adopting the "Do It Anyway" philosophy, using the power of constraint, and conducting daily excuse audits, you'll transform your relationship with challenges.

Instead of seeing obstacles as reasons to stop, you'll start seeing them as opportunities to grow, adapt, and overcome.

And that transformation—from excuse-maker to unstoppable executor—will change everything in your business and your life.

## Chapter Summary: Key Takeaways

- Excuses feel good temporarily but cost you everything you want long-term
- Most excuses fall into common categories and have specific fears behind them
- The Excuse Elimination System helps identify and neutralize your top excuses
- Creating constraints can force action and prevent procrastination
- Real obstacles require creative solutions, not surrender
- A daily excuse audit develops self-awareness and prevents excuses from becoming habits
- Execution, not excuses, builds successful businesses and meaningful lives

## Action Steps:

1. Identify your top three excuses and the fears behind them
2. Create an excuse-busting plan for each one
3. Implement at least one constraint that will force action
4. Set up your environment to support action over excuses
5. Begin a daily excuse audit practice
6. Adopt the "Do It Anyway" mantra for the next 30 days

If you're passionate about **impact, purpose, and real results,** we want to hear from you. **Partner with Neo**. Visit PartnerWithNeo.com/apply to explore how we can collaborate.

# CHAPTER 3

# THE ENVIRONMENT OF EXCELLENCE

There's a phrase that transformed my business and my life: *Get in the room and stay in the room.*

In the previous chapters, you made the decision to succeed and eliminated the excuses that have been holding you back. Now it's time to focus on perhaps the most overlooked factor in entrepreneurial success: your environment.

Your environment shapes you far more than you realize. No matter how strong your mindset or how disciplined you are, if you're surrounded by the wrong people, consuming the wrong information, and spending time in the wrong places, your growth will be stunted.

## The Proximity Principle

I'm going to share something personal with you.

Every single day, if I wanted to, I could have lunch with a different millionaire in Atlanta for the next 300 days straight. I could gather a group of entrepreneurs who collectively own more than $15 million worth of luxury cars for a meetup tomorrow. I can pick up the phone and get advice from people who run nine-figure businesses.

I'm not telling you this to impress you. I'm telling you because there was a time when I didn't know a single successful entrepreneur. There was a time when everyone in my circle was struggling financially. There was a time when the only "business advice" I received was to get a stable job.

What changed? My environment.

I made a conscious decision to place myself in proximity to success. This didn't happen by accident or good fortune. It happened because I understood a fundamental truth: *Proximity is power.*

Proximity gives you access to:

- Information that isn't available to the public
- Opportunities that aren't advertised
- Connections that can accelerate your growth
- Mindsets that challenge your limitations
- Standards that elevate your performance

When you're in proximity to success, what seems impossible to others becomes normal to you. When everyone around you is building seven-figure businesses, a six-figure goal doesn't seem so daunting. When you personally know people who have overcome the exact obstacles you're facing, those obstacles lose their power.

# Assessing Your Current Environment

Before we discuss how to upgrade your environment, let's take an honest look at where you are now. Rate your current environment in these key areas on a scale of 1-10:

## 1. Your Inner Circle (the 5-7 people you spend the most time with)

- What's their average income?
- What are their ambitions and goals?
- How do they respond when you share your dreams?
- Do they challenge you to grow or comfort you in mediocrity?

## 2. Your Information Diet

- What books, podcasts, and courses are you consuming?
- Who are your mentors (whether in person or through content)?
- What social media fills your feed?
- Where do you get your business education?

## 3. Your Physical Spaces

- Where do you work?
- Where do you network?
- Where do you spend your leisure time?
- Do these spaces inspire growth or reinforce comfort?

## 4. Your Digital Communities

- What online groups do you belong to?
- What's the caliber of conversation in these spaces?

- Are members achieving the results you want?
- Do you have access to decision-makers and high performers?

Be brutally honest with yourself. If you're the smartest, most successful, or most ambitious person in most of your environments, that's a problem. Not for your ego, but for your growth.

As motivational speaker Jim Rohn famously said, "You are the average of the five people you spend the most time with." I would add that you're also the average of the information you consume, the spaces you occupy, and the communities you join.

## The Investment Mindset

Now let's talk about how to upgrade your environment. This requires what I call the "investment mindset."

Most people look at personal development as an expense: "Can I afford this conference, this mastermind, this coach?" They compare it to other ways they could spend that money, like a vacation or home renovation.

Successful entrepreneurs see it differently. They ask: "What will it cost me NOT to be in that room? What opportunities, connections, and knowledge am I missing by staying where I am?"

Let me give you a personal example. In 2018, I spent $25,000 to join a high-level mastermind. This was a significant investment for me at the time. Many people in my life thought I was crazy. "You're paying $25,000 to talk to people?" they asked incredulously.

What they didn't understand was that I wasn't paying for conversations—I was investing in transformation.

In that mastermind, I met the person who would become my business partner in a venture that generated over $2 million in its first year. I learned a marketing strategy that doubled the conversion rate on my webinars. I found my first high-ticket clients who valued my expertise enough to pay premium prices.

That $25,000 "expense" generated a return of more than 20x in the first year alone. And that doesn't include the ongoing value of the relationships I built, the confidence I gained, or the limiting beliefs I shed.

This is the investment mindset: understanding that the right environments don't cost you money—they make you money.

## Calculating Environment ROI

Let's get practical about this. I want you to start thinking about your environment in terms of Return on Investment (ROI).

For any environment you're considering joining—whether it's a conference, mastermind, coaching program, or co-working space—ask yourself:

1. What is the direct financial investment required?
2. What is the time investment required?
3. What specific outcomes could result from this environment?
4. What is the potential financial return of those outcomes?
5. What is the non-financial value (relationships, well-being, etc.)?

Let's work through a real example. Say you're considering attending a three-day business conference that costs $2,000 plus travel expenses.

Direct financial investment: $3,000 total Time investment: 3 days plus travel time Potential outcomes:

- 2-3 new client relationships ($5,000+ each)
- 1 key strategy that improves your business
- 5-10 new network connections
- Exposure to new ideas and perspectives

Even if you only secure one new client from this event, you've already made a positive ROI. Everything else is a bonus.

Now contrast this with spending that same $3,000 on equipment, ads, or other business expenses without upgrading your knowledge or network. The ROI is often much lower.

The most valuable investments you can make are not in things but in growth environments.

# Types of Growth Environments

Now that you understand the value of your environment, let's explore the specific types of environments you should be seeking out:

## 1. Strategic Masterminds

A mastermind is a group of peers who meet regularly to tackle challenges and problems together. The right mastermind puts you in a room with people playing at or above your level.

Look for masterminds that:

- Are led by someone who has achieved what you want to achieve
- Have a careful vetting process (the harder it is to get in, often the better)
- Include members with diverse expertise but similar ambition levels
- Meet regularly enough to build real relationships
- Have a track record of member success

The mastermind I mentioned earlier transformed my business because it placed me in weekly contact with entrepreneurs who were generating the results I wanted. Their success demystified my goals and gave me practical pathways to achieve them.

## 2. High-Level Conferences and Events

While masterminds provide depth, conferences provide breadth. They expose you to new ideas, trends, and people outside your usual circle.

Look for events that:

- Attract the leaders in your industry
- Have a strong speaker lineup
- Include structured networking opportunities
- Are specifically focused on your field or goal
- Have a reputation for quality over quantity

One of my clients made a single connection at a digital marketing conference that led to a $430,000 joint venture deal. That would never have happened if she'd stayed in her comfort zone watching YouTube videos about marketing.

## 3. Coaching and Mentorship

Nothing accelerates growth like personalized guidance from someone who has already achieved what you want.

Look for coaches/mentors who:

- Have a proven track record (not just good marketing)
- Have helped others achieve the specific results you want
- Have a teaching style that resonates with you
- Hold you accountable rather than just cheering you on
- Are accessible to you in a meaningful way

I invest hundreds of thousands of dollars annually in coaching and mentorship. Why? Because I've learned that one insight from the right mentor can save you years of trial and error.

## 4. Coworking and Entrepreneurial Spaces

Where you work physically impacts how you think. Surrounding yourself with other ambitious entrepreneurs creates an environment of productivity and possibility.

Look for spaces that:

- Attract serious entrepreneurs (not just freelancers looking for cheap office space)
- Host regular events and networking opportunities
- Offer amenities that support your productivity
- Create a culture of excellence and ambition

When I moved my team to a premium coworking space in Atlanta, our productivity and creativity noticeably increased simply because we were surrounded by other successful companies.

## 5. Digital Communities

Not all valuable environments require physical presence. Online communities can provide access to people and ideas from around the world.

Look for digital communities that:

- Have active, engaged leadership
- Maintain high standards for membership
- Foster meaningful conversation (not just self-promotion)
- Include members who are transparent about their results
- Provide regular opportunities for deeper connection

I'm a member of several paid online communities that have provided valuable connections, partnerships, and insights—often at a fraction of the cost of in-person environments.

# Finding Your Way In

"This all sounds great, Nehemiah," you might be thinking, "but how do I actually get into these environments? I don't have the money/connections/credentials to join these spaces."

I understand this concern because I started with none of those things either. Here's what I've learned about gaining access to environments that might seem out of reach:

## 1. Start Where You Can, Then Upgrade

Don't wait for the perfect environment—start with what's accessible now.

When I couldn't afford premium masterminds, I joined free Facebook groups run by successful entrepreneurs. When I couldn't afford national conferences, I attended local meetups. I used these starter environments to learn, connect, and create results I could leverage to access higher-level spaces.

The key is to maximize whatever environment you're in. Be the most engaged, the most helpful, the most action-oriented person in the room. This gets you noticed by the leaders, who often have connections to higher-level environments.

## 2. Provide Value First

One of the most effective ways to enter premium environments is to become valuable to those environments.

Before I could afford certain conferences, I volunteered to help run them. Before I could pay for high-level coaching, I found ways to support coaches with their businesses. Before I could join exclusive masterminds, I created results that made those masterminds want me as a member.

Ask yourself: What skills, connections, or perspectives do I have that would be valuable to the environment I want to join? How can I serve first, rather than just seeking to extract value?

## 3. Leverage Relationships

Your network is your net worth. One connection can open doors to environments that would otherwise remain closed.

Identify people one or two levels ahead of you who have access to the environments you want to join. Build genuine relationships with them by providing value and showing your commitment. When the time is right, they can become your sponsors into higher-level spaces.

Several of my biggest opportunities came through introductions from people who recognized my potential and vouched for me in rooms I couldn't access on my own.

## 4. Create Your Own Environment

If you can't find the perfect environment, create it.

Some of the most valuable environments I've been in started with me inviting a small group of peers to meet regularly and support each other. As we all grew, so did the caliber of our meetings and the value of our network.

Don't underestimate the power of being the connector. When you bring valuable people together, you become valuable to them.

## 5. Invest Strategically

Sometimes the only way in is to pay the price of admission. In these cases, view it as a strategic investment rather than an expense.

I've taken out loans to join certain environments because I was confident in the ROI. I've prioritized experiences over possessions because I understood that being in the right room would create more long-term wealth than having the right car or house.

Be strategic about where you invest. One premium mastermind is often worth more than ten mediocre courses. One high-quality conference can yield more value than months of unfocused networking.

# Maintaining Environment Excellence

Getting into the right environments is only half the battle. Staying in them—and maximizing their value—is equally important.

Here are strategies to get the most from your growth environments:

## 1. Show Up Fully

Presence isn't just about physical attendance—it's about full engagement.

In masterminds, be the first to volunteer information and the last to leave discussions. At conferences, attend the early sessions and the after-hours events. In coaching relationships, come prepared with questions and progress updates.

Half-hearted participation yields half-measured results. Commit to being all in.

## 2. Give Before You Take

The most valuable people in any environment are those who create value for others.

Look for opportunities to contribute: make introductions, share resources, offer feedback, celebrate others' wins. When you become known as a giver rather than just a taker, people go out of their way to help you succeed.

Some of my biggest business breakthroughs came after I helped someone else solve their challenge, with no expectation of return.

## 3. Apply What You Learn

The right environments will flood you with ideas and opportunities. Your job is to implement them.

After every event, meeting, or coaching session, identify the 1-3 most important action items and prioritize their implementation. This not only creates results but demonstrates to others in the environment that you're serious about growth.

I've seen people get removed from premium environments not because they couldn't afford the investment, but because they never applied what they learned.

## 4. Track Your ROI

Regularly assess the value you're getting from each environment.

Keep a journal of insights, connections, and opportunities that come from each space. Estimate their tangible and intangible value. Use this information to make informed decisions about where to continue investing your time and money.

Not all environments will serve you forever. As you grow, your needs will change, and environments that were once perfect may become limiting.

## 5. Elevate Others As You Rise

As you achieve success, remember to create opportunities for others who are where you once were.

Some of the most fulfilling experiences in my career have come from sponsoring promising entrepreneurs into environments they couldn't access on their own. This not only creates goodwill but strengthens your position as a leader and connector.

The more you elevate others, the more valuable you become to every environment you're part of.

# Creating Your Environment Strategy

Now it's time to create your personal environment strategy—a deliberate plan for upgrading the rooms you're in over the next 12 months.

Here's a simple framework:

## Step 1: Define Your Environment Goals

What specific environments do you want to be part of in the next year? Be specific:

- Which masterminds or communities?
- Which conferences or events?
- Which coaching programs or mentorship opportunities?
- Which physical spaces?
- Which digital platforms?

For each environment, identify why it's valuable and what specific outcomes you hope to gain from it.

## Step 2: Assess the Requirements

For each desired environment, determine:

- The financial investment required
- The time commitment needed
- The entry requirements or qualifications
- The application or introduction process
- The timeline for joining

This gives you a clear picture of what you're working toward.

## Step 3: Create Your Investment Plan

Based on the requirements, develop a concrete plan for accessing each environment:

- How will you allocate or generate the necessary funds?
- How will you create the time in your schedule?
- What qualifications do you need to develop?
- Who can provide introductions or recommendations?
- What value can you offer to earn your place?

Be realistic but ambitious. Stretch yourself without setting impossible expectations.

## Step 4: Implement and Iterate

Begin executing your plan immediately. Start with the most accessible environments and use the results from those to access higher-level ones.

Regularly review and adjust your strategy based on:

- The ROI you're getting from current environments
- New opportunities that emerge
- Changes in your business goals
- Feedback from mentors and peers

Remember, the goal isn't to be in the most expensive or exclusive environments—it's to be in the most transformative ones for your specific journey.

# The Foundation Connection

I want to close this chapter by sharing how environment has played a crucial role in the work we do through the Nehemiah Davis Foundation.

One of our core programs provides mentorship and educational opportunities for underprivileged youth in Philadelphia. Why? Because we understand that environment shapes destiny. Many of these young people are surrounded by limiting beliefs, negative influences, and low expectations.

By placing them in environments of excellence—connecting them with successful professionals, exposing them to college campuses, introducing them to entrepreneurial thinking—we're changing what they believe is possible for their lives.

The same principle that transforms businesses transforms communities: get in the room and stay in the room.

As your business grows through the principles in this book, I encourage you to consider how you might create access for others. Could you:

- Sponsor someone who can't afford a conference you found valuable?
- Mentor an entrepreneur from an underserved community?
- Create a scholarship for your coaching program?
- Donate to organizations that create opportunity through environment change?

This is how we create lasting impact—by recognizing that many people aren't held back by lack of potential but by lack of access to environments where that potential can flourish.

## Chapter Summary: Key Takeaways

- Your environment shapes your thinking, actions, and results more than you realize
- Proximity is power—being close to success makes success more achievable
- View environment investments through the lens of ROI, not expense
- Strategic masterminds, high-level events, coaching, coworking spaces, and digital communities are key environments for growth
- Access to premium environments comes through starting where you can, providing value, leveraging relationships, creating your own spaces, and strategic investment

- Maximize environment value by showing up fully, giving before taking, applying what you learn, tracking ROI, and elevating others
- Creating access for others is both a responsibility and an opportunity as you succeed

## Action Steps:

1. Assess your current environments across all five categories
2. Identify the three environments that would most accelerate your growth
3. Research the requirements and investment needed for each
4. Create a 12-month environment strategy
5. Take one immediate action to upgrade your environment this week
6. Consider how you might create environment access for someone else

If you're passionate about **impact, purpose, and real results,** we want to hear from you. **Partner with Neo**. Visit PartnerWithNeo.com/apply to explore how we can collaborate.

# CHAPTER 4

# CERTAINTY SELLS

There's a moment before I speak—whether on a webinar, a virtual event, or a stage with thousands of people—when everything changes. My mind clears, distractions fade, and a profound sense of certainty washes over me.

This isn't arrogance. It's not blind confidence. It's a state I've deliberately cultivated because I understand a fundamental truth: *Certainty sells*.

In the previous chapters, you've committed to success, eliminated excuses, and begun upgrading your environment. Now we'll focus on a quality that separates wildly successful entrepreneurs from those who struggle: the ability to project absolute certainty in yourself, your offers, and the transformation you provide.

## The Psychology of Certainty

Think about the last time you made a significant purchase. Maybe it was an expensive program, a high-ticket item, or an important service. What ultimately convinced you to buy?

If you look deeper than the features and benefits, you'll likely find the same answer I've discovered through thousands of sales conversations: you bought because the person or brand made you feel certain about the decision.

Certainty is contagious. When you are absolutely convinced of your value, that conviction transfers to your audience, your clients, and your team. When you waver, they waver. When you doubt, they doubt.

This isn't about manipulation or false promises. It's about genuinely believing in the transformation you provide and communicating that belief with unwavering conviction.

Some entrepreneurs struggle with this concept. They think, "Isn't it more honest to acknowledge uncertainties? To admit that I don't have all the answers?"

Here's the truth: Your clients aren't paying for your doubts. They're paying for your clarity, your conviction, and your belief in what's possible for them.

Think about it: Would you hire a surgeon who tells you, "I'll try my best, but I'm not really sure if this will work"? Would you board a plane if the pilot announced, "I'm going to attempt to land this thing, but no guarantees"?

Of course not. In crucial moments, you want the people guiding you to project absolute certainty.

Your clients feel the same way about you.

# The Elements of Certainty

Certainty isn't a monolithic quality. It's composed of several elements that work together to create an unshakable presence. Let's break them down:

## 1. Physical Certainty

Your body communicates certainty or doubt before you even speak. Pay attention to:

- **Posture**: Stand or sit tall with your shoulders back and chest open.
- **Movement**: Move deliberately and purposefully, not nervously or randomly.
- **Gestures**: Use defined, intentional hand movements that emphasize key points.
- **Eye contact**: Maintain steady eye contact that connects rather than darts away.
- **Voice**: Speak from your diaphragm with a measured pace and deliberate pauses.

On virtual platforms, these principles still apply. Your camera position, lighting, background, and energy level all communicate certainty or uncertainty to your audience.

I make sure my video setup is professional, my posture is strong even when seated, and my energy is high from the moment I appear on screen. These physical cues telegraph certainty before I say a word.

## 2. Verbal Certainty

Your language patterns either reinforce or undermine your certainty. Eliminate:

- **Hedging words**: "Sort of," "kind of," "maybe," "I think," "I hope"
- **Permission seeking**: "If that's okay," "Does that make sense?"
- **Apologies**: "Sorry to bother you," "Sorry for the confusion"
- **Minimizers**: "Just," "only," "a little bit," "somewhat"

Replace these with phrases that demonstrate conviction:

- "I know" instead of "I think"
- "You will" instead of "You might"
- "This works" instead of "This could work"
- "Here's what I've found" instead of "Here's what I believe"

When I tell my audience, "What I'm about to show you will transform your business," I'm not hoping or wishing—I'm stating a fact based on the results I've seen repeatedly.

## 3. Emotional Certainty

This is the internal state that powers the external expressions. Emotional certainty comes from:

- Deep belief in your products and services
- Personal experience with the transformation you offer
- Evidence collected from client results
- Thorough preparation and mastery of your material

- Connection to your purpose beyond profit

I call this "knowing bone-deep" that what you're offering is valuable. When you have this level of emotional certainty, you can face any objection, criticism, or skepticism without being shaken.

## 4. Strategic Certainty

This is certainty about the path forward—the roadmap you're providing. Strategic certainty demonstrates that:

- You've been where they want to go
- You've helped others get there
- You understand the obstacles and how to overcome them
- You have a clear, proven system
- You've anticipated their needs and questions

When I present my digital product framework, I'm not just sharing ideas that might work—I'm revealing a battle-tested system that has generated millions for me and my clients. That's strategic certainty.

# Building Your Certainty Muscle

Like any quality, certainty can be developed and strengthened over time. Here are the most effective ways to build your certainty muscle:

## 1. Become a Master of Your Craft

Nothing breeds certainty like genuine expertise. Dive deep into your field through:

- Constant learning and skill development
- Testing and measuring what works
- Studying the masters in your industry
- Developing proprietary systems and frameworks
- Collecting and analyzing results data

I invest hundreds of thousands of dollars annually in my education because I know that knowledge fuels certainty. The more I learn, the more powerful my certainty becomes.

## 2. Document Your Successes

Evidence crushes doubt. Create a "certainty file" that contains:

- Screenshots of client testimonials
- Before-and-after results
- Case studies of transformations
- Revenue screenshots from successful launches
- Thank you messages from those you've helped

Review this file regularly, especially before important presentations or sales conversations. When doubt creeps in (and it will), your evidence will restore your certainty.

I keep a folder on my phone with screenshots of my biggest wins and most meaningful client transformations. Before every major presentation, I review it to anchor myself in the value I deliver.

## 3. Develop Pre-Performance Rituals

Elite athletes, performers, and speakers use rituals to enter a state of certainty. Create your own ritual that might include:

- Physical preparation (movement, breathing exercises, power poses)
- Mental preparation (visualization, affirmations, reviewing key points)
- Emotional preparation (connecting to your why, reviewing testimonials)
- Technical preparation (equipment checks, environment optimization)

My personal ritual includes 10 minutes of physical movement, reviewing my certainty file, standing in a power pose while reciting specific affirmations, and a brief prayer asking for guidance. This sequence transitions me into a state of absolute certainty.

## 4. Practice Progressive Desensitization

Gradually expose yourself to increasingly challenging situations:

- Start by recording videos just for yourself
- Then share content with a small, supportive audience
- Next, speak to small groups in low-pressure environments
- Finally, take on higher-stakes opportunities

Each successful experience builds your certainty for the next challenge. I began by speaking at local meetups, then small workshops, then industry events, and eventually international stages with thousands of attendees.

## 5. Invest in Your Presentation

Your environment and tools either support or undermine your certainty:

- Invest in quality equipment (camera, microphone, lighting)
- Create professional presentation materials
- Dress in a way that makes you feel confident
- Ensure your physical or virtual stage is optimized

I invested in a professional intro video that plays before I speak, quality slides that reinforce my message, and a personal appearance that communicates success. These external elements support my internal certainty.

# Certainty in Different Contexts

Let's explore how to apply certainty across various business situations:

## Certainty in Content Creation

Whether you're creating videos, writing posts, or recording podcasts, certainty transforms your content from interesting to compelling:

- Make definitive statements rather than wishy-washy suggestions
- Share specific outcomes rather than vague possibilities
- Use stories that demonstrate proven results
- Create frameworks that provide clear paths forward
- End with calls to action that assume engagement

My most successful content pieces aren't necessarily the most polished—they're the ones where my certainty in the message is absolute.

## Certainty in Sales Conversations

Nothing kills sales faster than uncertainty. In sales conversations:

- Listen fully, then diagnose with authority
- Present solutions as the clear answer, not one option among many
- Address objections as opportunities for clarification, not threats
- Guide the conversation toward a decisive conclusion
- Assume the close rather than hoping for it

I approach every sales conversation with the mindset that if the prospect is a good fit, it would be a disservice NOT to have them work with me. This certainty makes the enrollment process natural and non-pushy.

## Certainty in Team Leadership

Your team will never be more certain than you are. When leading others:

- Communicate vision with unwavering conviction
- Make decisions promptly and stand behind them
- Acknowledge challenges while maintaining certainty about overcoming them
- Celebrate wins to reinforce the certainty of future success
- Model the certainty you want to see in your team

When I faced a major business challenge that required restructuring our team, I called an emergency meeting. Instead of projecting worry, I stated clearly: "This is exactly what we needed to reach our next level. Three months from now, we'll look back and see this was the best thing that happened to us." That certainty carried us through the transition to a much stronger organization.

## Certainty in Public Speaking

Whether on stage or on a webinar, certainty is what moves audiences to action:

- Begin with a strong, definitive opening
- Make bold statements backed by evidence

- Use phrases like "I guarantee" and "I promise" (when you can truly deliver)
- Address skepticism head-on
- Close with absolute clarity about the next step

When I speak at events, I often begin with: "What I'm about to share will transform the way you think about digital business. This isn't theory—this is the exact framework that has generated millions for me and my clients." This certainty immediately captures attention and creates openness to the message that follows.

## Authenticity vs. False Confidence

At this point, you might be wondering: "Isn't this just about faking it till you make it? Isn't this encouraging false confidence?"

Let me be clear: I'm not advocating pretending to know things you don't or promising results you can't deliver. That's not certainty—that's fraud.

The certainty I'm describing comes from:

1. Only making claims you can back up with evidence
2. Only offering solutions you genuinely believe in
3. Only promising what you know you can deliver
4. Being prepared to stand behind your work 100%

The difference between authentic certainty and false confidence is integrity. Authentic certainty is grounded in truth and reinforced by evidence. False confidence crumbles under scrutiny because it lacks foundation.

I never teach strategies I haven't personally tested. I never promise results that aren't realistic. I never claim expertise in areas where I'm still learning. This integrity makes my certainty unshakable because it's built on truth.

# Dealing with Doubt

Even with all these practices, doubt will occasionally creep in. This is normal and human. The key is not to eliminate doubt entirely but to develop strategies for managing it:

## 1. Recognize Doubt as a Visitor, Not a Resident

When doubt appears, acknowledge it: "I notice I'm feeling uncertain right now." This simple recognition prevents doubt from hijacking your thoughts.

## 2. Return to Evidence

Immediately review your certainty file or recall specific success stories. Evidence is the antidote to doubt.

## 3. Utilize Pattern Interrupts

Physical movement, deep breathing, or even a quick change of environment can break the pattern of doubtful thinking.

## 4. Reframe Doubt as Excitement

The physiological signatures of doubt and excitement are nearly identical. Try relabeling your feelings: "I'm not nervous—I'm excited about the impact I'm about to make."

## 5. Connect to Service

Shift focus from yourself to those you help. When you're focused on serving others, self-doubt diminishes.

Before a major presentation where I was feeling unusually nervous, I stepped away to a quiet place and scrolled through messages from clients whose lives had been changed through our work. Within minutes, my doubt was replaced by certainty because I reconnected to the impact we create.

# Certainty and the Greater Good

Certainty becomes even more powerful when connected to purpose beyond profit. When your business serves a greater mission, your certainty isn't just about products and services—it's about the change you're creating in the world.

Through the Nehemiah Davis Foundation, we provide resources, mentorship, and opportunities to underserved communities in Philadelphia. This mission infuses everything we do with deeper purpose.

When I speak about our foundation work, my certainty reaches another level. It's no longer just about business strategies or digital products—it's about transforming lives and communities. This certainty resonates differently with audiences because they feel the authentic passion behind it.

Your certainty will reach its peak when your business success becomes a vehicle for meaningful impact. When you know that every sale not only serves your client but also contributes to a greater good, your conviction becomes unshakable.

Consider how your business could serve a greater purpose. Could you:

- Allocate a percentage of profits to causes you care about?
- Create scholarship opportunities for underserved populations?
- Develop programs that address community needs?
- Mentor young entrepreneurs from disadvantaged backgrounds?
- Use your platform to raise awareness for important issues?

When your certainty is fueled by purpose, it becomes a powerful force for positive change.

## The Ultimate Certainty Exercise

Let's close this chapter with a powerful exercise that will immediately strengthen your certainty muscle. I call it the "Certainty Declaration."

1. Find a quiet space where you can speak at full volume without interruption.
2. Stand in a power pose: feet shoulder-width apart, shoulders back, chin slightly raised.
3. Take three deep breaths, inhaling through your nose for four counts and exhaling through your mouth for six counts.

4. In a strong, clear voice, declare the following (filling in your specific details):

"I am [YOUR NAME], and I help [YOUR IDEAL CLIENTS] achieve [SPECIFIC TRANSFORMATION] through [YOUR SOLUTION].

I know this works because [SPECIFIC EVIDENCE].

Every day, I become more certain of the value I provide.

My certainty is not arrogance—it's responsibility.

My clients need my certainty. My team needs my certainty. My community needs my certainty.

Today, I choose certainty over doubt. I choose conviction over hesitation. I choose impact over fear.

I am [YOUR NAME], and I am absolutely certain of the transformation I provide."

5. Repeat this declaration daily for 30 days, ideally before important meetings, calls, or presentations.

This may feel uncomfortable at first. That's normal. Push through the discomfort and notice how your certainty strengthens with repetition.

I've used variations of this exercise for years, and it has transformed my ability to communicate with conviction, close high-ticket sales, and lead teams through challenges.

# Chapter Summary: Key Takeaways

- Certainty is contagious—when you believe absolutely in your value, others will too
- Certainty has physical, verbal, emotional, and strategic components
- You can build your certainty muscle through mastery, evidence, rituals, practice, and presentation
- Apply certainty across content creation, sales, leadership, and speaking
- Authentic certainty differs from false confidence through integrity and evidence
- Manage doubt through recognition, evidence, pattern interrupts, reframing, and service
- Connect your certainty to a greater purpose for maximum impact
- Practice the Certainty Declaration daily to strengthen your conviction

# Action Steps:

1. Create your certainty file with evidence of your impact and success
2. Develop a pre-performance ritual that transitions you into a state of certainty
3. Audit your language patterns and eliminate uncertainty phrases
4. Invest in at least one element of your presentation (equipment, materials, appearance)
5. Identify a greater purpose that your business success can serve

6. Practice the Certainty Declaration daily for 30 days
7. Record yourself speaking about your business, then analyze your certainty cues

If you're passionate about **impact, purpose, and real results,** we want to hear from you. **Partner with Neo**. Visit PartnerWithNeo.com/apply to explore how we can collaborate.

# CHAPTER 5

# FROM ONE-TO-ONE TO ONE-TO-MANY

I was standing in the hot Philadelphia sun, loading furniture into a moving truck for the third time that day. My back ached. My hands were blistered. I had been working since 5 AM, and I still had two more jobs to complete before I could rest.

As I hefted a couch up the ramp, a realization hit me with more force than the physical exhaustion: *I had created another job for myself, not a business.*

Yes, I was an entrepreneur on paper. I owned the moving company. But in reality, I was simply trading hours for dollars—and my body was paying the price.

That moment was my first encounter with a principle that would transform my financial life: the shift from one-to-one to one-to-many.

In the previous chapters, we've laid the groundwork for success through commitment, eliminating excuses, upgrading your environment, and developing certainty. Now we're going to focus on a concept that will fundamentally change how you think about business and income.

# The One-to-One Trap

Most entrepreneurs, especially service providers, start in a one-to-one model:

- The hairstylist serving one client at a time
- The consultant working with one company at a time
- The personal trainer coaching one person at a time
- The real estate agent selling one property at a time

This model has severe limitations that become more apparent the more successful you become:

## 1. Time Ceiling

There are only 24 hours in a day. No matter how efficiently you work or how much you charge per hour, there's a hard ceiling on how much you can earn in a one-to-one model.

Let's do the math. Say you charge $100 per hour (which is more than most service providers):

- Working 8 billable hours a day = $800
- Working 5 days a week = $4,000
- Working 50 weeks a year = $200,000

That might seem like a good income, but it requires you to:

- Never get sick
- Never take vacation
- Find clients to fill every available hour
- Maintain peak performance with no breaks
- Have zero administrative time

The reality is usually much less: most service providers are lucky to bill 20-25 hours weekly, bringing that theoretical $200,000 down to $100,000-$125,000—with no room for growth.

## 2. Physical Limitations

Your body can only handle so much, as I learned in my moving business. Whether you're a hairstylist standing all day, a massage therapist using your hands, or a consultant traveling to clients, your physical limitations will eventually assert themselves.

Many one-to-one entrepreneurs end up with:

- Repetitive stress injuries
- Chronic fatigue
- Burnout
- Health problems from stress and overwork

Is this the freedom you envisioned when you became an entrepreneur?

## 3. Scale Limitations

In a pure one-to-one model, the only ways to grow are to:

- Raise your prices (which has a ceiling in most markets)
- Work more hours (which you can't do indefinitely)

Eventually, you hit what I call the "service ceiling"—the maximum you can earn no matter how talented or hardworking you are.

I hit this ceiling multiple times in my early businesses. My moving company could only handle so many jobs per day. My event space could only host so many events. I was working harder and harder for incremental gains until I discovered the one-to-many model.

# The One-to-Many Revolution

The one-to-many model changes everything. Instead of serving clients individually, you create systems to serve multiple clients simultaneously. This isn't about working harder—it's about working differently.

There are many forms of one-to-many models, but digital products represent one of the most accessible and scalable versions. With digital products, you can:

1. Create Once, Sell Repeatedly: Unlike physical products or services, digital products have no inventory costs or production limitations.
2. Remove Time and Location Constraints: Your products can be selling while you sleep, across time zones, to people you'll never meet in person.

3. Maintain High Profit Margins: Without physical production costs, your margins can be 80-95% after initial creation and marketing costs.
4. Build Passive and Recurring Revenue: The right digital products can create income streams that continue with minimal ongoing effort.
5. Reach Global Markets: Your potential audience expands from local to worldwide.

The financial transformation can be staggering. Let me share a real example from my own journey.

My moving company, at its peak, generated about $30,000 monthly in revenue. But that required:

- A team of 6 people
- 3 trucks with maintenance costs
- Insurance and liability coverage
- 60-70 hour work weeks for me
- Physical toll on my body
- Constant customer service issues

After expenses, my take-home was around $10,000 monthly. Not bad, but hardly the freedom I wanted.

Contrast that with my first digital product—an e-book called "Seven Steps to Turning Your Instagram into a Cash Machine."

- Creation time: One weekend
- Production cost: $0 (I wrote it myself)
- Selling price: $47
- Marketing: Instagram and email list

In its first month, it generated $13,000 in sales. By month three, it was consistently bringing in $30,000 monthly—the same as my entire moving company, but with:

- No employees
- No physical inventory
- No equipment
- No geographical limitations
- Minimal customer service
- 95% profit margin

That single product has now generated over $1 million in revenue. But more importantly, it freed me from the one-to-one trap and showed me what was possible when you leverage your knowledge, experience, and expertise.

## Digitizing Your Expertise

"But Nehemiah," you might be thinking, "my business can't be digitized. What I do requires my physical presence."

I hear this objection constantly, and I understand it. But here's what I've learned working with thousands of entrepreneurs: *Almost any expertise can be digitized—not to replace your core business, but to amplify it.*

Let's explore how various businesses can move from one-to-one to one-to-many through digitization:

## Hairstylist/Barber

One-to-One: Cutting/styling hair for individual clients
One-to-Many Possibilities:

- Digital course on hair care techniques for specific hair types
- Subscription box of recommended products with tutorial videos
- Online community with monthly styling tips
- Training program for aspiring stylists

Real Example: My client Tasha was a hairstylist working 50-hour weeks. She created a digital course teaching women with natural hair how to care for it between salon visits. Within six months, her course was generating more income than her salon work, allowing her to reduce her client hours by 60%.

## Personal Trainer

One-to-One: In-person training sessions
One-to-Many Possibilities:

- Specialized workout program for specific goals
- Nutrition guide with meal plans
- Monthly membership with new workouts
- Certification program for specialized training methods

Real Example: Marcus was a personal trainer making $45,000 annually. He created a 12-week program for men over 40, priced at $297. With just 30 sales per month, he added $107,000 in annual income while reducing his in-person training hours.

## Real Estate Agent

One-to-One: Helping individuals buy/sell homes
One-to-Many Possibilities:

- First-time homebuyer's digital guide
- Investment property analysis calculator
- Course on house flipping in specific markets
- Membership site for real estate investors

Real Example: Jessica was a successful agent spending countless hours educating first-time buyers. She created a comprehensive course for $497 that walked them through the entire process. She now enrolls her potential clients in the course first, which both educates them and pre-qualifies the most serious buyers.

## Restaurant Owner

One-to-One: Serving meals to individual diners

One-to-Many Possibilities:

- Signature recipe cookbook
- Cooking master class
- Specialty food products that ship nationwide
- Restaurant startup consulting program

Real Example: Chef Andre's small bistro had limited seating and high demand. He created a membership where fans received video tutorials of his most popular dishes, ingredient recommendations, and monthly Q&A sessions. The membership now generates more profit than his restaurant with none of the overhead.

## Consultant/Coach

One-to-One: Individual client sessions
One-to-Many Possibilities:

- Implementation program for specific outcomes
- Templates and frameworks package
- Group coaching program
- Certification program for your methodology

Real Example: Carlos was a business consultant charging $3,000 monthly per client, limited to 10 clients. He developed a group program at $1,000 monthly that served 50 clients simultaneously, increasing his income from $30,000 to $50,000 monthly while actually reducing his working hours.

The key insight is that digitizing your expertise doesn't mean abandoning your core business—it means leveraging what you already know to create additional income streams while helping more people.

# Finding Your Digital Sweet Spot

The most successful digital products exist at the intersection of three elements:

1. Your Expertise: What you know deeply and can teach effectively
2. Market Demand: What people are actively seeking and willing to pay for
3. Your Passion: What you genuinely care about and enjoy sharing

Let's explore how to identify each element:

## Identifying Your Expertise

Your expertise isn't always what you're formally trained in. It might be:

- Something you've overcome (weight loss, debt, relationship challenges)
- A skill you've mastered (public speaking, negotiation, technical ability)
- A process you've optimized (productivity, organization, system-building)
- Knowledge you've accumulated (industry insights, historical understanding, cultural awareness)

Ask yourself:

- What do people consistently ask for my help with?
- What seems obvious to me but mystifies others?
- What have I figured out through trial and error?
- What results have I achieved that others want?

One of my clients, Michelle, was a corporate accountant who thought her only expertise was tax preparation. Through our work together, she realized her real expertise was helping creatives understand their finances and make better business decisions—something she did naturally for friends. This realization led to a six-figure course called "Financial Clarity for Creatives."

## Gauging Market Demand

The best digital product in the world won't sell if nobody wants it. Research demand by:

- Studying popular questions in your industry forums and social media groups
- Using keyword research tools to identify search volume
- Analyzing successful competitors to see what's selling
- Directly asking your audience what they're struggling with
- Testing concepts with small offers before building the full product

When developing my Instagram Cash Machine e-book, I first posted a series of Instagram tips and tracked which ones got the most engagement. The posts about monetization consistently outperformed all others—a clear signal of market demand that guided my product development.

## Connecting With Your Passion

Sustainable success requires genuine interest in what you're teaching. Ask yourself:

- What topics can I talk about for hours without getting bored?
- What aspects of my expertise do I most enjoy sharing?
- What transformation gives me the greatest satisfaction to facilitate?
- What problems am I personally motivated to solve?

Your passion creates authenticity that customers can feel. It also ensures you'll stay committed when challenges arise.

When these three elements—expertise, demand, and passion—align, you've found your digital sweet spot. This is where your most successful products will emerge.

# Digital Product Types for Beginners

If you're just starting your journey from one-to-one to one-to-many, here are the most accessible digital product types to consider:

## 1. E-Books and Guides

Pros:

- Quick to create (can be done in a weekend)
- Low technical requirements

- Easy to deliver
- Low price point makes selling easier

Cons:

- Lower perceived value than other formats
- Typically lower price point
- May have higher refund rates if not delivered well

Best For:

- Entrepreneurs just starting with digital products
- Testing market demand before creating more extensive products
- Establishing authority in your field

Example Price Points: $27-97

My Instagram Cash Machine e-book started at $47 and has been my gateway product, leading customers to higher-ticket offers.

## 2. Online Courses

Pros:

- Higher perceived value than e-books
- Can command premium prices
- Multiple content formats (video, audio, text)
- Structured learning experience

Cons:

- Requires more production time
- May need video/audio equipment
- More technical setup (hosting, delivery)

Best For:

- Teaching step-by-step processes
- Skills that benefit from demonstration
- Topics requiring deeper explanation

Example Price Points: $297-1,997

My Digital Product Mastery course sells for $997 and includes video lessons, worksheets, and implementation guides, creating higher perceived value than text-only products.

## 3. Templates and Toolkits

Pros:

- Relatively easy to create
- High utility value for customers
- Can be used immediately (instant gratification)
- Great for establishing expertise

Cons:

- May require design skills or software
- Can become outdated and need updates
- Often lower price point than courses

Best For:

- Saving customers time on creation
- Providing frameworks that can be customized
- Helping customers implement strategies

Example Price Points: $47-497

My Funnel Framework Templates package sells for $297 and includes ready-to-use marketing funnel designs that customers can implement immediately.

# 4. Membership Programs

Pros:

- Recurring revenue model
- Ongoing relationship with customers
- Can start small and add content over time
- Community aspect creates retention

Cons:

- Requires consistent content creation
- More complex to set up and maintain
- Needs ongoing management and engagement

Best For:

- Topics requiring consistent updates
- Experts with breadth of knowledge to share
- Businesses with engaged audiences

Example Price Points: $27-197/month

My Inner Circle membership is $97/month and includes weekly training, monthly Q&A calls, and a community forum where members support each other.

## 5. Digital Workshops and Masterclasses

Pros:

- Can be created and launched quickly
- Live element creates urgency and higher engagement
- Can test concepts before building more extensive programs
- Often leads to higher-ticket sales

Cons:

- Requires confident presentation skills
- Technical considerations for live delivery
- Limited scalability in the live format

Best For:

- Testing new content areas
- Creating launch momentum
- Building relationships with your audience

Example Price Points: $97-497

I regularly host Digital Product Masterclasses for $197 that teach one specific aspect of digital business. These often lead to sales of my more comprehensive programs.

# Creating Your First Digital Product

Now that you understand the possibilities, let's walk through the process of creating your first digital product:

## Step 1: Identify Your Topic

Based on the intersection of your expertise, market demand, and passion, select a specific problem you'll solve or transformation you'll facilitate.

The more specific, the better. Instead of "Instagram Marketing," choose "Instagram Story Strategies That Convert Followers to Customers." Instead of "Weight Loss," choose "14-Day Reset for Busy Professionals."

My first successful product focused specifically on monetizing Instagram, not general social media growth or marketing.

## Step 2: Define Your Unique Approach

What makes your solution different from others in the market? This could be:

- A unique framework or system
- A specific methodology
- Your personal experience and results
- A particular philosophy or perspective

Document your approach as a step-by-step process that delivers results. This becomes the backbone of your product.

For my Instagram Cash Machine, I created a 7-step framework that differed from other Instagram courses by focusing exclusively on monetization rather than growth tactics.

## Step 3: Choose Your Format

Based on your content and audience preferences, select the format that best delivers your transformation:

- Written (e-book, PDF guide)
- Video (course, tutorial series)
- Audio (program, guided implementation)
- Mixed media (comprehensive course)

Consider your comfort level with different media and your audience's learning preferences.

I started with an e-book because it played to my strengths as a writer and required minimal technical setup.

## Step 4: Outline Your Content

Create a detailed outline of your product:

- Introduction (problem, promise, positioning)
- Core content modules or chapters
- Specific lessons, strategies, or techniques
- Implementation guidance
- Resources and support materials

Be thorough but focused. It's better to solve one problem completely than to address multiple problems superficially.

My Instagram Cash Machine outline covered seven specific strategies, each with detailed implementation steps and examples.

## Step 5: Create Your Content

This is where most people get stuck—but it doesn't have to be complicated. You can:

- Write directly in Google Docs or Word
- Record videos with your smartphone
- Create slides in PowerPoint or Google Slides
- Use AI tools like ChatGPT to help organize and refine your ideas

The key is to start creating without perfectionism. Done is better than perfect, especially for your first product.

I wrote the first draft of my e-book in a single weekend by blocking out all distractions and focusing solely on delivering value.

## Step 6: Package Your Product

Give your product professional presentation:

- Create a compelling title
- Design a cover or graphic representation
- Organize content in a user-friendly way
- Add relevant images, graphics, or diagrams

- Include practical exercises or worksheets

You can use tools like Canva for design elements or hire freelancers on platforms like Fiverr or Upwork for professional touches.

I invested $250 in professional e-book formatting and cover design, which significantly increased perceived value.

## Step 7: Set Up Delivery

Establish the technical infrastructure to deliver your product:

- Payment processing (PayPal, Stripe, etc.)
- Delivery mechanism (email, membership site, course platform)
- Access security
- Customer support system

Many all-in-one platforms like Kajabi, Teachable, or Podia handle these elements for you.

I started with a simple setup: PayPal for payment and automatic e-book delivery through my email service provider.

# Pricing Your Digital Product

Pricing is where many entrepreneurs significantly undervalue their expertise. Here are key principles for effective pricing:

## 1. Price Based on Value, Not Time

Calculate the value of the transformation you provide, not the hours it took to create the product. If your course helps someone make an extra $5,000, a price of $997 represents tremendous value.

## 2. Consider Your Positioning

Higher prices often position you as a premium provider. Lower prices can suggest lower quality. Where do you want to be positioned in your market?

## 3. Start with Tiered Pricing

Offer multiple price points to capture different segments of your market:

- Basic (core content only)
- Premium (core content plus additional resources)
- VIP (everything plus personalized support)

This approach gives customers options while maximizing your revenue.

## 4. Use Strategic Price Points

Psychological pricing points make a difference:

- $27 feels significantly less than $30
- $97 feels significantly less than $100
- $497 feels significantly less than $500
- $1,997 feels significantly less than $2,000

These strategic price points often convert better than round numbers.

## 5. Test Different Prices

Don't be afraid to test different price points to find the optimal balance between conversion rate and revenue.

When I first launched my Instagram Cash Machine, I tested $37, $47, and $67 price points. The $47 price point produced the highest overall revenue and became my standard price.

# From First Product to Digital Ecosystem

One successful digital product is just the beginning. The real power comes from building a digital ecosystem—a suite of complementary products that serve customers at different stages of their journey.

Here's how I structure my digital ecosystem:

## 1. Free Lead Magnets

- Instagram audit checklist
- Social media content calendar
- Webinar training snippets

Purpose: Attract potential customers and demonstrate value

## 2. Low-Ticket Products ($27-97)

- Instagram Cash Machine e-book
- Content Creation Templates
- 14-Day Challenge programs

Purpose: Convert leads to customers and identify buyers

## 3. Mid-Ticket Products ($297-997)

- Digital Product Mastery course
- Funnel Framework program
- Group coaching programs

Purpose: Deliver comprehensive solutions to committed customers

## 4. High-Ticket Products ($1,997-10,000+)

- Inner Circle mastermind
- VIP implementation days
- Done-for-you services

Purpose: Provide premium support to ideal clients

This ecosystem creates a natural ascension path for customers:

- Some will only engage with free content
- Others will purchase low-ticket products
- A percentage will move to mid-ticket offerings
- A select few will invest in high-ticket programs

Instead of trying to sell a $5,000 program to cold prospects, you build trust through increasingly valuable interactions.

# Leveraging Your Success for Greater Impact

As your digital business grows, you gain two precious resources: time and money. This is where the true power of the one-to-many model reveals itself—in the freedom it creates to make a difference.

Through the Nehemiah Davis Foundation, we've been able to:

- Build basketball courts in underserved neighborhoods
- Provide thousands of meals to families in need
- Award scholarships to promising students
- Create entrepreneurship programs for young people
- Support community development initiatives

None of this would have been possible if I was still loading furniture into moving trucks 60 hours a week.

The transition from one-to-one to one-to-many isn't just about making more money with less effort—though that's certainly a benefit. It's about creating the freedom to pursue your greater purpose.

As you develop your digital products, I encourage you to consider:

- How might your financial freedom enable you to give back?
- What causes or communities could benefit from your support?
- How could your expertise help those who can't afford your services?
- What legacy do you want to leave beyond business success?

Your digital business can become the foundation for meaningful impact that extends far beyond your customers.

## Chapter Summary: Key Takeaways

- The one-to-one model creates inherent limitations on your time, income, and impact
- The one-to-many model through digital products removes these limitations
- Almost any expertise can be digitized, regardless of your industry
- Your digital sweet spot lies at the intersection of expertise, market demand, and passion
- Begin with accessible formats like e-books, courses, or templates
- Follow a structured process to create your first digital product
- Price based on value, not time or effort
- Build a digital ecosystem that serves customers at different stages
- Use your success to create meaningful impact beyond business

## Action Steps:

1. Identify three aspects of your expertise that could be digitized
2. Research market demand for these topics through social media, forums, and keyword tools
3. Select one specific problem you'll solve with your first digital product
4. Choose the format that best delivers your solution
5. Create a detailed outline of your product content
6. Block time in your calendar for content creation
7. Determine your pricing strategy with at least two price tiers
8. Consider how your digital business could eventually support causes you care about

If you're passionate about **impact, purpose, and real results,** we want to hear from you. **Partner with Neo**. Visit PartnerWithNeo.com/apply to explore how we can collaborate.

# CHAPTER 6

# DISCOVERING YOUR DIGITAL PRODUCT

The woman was in tears as she approached me after my presentation at a small business conference in Atlanta.

"Nehemiah, everything you said about digital products makes perfect sense. I'm working 70 hours a week as a wedding photographer, my body is breaking down, and I've hit an income ceiling. But I have no idea what digital product I could create. What would anyone want to learn from me?"

This wasn't the first time I'd heard this concern. In fact, it's the most common objection I hear when introducing the concept of digital products to successful service providers and entrepreneurs.

What this photographer couldn't see—and what you might not see in yourself—is the incredible wealth of knowledge, experience, and expertise she had accumulated over 15 years in her profession. She couldn't see it precisely because it had become second nature to her. What was obvious to her was mysterious to others.

By the end of our conversation, we had identified at least seven potential digital products she could create—from a guide on natural lighting techniques to a course on building a referral-based photography business. Six months later, she launched her first course teaching photographers how to streamline their editing workflow. It generated $43,000 in the first launch.

In the previous chapter, we explored why the shift from one-to-one to one-to-many is essential for breaking through income ceilings and creating true freedom. Now we'll dive deep into discovering exactly what digital product you should create first—even if you currently believe you have nothing to offer.

# The Value Blindness Phenomenon

Most entrepreneurs suffer from what I call "value blindness"—the inability to recognize the value in their own knowledge, skills, and experiences. This blindness stems from three cognitive biases:

## 1. The Curse of Knowledge

Once you know something, it's nearly impossible to remember what it was like not to know it. The skills and insights you've developed over years of experience seem obvious or trivial to you, when in reality they're valuable assets others would gladly pay to acquire.

## 2. The Expert's Paradox

The more expertise you develop in a field, the less qualified you feel to teach it because you become increasingly aware of how much more there is to learn. Beginners often have more confidence teaching than true experts because they don't yet know what they don't know.

## 3. The Proximity Effect

You're too close to your own knowledge to see its value clearly. Just as you can't see your own face without a mirror, you can't fully appreciate your expertise without external reflection.

These biases create a perfect storm that keeps many talented entrepreneurs from packaging and selling their knowledge. The first step in discovering your digital product is recognizing and overcoming this value blindness.

# The Four Sources of Digital Product Value

To discover your most valuable digital product opportunities, let's explore the four primary sources of value you can provide:

## 1. Expertise-Based Value

This is knowledge you've acquired through formal education, professional experience, and deliberate practice. It's what most people think of first when considering what they might teach.

**Examples:**

- Technical skills (photography, coding, design)
- Professional knowledge (legal, financial, medical)
- Academic knowledge (history, science, literature)
- Procedural knowledge (how to perform specific tasks)

**Identification Questions:**

- What have you been formally trained to do?
- What skills have you mastered through years of practice?
- What specialized knowledge do you possess that others don't?
- What processes have you refined through repetition?

One of my clients, Dr. Sarah, was a clinical psychologist who created a digital course teaching therapists how to build a private practice. She drew on her expertise in both psychology and business operations to create a program that now generates over $300,000 annually.

## 2. Experience-Based Value

This comes from your personal journey, challenges you've overcome, and lessons learned through trial and error. Often more relatable and compelling than pure expertise.

**Examples:**

- Personal transformation stories (health, relationships, spirituality)
- Overcoming specific challenges (debt, illness, adversity)

- Achieving noteworthy results (athletic accomplishment, business milestones)
- Navigating complex systems or situations

**Identification Questions:**

- What significant challenges have you overcome?
- What personal transformations have you achieved?
- What journeys have you completed that others are just beginning?
- What mistakes have you made that taught you valuable lessons?

My own first digital product—the Instagram Cash Machine e-book—was primarily experience-based. I shared exactly what worked for me to monetize Instagram, including the mistakes and dead ends I encountered along the way.

## 3. Curation-Based Value

This involves organizing, synthesizing, and presenting existing information in ways that save others time and confusion. Don't underestimate this; in an age of information overload, curation is incredibly valuable.

**Examples:**

- Resource compilations (tools, templates, websites)
- Research summaries (studies, data, trends)
- Frameworks that organize complex topics
- Comparison guides and decision matrices

**Identification Questions:**

- What information do you regularly organize for yourself or others?
- What resources do you consistently recommend to people?
- What complex topics do you help people navigate?
- What overwhelming choices do you help simplify?

My client Michael created a digital product that was simply a curated collection of legal templates for small business owners, along with guidance on when and how to use each one. This collection saves his customers thousands in legal fees and hours of research.

## 4. Access-Based Value

This provides connections, opportunities, or entry points that others can't easily obtain on their own. Your network, relationships, and positioning can be monetized through digital products.

**Examples:**

- Introductions to key people or communities
- Shortcuts to opportunities (auditions, submissions, applications)
- Insider knowledge of hidden processes
- Pathways into exclusive spaces

**Identification Questions:**

- What groups or communities do you have access to?
- What "insider" knowledge do you possess about how things really work?

- What connections could you facilitate for others?
- What opportunities could you help others access?

Celebrity stylist Marcus created a digital course revealing how to break into celebrity styling—including which events to attend, how to approach potential clients, and how to structure initial offers. His access-based knowledge allowed complete outsiders to enter an otherwise closed industry.

Most successful digital products combine multiple value sources. For example, a course on building a six-figure photography business might include:

- Expertise-based value (technical photography skills)
- Experience-based value (your journey from struggling to successful)
- Curation-based value (compiled resources and tools)
- Access-based value (introductions to vendors and potential clients)

## Market Research: Finding the Profit Intersection

Now that you understand your potential value sources, it's time to ensure there's market demand for what you can offer. The most successful digital products exist at the intersection of what you can teach and what people want to learn.

Here are six methods to research market demand:

## 1. The Question Inventory Method

Start paying attention to questions people regularly ask you. These are direct indicators of market interest.

**Implementation:**

- Keep a notebook or digital file specifically for tracking questions
- Record questions from clients, colleagues, friends, and social media
- Look for patterns and recurring themes
- Note the emotional intensity behind different questions

My client Rebecca, a relationship coach, used this method to discover her most valuable digital product topic. She realized clients continuously asked about dating app strategies, despite it being a small part of her coaching. Her "Dating App Success System" became her highest-selling digital product.

## 2. The Social Listening Approach

Research what your target audience is already discussing online to identify their needs, challenges, and desires.

**Implementation:**

- Join Facebook groups where your target audience gathers
- Follow relevant hashtags on Instagram and Twitter

- Browse subreddits related to your field
- Participate in industry forums and communities

Pay special attention to:

- Questions that receive many responses
- Topics that generate heated discussion
- Complaints and frustrations
- Aspirational posts about desired outcomes

When developing my digital products on speaking and presenting, I spent weeks in entrepreneurial Facebook groups noting every comment about fear of public speaking, presentation anxiety, and sales conversion challenges. This research shaped my product to address the specific language and concerns of my audience.

## 3. The Keyword Research Strategy

Use search data to identify what people are actively looking for in your area of expertise.

**Implementation:**

- Use free tools like Google Keyword Planner or Ubersuggest
- Research search volume for topics in your field
- Look for "how to" and question-based searches
- Note the competition level for different keywords

Focus on:

- Medium-volume, lower-competition keywords
- Questions people are asking

- Problem-focused search terms
- Specific rather than general topics

One client discovered through keyword research that while "weight loss for women" was highly competitive, "weight loss for women over 50 with hypothyroidism" had significant search volume with much less competition. This specific focus helped her digital product stand out in a crowded market.

## 4. The Competitor Analysis Technique

Study successful competitors to identify proven market demand and potential differentiation opportunities.

**Implementation:**

- Identify 3-5 competitors offering similar digital products
- Purchase their products if possible (consider it market research)
- Study their marketing, positioning, and offers
- Read customer reviews and testimonials carefully

Look for:

- What customers praise about existing products
- What complaints or disappointments appear in reviews
- Gaps in what's being offered
- Opportunities to provide something better or different

I regularly purchase competitors' products not to copy them but to understand the market landscape and identify unmet needs. This research has helped me position my digital products to fill specific gaps rather than competing directly with established offers.

## 5. The Direct Survey Method

Ask your audience directly about their challenges, needs, and interests.

**Implementation:**

- Create a simple survey using Google Forms or Typeform
- Ask open-ended questions about challenges and goals
- Include questions about willingness to invest in solutions
- Distribute to your email list, social followers, or clients

Effective survey questions include:

- "What's your biggest challenge with [topic]?"
- "What have you tried to solve this problem?"
- "What would solving this problem be worth to you?"
- "What specific outcomes are you looking to achieve?"

Before creating my course on digital marketing for service providers, I surveyed my email list of 5,000 people. The responses highlighted specific pain points I hadn't anticipated, allowing me to create a much more targeted and effective product.

## 6. The Prototype Test Approach

Create a minimal version of your digital product and test market response before full development.

**Implementation:**

- Develop a small portion of your planned product (one module, chapter, or tool)
- Offer it at a reduced price or as a free lead magnet
- Gather feedback and measure engagement
- Use insights to refine your full product concept

This approach:

- Validates market interest before major investment
- Provides real user feedback early in the process
- Builds an initial customer base for your full launch
- Reduces the risk of creating something unwanted

I tested my speaking program by offering a single training module as a standalone webinar for $97. The strong response and specific feedback guided the development of my comprehensive $1,997 program, ensuring it addressed exactly what my market wanted.

# Digital Product Idea Generation

Now that you understand your value sources and have methods to research market demand, let's generate specific digital product ideas for your business. We'll approach this through industry-specific lenses:

## For Service Providers (Coaches, Consultants, Freelancers)

### Potential Digital Products:

1. Client Attraction System: Teaching your specific method for finding and securing clients
2. Service Delivery Framework: Your process for delivering results systematically
3. Productivity Suite: Tools and methods for managing multiple clients efficiently
4. Pricing and Packaging Guide: How to structure offers for maximum profit
5. Client Management System: Templates and processes for onboarding and retaining clients

**Success Example:** Maya was a business coach charging $300/hour for one-on-one sessions. She created a group program teaching her client attraction system for $997. In her first launch, she enrolled 43 students, generating $42,871—more than she could make in a month of individual sessions.

# For Creators and Artists (Photographers, Writers, Designers)

**Potential Digital Products:**

1. Technical Mastery Course: Teaching specific techniques in your medium
2. Business of Creativity Guide: How to monetize creative skills
3. Creative Process Framework: Your system for consistently producing quality work
4. Portfolio Development System: How to create work that attracts ideal clients
5. Productivity System for Creatives: Overcoming blocks and managing creative energy

**Success Example:** James was a freelance writer specializing in email copywriting. He packaged his email templates and writing formulas into a digital product priced at $297. With minimal marketing, he sells 15-20 copies monthly, adding $4,500+ in passive income while actually generating leads for his high-ticket services.

# For Physical Business Owners (Retail, Restaurant, Local Service)

**Potential Digital Products:**

1. Business Setup Blueprint: How to open a successful [type of business]
2. Operations Manual Template: Systems for running your type of business efficiently

3. Staff Training Program: How to hire and develop effective employees

4. Marketing Playbook: Local marketing strategies that worked for your business

5. Vendor Negotiation Guide: How to secure the best terms with suppliers

**Success Example:** Robert owned three successful barbershops. He created a course teaching barbers how to open their own shops, covering location selection, equipment, licensing, staffing, and marketing. Priced at $1,497, the course generates approximately $30,000 monthly while simultaneously creating potential franchisees for his expanding brand.

## For Health and Wellness Professionals

**Potential Digital Products:**

1. Specialized Protocol: Your approach for addressing specific health concerns

2. Home Assessment Tool: Helping people identify issues themselves

3. Maintenance Program: What to do between professional sessions

4. Equipment Guide: Helping clients select and use tools for home care

5. Lifestyle Integration System: How to incorporate health practices into daily life

**Success Example:** Dr. Lisa was a chiropractor limited by the number of patients she could see daily. She created a digital program teaching her specific method for addressing lower back pain through targeted exercises and lifestyle modifications. Priced at $197, the program helps patients maintain results between visits while attracting new clients to her practice.

## For Educators and Subject Matter Experts

**Potential Digital Products:**

1. Accelerated Learning System: Your method for mastering specific subjects quickly
2. Resource Compilation: Organized collection of the best tools and materials
3. Practice Program: Structured exercises for skill development
4. Assessment Framework: How to evaluate progress and identify improvement areas
5. Advanced Application Guide: Moving beyond basics to mastery

**Success Example:** Professor Williams taught statistics at a local university. He created a digital course specifically helping graduate students complete their research methods requirements. His step-by-step system, priced at $497, helps hundreds of students annually while generating more income than his university position.

# The Product-Market Fit Matrix

After generating potential product ideas, you need to evaluate which one to pursue first. The Product-Market Fit Matrix helps you make this critical decision by assessing two key factors:

1. **Market Demand**: How strongly people want this solution
2. **Your Advantage**: How well-positioned you are to provide it

Here's how to use the matrix:

1. List your top 3-5 digital product ideas
2. For each idea, rate market demand on a scale of 1-10 based on your research
3. For each idea, rate your advantage on a scale of 1-10 based on your expertise, experience, and differentiation
4. Multiply these scores to get a Product-Market Fit score
5. Prioritize the idea with the highest score

Let's see this in action with an example:

**Sarah's Digital Product Ideas:**

1. Weight Loss for Busy Professionals
    - Market Demand: 9
    - Her Advantage: 6
    - Product-Market Fit Score: 54
2. Stress Management Through Nutrition
    - Market Demand: 7
    - Her Advantage: 9
    - Product-Market Fit Score: 63

3. Food Prep Systems for Families
   - Market Demand: 8
   - Her Advantage: 4
   - Product-Market Fit Score: 32

Based on this analysis, Sarah should pursue the "Stress Management Through Nutrition" product first, despite "Weight Loss for Busy Professionals" having higher market demand. Her stronger advantage in the stress management area gives her a better overall product-market fit.

# Positioning Your Digital Product

Once you've selected your digital product idea, you need to position it effectively in the market. Positioning answers the critical question: "Why should customers choose your product over alternatives?"

Strong positioning has five key elements:

## 1. Specific Target Audience

Narrow your focus to a clearly defined customer segment. The more specific, the better.

**Generic**: "For small business owners" **Specific**: "For female service-based business owners making $75K-150K annually who want to scale without working more hours"

## 2. Clear Transformation Promise

Articulate exactly what outcome your product delivers.

**Generic**: "Learn email marketing" **Specific**: "Generate your first $10,000 in sales using our 5-step email sequence framework"

## 3. Unique Methodology

Name and explain your distinctive approach or system.

**Generic**: "A course about weight loss" **Specific**: "The Metabolic Reset Method: A 3-phase system for women over 40 to reactivate natural fat-burning mechanisms"

## 4. Credibility Markers

Incorporate elements that establish your authority and trustworthiness.

**Generic**: "I've helped many people" **Specific**: "Creator of the 8-Figure Launch Framework used by 127 businesses including [recognizable names]"

## 5. Risk Reversal

Address potential objections and reduce perceived risk.

**Generic**: "30-day refund policy" **Specific**: "Implement our client attraction system for 60 days. If you don't secure at least 3 new high-ticket clients, we'll refund your investment and give you a free 1-on-1 strategy session to identify what's not working."

Let's see how these elements come together in a complete positioning statement:

"The Client Attraction Blueprint is for coaches and consultants earning $5K-10K monthly who want a predictable system for enrolling premium clients without relying on referrals or complicated funnels. Our proprietary 3-Part Visibility Method has helped over 300 service providers double their income in 90 days or less, including featured case studies in Forbes and Entrepreneur. Implement the system for 60 days—if you don't secure at least 3 new clients, we'll refund your investment and personally analyze where the process broke down."

This positioning clearly communicates who the product is for, what it will deliver, how it works, why it's credible, and how the purchase is de-risked.

# The Digital Product Value Ladder

While we're focusing on creating your first digital product, it's important to understand how it fits into a larger ecosystem. The Digital Product Value Ladder is a strategic framework for offering multiple products at different price points to serve customers throughout their journey.

Here's how to structure your value ladder:

## Level 1: Free Lead Magnets ($0)

**Purpose**: Attract prospects and build your audience **Examples**: Checklists, templates, mini-courses, challenges, webinars **Value Characteristics**: Quick wins, specific solutions, easy implementation

## Level 2: Entry-Level Products ($27-97)

**Purpose**: Convert prospects to customers and identify buyers **Examples**: E-books, short courses, template collections, assessments **Value Characteristics**: Focused solutions, standalone value, minimal support

## Level 3: Core Products ($297-997)

**Purpose**: Deliver comprehensive solutions to committed customers **Examples**: Full courses, extensive programs, robust systems **Value Characteristics**: Complete frameworks, moderate support, community elements

## Level 4: Premium Offers ($1,997-9,997)

**Purpose**: Provide high-touch solutions to ideal clients **Examples**: Group coaching programs, masterminds, implementation programs **Value Characteristics**: Personalized support, accountability, advanced strategies

## Level 5: Elite Experiences ($10,000+)

**Purpose**: Serve top clients with white-glove solutions **Examples**: VIP days, done-for-you services, exclusive retreats **Value Characteristics**: Direct access, customization, highest level of support

Your first digital product will likely be at Level 2 or 3. However, understanding the entire value ladder helps you strategically position this product within your long-term business vision.

For example, my Instagram Cash Machine e-book at $47 (Level 2) naturally leads customers to my Digital Business Accelerator at $997 (Level 3), which then introduces some to my Inner Circle Mastermind at $25,000 annually (Level 5).

# Digital Product Validation Techniques

Before investing significant time and resources into fully developing your digital product, it's wise to validate your concept with the market. Here are four effective validation approaches:

## 1. The Pre-Sale Method

Sell your product before creating it, with clear communication about delivery timeline.

**Process:**

- Create a compelling sales page describing your product
- Set a launch date 30-60 days in the future
- Offer early-bird pricing or bonuses for pre-orders
- Start creating the product only after receiving orders

**Benefits:**

- Generates real market validation (people voting with dollars)
- Provides funding for product development
- Creates deadline pressure for completion
- Builds a list of committed buyers

I pre-sold my Digital Product Mastery course eight weeks before delivery, generating $87,000 in revenue that funded the production process and confirmed strong market interest.

## 2. The Minimum Viable Product (MVP) Approach

Create the simplest version of your product that delivers value, then iterate based on feedback.

**Process:**

- Identify the core promise of your product
- Develop only the essential elements needed to fulfill that promise
- Release to a small group of customers at a reduced price
- Gather extensive feedback and improve iteratively

**Benefits:**

- Requires minimal initial investment
- Provides real user feedback early
- Allows pivoting before major resource commitment
- Creates testimonials and case studies for full launch

My client David created an MVP version of his real estate investing course with just three modules instead of the planned ten. He offered it to 25 students at half price in exchange for detailed feedback, which dramatically improved the full version and generated his first success stories.

## 3. The Pilot Program Strategy

Deliver your digital product content live to a small group before creating the recorded/packaged version.

**Process:**

- Outline your complete product content
- Invite a limited group to join a live implementation program
- Deliver the content through live sessions over several weeks
- Record sessions for future product creation

**Benefits:**

- Tests content in real-time with actual users
- Creates valuable recordings for the final product
- Generates testimonials and case studies
- Allows refinement based on questions and challenges

I used this approach with my Speaking for Impact program, running a 6-week live cohort with 18 participants before creating the self-paced digital version. The questions and challenges that emerged shaped the final product significantly.

## 4. The Free Beta Test Method

Offer your product for free to a select group in exchange for feedback and testimonials.

**Process:**

- Create a basic version of your digital product
- Invite 10-20 ideal customers to access it for free
- Require completion and detailed feedback
- Use successful results for testimonials and refinement

**Benefits:**

- Low risk for both you and participants
- Creates goodwill in your community
- Generates before-and-after stories
- Highlights potential improvements

My client Sarah used this approach for her productivity system for creative entrepreneurs. Ten beta testers received the program for free but had to complete implementation and provide video testimonials if they achieved results. Eight completed the program successfully, providing powerful social proof for her launch.

# Creating Your Digital Product Action Plan

Now it's time to create a concrete action plan for discovering, validating, and creating your first digital product. Follow these steps:

## Step 1: Value Inventory (Week 1)

- Complete a self-assessment of your expertise, experience, curation capabilities, and access value

- Interview 3-5 people who know you well about what they see as your unique value
- Document all potential areas where you could provide valuable information or transformation

## Step 2: Market Research (Weeks 2-3)

- Implement at least three of the market research methods we discussed
- Identify 5-10 specific pain points or desires in your target audience
- Research competitors and existing solutions in your potential market
- Create a list of 3-5 potential digital product ideas

## Step 3: Product Selection (Week 4)

- Apply the Product-Market Fit Matrix to your ideas
- Choose your first digital product to pursue
- Develop your unique positioning using the five key elements
- Create a one-page product concept document

## Step 4: Validation (Weeks 5-8)

- Select and implement one validation technique
- Gather market feedback and make necessary adjustments
- Secure initial customers or beta testers
- Refine your product concept based on validation results

## Step 5: Creation Planning (Week 9)

- Outline your complete product content
- Identify required resources (equipment, software, support)
- Create a production timeline with specific milestones
- Develop a content creation schedule

Remember, the goal is progress, not perfection. Many entrepreneurs get stuck in endless planning and never launch their digital products. Commit to this timeline and hold yourself accountable to these milestones.

# The Impact Dimension

As we conclude this chapter, I want to bring our discussion full circle to the greater purpose behind creating digital products. While financial freedom is a worthy goal, the most fulfilling aspect of this business model is the impact it enables you to create.

Digital products allow you to:

1. **Reach People You Could Never Serve Individually** Your knowledge can help thousands rather than dozens, expanding your impact exponentially.
2. **Create Accessibility Through Price Points** Not everyone can afford your one-on-one services, but digital products make your expertise available at various investment levels.
3. **Generate Resources for Philanthropic Work** The income from digital products can fund causes and initiatives you care about.

4. **Build a Platform for Important Messages** A successful digital product business gives you visibility to advocate for issues that matter.

Through the Nehemiah Davis Foundation, we've been able to provide resources, opportunities, and support to underserved communities in Philadelphia. None of this would have been possible without the freedom and resources generated by our digital product ecosystem.

As you discover your digital product, consider:

- How might your product improve lives beyond your immediate customers?
- What portion of proceeds could support causes you care about?
- Could your product create opportunities for underserved populations?
- How might your success enable greater giving and impact?

The transition from one-to-one to one-to-many isn't just about making more money with less effort—though that's certainly a benefit. It's about expanding your impact and creating a foundation for significance that extends far beyond business success.

## Chapter Summary: Key Takeaways

- Most entrepreneurs suffer from "value blindness" that prevents them from recognizing their marketable expertise
- Digital product value comes from four sources: expertise, experience, curation, and access

- Effective market research uses multiple methods to identify demand and pain points
- Industry-specific digital product ideas can be generated based on your unique background
- The Product-Market Fit Matrix helps select your most promising first product
- Strong positioning includes specific audience, transformation, methodology, credibility, and risk reversal
- Your first digital product should fit within a larger value ladder strategy
- Validation techniques reduce risk and improve product-market fit
- A structured action plan keeps your digital product development on track
- Digital products enable expanded impact and philanthropic possibilities

## Action Steps:

1. Complete the Value Inventory self-assessment
2. Implement at least two market research methods this week
3. Identify and list at least three potential digital product ideas
4. Evaluate your ideas using the Product-Market Fit Matrix
5. Create a positioning statement for your top digital product concept
6. Select one validation technique to test your concept
7. Develop a 9-week action plan with specific milestones
8. Consider how your digital product could support causes you care about

If you're passionate about **impact, purpose, and real results,** we want to hear from you. **Partner with Neo**. Visit PartnerWithNeo.com/apply to explore how we can collaborate.

# CHAPTER 7

# CREATING YOUR DIGITAL PRODUCT

**"I** know exactly what digital product I want to create, but I have no idea how to actually create it."

I hear this sentiment constantly from entrepreneurs who understand the potential of digital products but feel overwhelmed by the creation process. They worry about technology, design, content organization, and a host of other details that seem to require expertise they don't possess.

If you're feeling this way, I have good news: creating a high-quality digital product is far simpler than you might think. You don't need advanced technical skills, expensive equipment, or a team of specialists. What you need is a clear process and the willingness to take action, even when it's imperfect.

In the previous chapter, we identified your digital product idea and validated its market potential. Now we'll focus on transforming that idea into a tangible product that delivers real value to your customers—without getting stuck in perfectionism or technical complications.

# The 80/20 Principle of Digital Product Creation

Before we dive into specific creation strategies, I want to introduce a guiding principle that will save you countless hours and significant frustration: the 80/20 rule of digital product creation.

This principle states that 80% of your product's value comes from 20% of its content and features. Understanding this transforms your approach to creation by helping you:

1. **Focus on high-impact elements first**
2. **Avoid perfectionism that delays launch**
3. **Create a minimum viable product you can improve over time**
4. **Launch faster with confidence your product will deliver results**

I've seen too many entrepreneurs spend months (even years) perfecting their digital products, only to discover that most of what they labored over doesn't significantly impact customer results.

For example, my client Jessica spent three months creating elaborate graphics for her real estate investment course, believing they were essential to her product's value. When we surveyed her first customers about what they found most valuable, not a single person mentioned the graphics. Instead, they highlighted her deal analysis spreadsheet (which took her just four hours to create) and her step-by-step acquisition process (which she taught through simple screen recordings).

This doesn't mean aesthetics and supplementary materials don't matter—they do. But they should never delay getting your core value into the hands of customers who need it.

# The Four Types of Digital Products

Before we explore creation strategies, let's clarify the four main types of digital products and their creation requirements:

## 1. Information Products

These primarily deliver knowledge and insights, often in written or audio format.

**Examples:**

- E-books
- Guides
- Reports
- Audiobooks
- Whitepapers

**Creation Requirements:**

- Writing or recording skills
- Basic editing capabilities
- Simple design elements
- PDF or audio file creation

**Ideal For:**

- First-time product creators
- Those with strong written communication
- Testing market demand with minimal investment

My Instagram Cash Machine e-book falls into this category. I created it in a weekend using Google Docs, then converted it to a professional-looking PDF. Despite its simplicity, it has generated over $1 million in revenue because the content delivers genuine value.

## 2. Educational Products

These teach specific skills or processes through structured learning experiences.

**Examples:**

- Online courses
- Workshops
- Masterclasses
- Training programs
- Tutorial series

**Creation Requirements:**

- Content organization skills
- Video and/or audio recording
- Slide creation (optional)
- Learning platform or delivery system

**Ideal For:**

- Teaching step-by-step processes
- Skills that benefit from visual demonstration
- Building authority in your field

My Digital Business Accelerator program is an educational product with video lessons, worksheets, and implementation guides. While it took longer to create than my e-book, it commands a higher price point ($997) and has become my flagship digital offering.

## 3. Tool-Based Products

These help customers implement strategies or achieve results through practical tools.

**Examples:**

- Templates
- Calculators
- Spreadsheets
- Swipe files
- Scripts

**Creation Requirements:**

- Functional design skills
- Software knowledge (often just Google Sheets or Word)
- Clear instructions for use
- Results-oriented thinking

**Ideal For:**

- Practical implementation of strategies
- Saving customers time on creation
- Complementing information or educational products

My Client Acquisition Calculator is a tool-based product that helps entrepreneurs forecast and plan their marketing efforts. Created in Google Sheets, it took just two days to build but provides immense practical value to users.

# 4. Community-Based Products

These deliver value through connection, accountability, and shared experiences.

**Examples:**

- Membership sites
- Group coaching programs
- Mastermind communities
- Accountability circles
- Forums

**Creation Requirements:**

- Community management skills
- Communication platforms
- Engagement strategies
- Content calendar

**Ideal For:**

- Ongoing customer relationships
- Topics benefiting from peer support
- Building a loyal customer base

My Inner Circle is a community-based product that combines educational content with group interaction. While it requires ongoing management, it generates predictable recurring revenue and creates deep customer relationships.

Most successful digital entrepreneurs eventually create products in multiple categories, building a comprehensive ecosystem. However, for your first product, I recommend starting with either an information product or a tool-based product, as these typically have the lowest creation barriers and fastest time to market.

# Simple Creation Pathways by Product Type

Now let's explore the simplest creation path for each type of digital product:

## Creating an Information Product (E-book, Guide, or Report)

1. **Outline Your Content**
   - Create a detailed table of contents
   - Break main topics into specific subtopics

    ○  Identify key examples, stories, and supporting evidence

2. **Write Your First Draft**
   - Set aside dedicated writing blocks (2-3 hours each)
   - Focus on content value, not perfect writing
   - Use conversational language as if speaking to one person
   - Include personal stories and examples for engagement

3. **Edit for Clarity and Impact**
   - Remove unnecessary words and redundant ideas
   - Ensure logical flow between sections
   - Add subheadings, bullet points, and formatting for readability
   - Consider having someone else review for clarity

4. **Design Your Final Product**
   - Create a professional cover (use Canva or hire on Fiverr)
   - Format interior pages with consistent styling
   - Add visuals where they enhance understanding
   - Convert to PDF with proper bookmarking and navigation

5. **Prepare for Delivery**
   - Create a welcome/instruction page
   - Consider adding bonus resources
   - Set up digital delivery system
   - Test the download process

**Recommended Tools:**

- Writing: Google Docs, Microsoft Word
- Design: Canva, PowerPoint

- PDF Creation: Adobe Acrobat, Google Docs export
- Graphics: Canva, Fiverr freelancers

**Timeline Expectation:** 2-4 weeks for a comprehensive guide or e-book

# Creating an Educational Product (Course or Training Program)

1. **Structure Your Curriculum**
   - Identify learning outcomes for each module
   - Organize content in logical progression
   - Plan exercises and implementation activities
   - Determine assessment or feedback mechanisms

2. **Prepare Your Presentation Materials**
   - Create slide templates for consistency
   - Outline key points for each lesson
   - Develop examples and case studies
   - Prepare demonstration materials

3. **Record Your Content**
   - Set up basic recording environment
   - Record in 15-30 minute segments
   - Focus on clarity and energy, not perfection
   - Re-record only if content is unclear (not for minor mistakes)

4. **Create Supporting Materials**
   - Develop worksheets and action guides
   - Create checklists for implementation
   - Compile resources and references
   - Design certificates of completion (optional)

5. **Set Up Your Delivery Platform**

- Choose a hosting platform (Teachable, Kajabi, Thinkific)
- Organize content in user-friendly modules
- Create engagement elements (quizzes, comments)
- Test the student experience

**Recommended Tools:**

- Recording: Zoom, Loom, Camtasia
- Slides: PowerPoint, Google Slides, Canva
- Hosting: Teachable, Kajabi, Thinkific
- Supporting Materials: Google Docs, Canva

**Timeline Expectation:** 4-8 weeks for a comprehensive course

# Creating a Tool-Based Product (Templates, Calculators, Resources)

1. **Define the Functional Requirements**
   - Identify exactly what the tool needs to accomplish
   - Determine user inputs and desired outputs
   - Define automation and calculation elements
   - Consider different use cases and variations
2. **Build the Core Functionality**
   - Create the basic structure and layout
   - Implement calculations or automation
   - Test with various scenarios
   - Refine based on functionality testing
3. **Develop User Instructions**
   - Write clear step-by-step usage guidelines

- Create example scenarios
- Address common questions or challenges
- Include troubleshooting advice

4. **Add Professional Elements**
   - Implement consistent formatting and design
   - Create user-friendly navigation
   - Add protection for proprietary elements
   - Include your branding

5. **Package for Delivery**
   - Create demonstration videos if needed
   - Prepare download instructions
   - Set up support mechanisms
   - Plan for updates and improvements

**Recommended Tools:**

- Spreadsheets: Google Sheets, Microsoft Excel
- Documents: Google Docs, Microsoft Word
- Design: Canva, PowerPoint
- Demonstration: Loom, Zoom recordings

**Timeline Expectation:** 1-3 weeks depending on complexity

# Creating a Community-Based Product (Membership or Group Program)

1. **Define Your Community Structure**
   - Determine engagement frequency and formats
   - Plan content delivery schedule
   - Establish community guidelines

      ○  Design onboarding experience

2. **Set Up Your Community Platform**
   - Select appropriate technology (Facebook Groups, Circle, Mighty Networks)
   - Create branded elements and welcome materials
   - Set up content organization system
   - Establish moderation processes

3. **Develop Core Content Calendar**
   - Plan first 30-90 days of content
   - Create recurring engagement activities
   - Develop special events or highlights
   - Prepare initial resources and trainings

4. **Establish Management Systems**
   - Create membership tracking processes
   - Set up payment and renewal systems
   - Develop communication protocols
   - Plan for scaling and growth

5. **Launch and Onboarding Preparation**
   - Create welcome sequences
   - Develop orientation materials
   - Prepare initial engagement activities
   - Establish feedback mechanisms

**Recommended Tools:**

- Community Platforms: Facebook Groups, Circle, Mighty Networks
- Content Delivery: Kajabi, Teachable, WordPress
- Communication: Email service provider, Slack
- Management: Membership software, spreadsheet systems

**Timeline Expectation:** 2-4 weeks for setup, ongoing management thereafter

# The Production Mindset Shift

Before we dive deeper into creation strategies, we need to address a critical mindset shift that will determine your success: moving from a perfectionist approach to a production approach.

Many entrepreneurs get stuck in what I call "perfection paralysis"—the inability to complete and launch their digital products because they're constantly refining, improving, and second-guessing their work. This leads to products that never reach the market or take so long to create that the entrepreneur loses momentum and motivation.

The production mindset focuses on:

1. **Progress over perfection**
2. **Completion over endless improvement**
3. **Customer results over creator preferences**
4. **Iteration based on feedback rather than assumption**

One of my mentors shared advice that transformed my approach: "Your first product won't be your best product—but you can't create your best product until you create your first."

Here are practical strategies to cultivate the production mindset:

## Set Hard Deadlines with External Accountability

Announce your launch date to your audience or commit to a specific delivery date with pre-order customers. External accountability creates productive pressure that overcomes perfectionism.

## Embrace the Concept of Minimum Viable Product (MVP)

Define the absolute core elements needed to deliver on your product's promise. Create those first, then consider additional elements as enhancements rather than essentials.

## Implement the 80% Rule

Release your product when it's 80% ready. The final 20% of refinements can come through post-launch updates based on real customer feedback rather than your assumptions.

## Create Modular Content

Design your product so you can easily add, remove, or update sections without rebuilding the entire product. This makes ongoing improvement manageable.

## Use Progressive Release Strategies

Consider releasing your product in phases to early customers, adding new modules or features over time. This creates momentum and allows you to improve based on real usage.

The production mindset doesn't mean creating low-quality products. It means recognizing that a good product delivered is infinitely more valuable than a perfect product that never launches.

# Rapid Content Creation Techniques

Now let's explore specific techniques to create your digital product content efficiently without sacrificing quality:

## 1. The Brain Dump Method

This technique quickly extracts your knowledge on a topic and transforms it into structured content.

**Process:**

1. Set a timer for 25 minutes
2. Write or record everything you know about a specific subtopic without editing
3. Take a 5-minute break
4. Repeat for each subtopic in your outline
5. Organize and refine the content afterward

**Best For:** Information products, educational content outlines

I used this method to create the first draft of my Instagram Cash Machine e-book, completing the content extraction phase in just two days of focused work.

## 2. The Interview Technique

This approach uses questions to pull content from your expertise in a conversational format.

**Process:**

1. Create a comprehensive list of questions covering your topic
2. Record yourself answering each question as if explaining to a client
3. Transcribe the recordings using AI tools
4. Edit and organize the transcriptions into coherent sections
5. Add transitions and supporting elements

**Best For:** Educational products, information products

My client Devon used this approach for his legal protection course for small businesses. He recorded himself answering 27 common legal questions, then transformed the transcripts into a comprehensive course in just two weeks.

## 3. The Template Transformation Method

This technique adapts existing structures to quickly create new content.

**Process:**

1. Identify successful formats in your field (frameworks, structures, outlines)
2. Adapt these templates to your specific topic and audience
3. Fill in each section with your unique expertise and examples
4. Customize the language and presentation for your brand
5. Add proprietary elements that differentiate your product

**Best For:** Tool-based products, structured guides

I frequently use this method for creating implementation guides and workbooks, saving weeks of development time while ensuring proven structures.

## 4. The Content Recycling Approach

This strategy leverages content you've already created in other formats.

**Process:**

1. Inventory all existing content (posts, videos, presentations, emails)
2. Organize by topics related to your product
3. Identify gaps that need new content
4. Adapt and enhance existing material for your product format
5. Create connective elements for coherent flow

**Best For:** Information products, educational courses

Many of my clients discover they already have 50-70% of their product content created in other formats. By systematically organizing and enhancing this material, they can launch much faster than starting from scratch.

## 5. The Collaborative Creation Method

This approach leverages other people's expertise or skills to accelerate creation.

**Process:**

1. Identify specific areas where you need support (design, editing, technology)
2. Find collaborators with complementary skills
3. Create clear guidelines and expectations
4. Maintain creative direction while delegating execution
5. Offer compensation or reciprocal value

**Best For:** Complex products requiring diverse skills

I frequently use this method for comprehensive courses, partnering with designers, editors, and technical specialists to create products that exceed what I could produce alone.

# Using AI Tools Effectively

Artificial intelligence tools like ChatGPT, Claude, and others have transformed digital product creation. When used properly, these tools can dramatically accelerate your creation process without sacrificing authenticity or value.

Here are strategic ways to leverage AI in your digital product creation:

# 1. Content Expansion

Provide AI with your core ideas and have it generate expanded explanations, examples, and supporting points.

**Example Prompt:** "I'm creating a digital course on Instagram marketing. One key concept is the importance of carousel posts for engagement. Please expand this idea into a 500-word explanation including benefits, best practices, and common mistakes to avoid."

# 2. Structure Development

Use AI to help organize your content into logical frameworks and learning sequences.

**Example Prompt:** "I'm creating a guide on personal finance for entrepreneurs. Please help me develop a comprehensive chapter structure that covers essential topics in a logical progression, with 3-5 subtopics for each main chapter."

# 3. Example Generation

Have AI create diverse examples that illustrate your concepts for different audiences or situations.

**Example Prompt:** "I'm teaching entrepreneurs how to create effective elevator pitches. Please generate 5 diverse examples of 30-second elevator pitches for different types of businesses (service business, physical product, software, coaching, creative service)."

## 4. Exercise Creation

Use AI to develop implementation activities, worksheets, and practice exercises.

**Example Prompt:** "I'm creating a course on productivity for creative professionals. Please design a reflective exercise that helps students identify their peak performance times and energy patterns, including 10 specific questions they should answer."

## 5. Resource Compilation

Leverage AI to generate resource lists, tools, and supplementary materials.

**Example Prompt:** "I'm creating a digital product on SEO for small businesses. Please compile a list of 20 essential SEO tools, organized by category (keyword research, technical SEO, content optimization, analytics), with a brief description of each and typical price range."

## Important AI Usage Guidelines:

While AI can dramatically accelerate your creation process, follow these guidelines to maintain authenticity and value:

1.  **Use AI for enhancement, not replacement** - Your unique expertise and voice should remain central.

2. **Always review and personalize AI output** - Add your own examples, insights, and language patterns.

3. **Focus AI on structure more than content** - Let it help organize your knowledge rather than substitute for it.

4. **Keep your proprietary methodologies private** - Don't share your unique frameworks or approaches with AI tools.

5. **Disclose AI usage appropriately** - Be transparent with your audience about how you've leveraged these tools.

When used correctly, AI accelerates the mechanical aspects of content creation, allowing you to focus on your unique insights, experiences, and transformational elements that truly differentiate your product.

# Production Quality Considerations

A common concern among new digital product creators is production quality—how "professional" their product needs to look and feel. Let's address this directly:

## What Actually Matters to Customers

After helping hundreds of entrepreneurs create successful digital products, I've found these are the elements that truly determine customer satisfaction:

1. **Clarity of Instruction** - Can they easily understand and follow your guidance?

2. **Results Achieved** - Does the product deliver the promised transformation?

3. **Ease of Implementation** - How straightforward is the path from learning to application?
4. **Relevance to Their Situation** - Does the content address their specific challenges?
5. **Uniqueness of Insight** - Are you sharing perspectives they can't find elsewhere?

Notice that "Hollywood-level production" isn't on this list. That's because customers overwhelmingly value substance over style, especially for your first products.

## Production Standards by Product Type

Here are appropriate production standards for different digital products:

**Information Products (E-books, Guides)**

**Minimum Standards:**

- Clear, readable text formatting
- Basic organization with headings and subheadings
- Error-free writing (grammar, spelling)
- Professional cover design
- Consistent styling throughout

**Nice-to-Have Enhancements:**

- Custom graphics and illustrations
- Interactive elements (if in digital format)
- Professional layout design
- Supplementary worksheets or resources

## Educational Products (Courses, Trainings)

## Minimum Standards:

- Clear audio quality (no significant background noise)
- Visible demonstrations when needed
- Organized content structure
- Readable slides or supporting visuals
- Consistent lesson format

## Nice-to-Have Enhancements:

- Professional lighting and camera setup
- Branded slide templates
- Music and professional transitions
- Multiple camera angles
- Custom animations or graphics

## Tool-Based Products (Templates, Calculators)

## Minimum Standards:

- Functional accuracy (calculations, formulas, etc.)
- Clear instructions for use
- Intuitive organization and labeling
- Basic professional formatting
- Error-free operation

## Nice-to-Have Enhancements:

- Advanced automation features
- Custom branding and design

- Interactive elements
- Video demonstrations
- Multiple formats or versions

**Community-Based Products (Memberships, Groups)**

**Minimum Standards:**

- Reliable platform accessibility
- Clear navigation and organization
- Consistent communication schedule
- Engaged facilitation presence
- Valuable content delivery

**Nice-to-Have Enhancements:**

- Custom community platform
- Branded visual elements
- Advanced engagement features
- Personalized member experiences
- Integrated content library

## The Equipment Question

Many potential creators get stuck on equipment concerns. Here's what you actually need:

**For Writing-Based Products:**

- A computer with basic word processing software
- That's it. Seriously.

**For Video-Based Courses:**

- A smartphone with a decent camera (all modern phones qualify)
- A $20-30 lavalier microphone that plugs into your phone
- A simple tripod or stable surface
- Natural lighting from a window or basic ring light ($20-40)

**For Screen Recording Products:**

- A computer with Zoom, Loom, or similar free/low-cost recording software
- Optional: A USB microphone ($50-100) for better audio quality

**For Audio-Based Products:**

- A smartphone with voice recording capability
- A quiet room (closets with clothes work well for sound dampening)
- Optional: A USB microphone ($50-100) for better quality

Don't let equipment concerns delay your launch. I've seen entrepreneurs create million-dollar digital product businesses starting with nothing more than their smartphone and basic computer.

# Technical Implementation Simplified

The technical aspects of digital product creation often cause unnecessary anxiety. Here's how to handle the technical side without specialized skills:

## Hosting and Delivering Your Digital Product

Several user-friendly platforms make hosting and delivering your digital products simple:

**All-in-One Platforms:**

- Kajabi: Comprehensive platform for courses, memberships, and digital products
- Teachable: Straightforward course and digital product platform
- Thinkific: User-friendly course and membership site platform
- Podia: Simple platform for multiple digital product types

**Simpler Options:**

- Gumroad: Extremely easy platform for selling digital downloads
- SendOwl: Simple digital delivery with marketing features
- ThriveCart: One-time fee platform with digital product delivery
- SamCart: User-friendly checkout and delivery system

For your first digital product, I recommend starting with the simplest technical option, even if it has slightly higher fees. The most important goal is getting your product to market—you can optimize platforms later.

## Payment Processing

Most platforms mentioned above include integrated payment processing. The most common options are:

- Stripe: Processes credit cards with approximately 2.9% + $0.30 per transaction
- PayPal: Familiar to most customers, similar fee structure to Stripe
- Apple Pay/Google Pay: Increasingly common options offered through major processors

For your first product, focus on offering 1-2 trusted payment methods rather than trying to accommodate every possible option.

## Delivery Automation

The most efficient digital products deliver automatically after purchase. This typically involves:

1. Integration between your payment processor and delivery platform
2. Automated email sequences to welcome customers
3. Immediate access to product materials

Most platforms mentioned earlier handle this automation with minimal setup. The key is testing your purchase and delivery process thoroughly before launch to ensure a smooth customer experience.

# The Launch Timeline

With your digital product created, it's time to prepare for launch. Here's a simplified timeline to get your product to market:

## 2 Weeks Before Launch

1. **Finalize Product Materials**
   - Complete all essential content
   - Test functionality and delivery
   - Implement basic tracking (purchases, engagement)
2. **Create Sales Materials**
   - Write compelling sales page copy
   - Develop basic promotional graphics
   - Set up purchase mechanisms
3. **Prepare Launch Communications**
   - Draft email sequences for your list
   - Create social media announcements
   - Develop direct outreach messages

## 1 Week Before Launch

1. **Test End-to-End Experience**
   - Make test purchases yourself
   - Review the customer journey
   - Fix any technical issues
2. **Brief Partners and Supporters**
   - Share promotional materials with affiliates
   - Brief team members on launch process

      ○  Activate your support network

3.  **Set Up Customer Support**
   - Create FAQ resources
   - Establish support channels
   - Prepare for common questions

## Launch Day

1.  **Activate Communications**
   - Send announcement emails
   - Post on social platforms
   - Make direct outreach to hot prospects

2.  **Monitor Systems**
   - Watch for technical issues
   - Track initial purchases
   - Be available for customer questions

3.  **Celebrate First Sales**
   - Acknowledge and thank early customers
   - Celebrate your achievement internally
   - Document what's working for future launches

## Post-Launch Week

1.  **Gather Initial Feedback**
   - Reach out to early customers
   - Request testimonials from satisfied users
   - Identify potential improvements

2.  **Optimize Based on Data**
   - Adjust sales copy based on questions

     ○   Fix any user experience issues

     ○   Enhance product based on feedback

3. **Plan Ongoing Promotion**

     ○   Develop continued marketing strategy

     ○   Schedule follow-up communications

     ○   Create content highlighting results

This simplified timeline focuses on the essentials. Your first launch doesn't need elaborate webinars, complex affiliate structures, or extensive paid advertising. Start simple, learn from the experience, and scale your launch strategies with future products.

# The Post-Launch Improvement Cycle

The real magic of digital products happens after launch when you can improve based on actual customer experience rather than assumptions. Here's how to implement a continuous improvement cycle:

## 1. Collect Structured Feedback

Create systems to gather specific feedback about your product:

- Post-purchase surveys at key milestones
- Implementation checkpoint emails
- Progress tracking mechanisms
- Direct outreach to active users

Ask targeted questions like:

- "What's been most valuable so far?"

- "Where have you encountered challenges?"
- "What would make implementation easier?"
- "What additional resources would help you succeed?"

## 2. Identify High-Impact Improvements

Not all enhancement opportunities are created equal. Prioritize improvements that:

- Address obstacles to customer results
- Solve problems mentioned by multiple customers
- Enhance the most-used elements of your product
- Create disproportionate value relative to implementation effort

## 3. Implement Iterative Enhancements

Rather than overhaul your entire product, make strategic improvements through:

- Additional resources for common sticking points
- Enhanced explanations where confusion exists
- Alternative approaches for various learning styles
- New examples for different use cases

## 4. Communicate Improvements

Let customers know about enhancements through:

- Update announcements highlighting new features
- Inside-product notifications about changes

- Emails highlighting specific improvements
- Celebration of customer-inspired enhancements

## 5. Measure Impact

Track whether your improvements are making a difference through:

- Completion rate changes
- Customer result improvements
- Reduction in support inquiries
- Testimonial and feedback shifts

This improvement cycle transforms your initial product into a highly refined offering while simultaneously giving you customer insights that inform future products.

# Digital Products With Purpose

As we conclude this chapter, I want to return to the greater purpose behind digital product creation—the opportunity to scale both income and impact.

Through the Nehemiah Davis Foundation, we've seen how digital product revenue can fund transformative community initiatives:

- Our after-school programs teach entrepreneurship to underserved youth
- Our scholarship programs provide educational opportunities
- Our community events create connection and support
- Our mentorship initiatives build leadership capacities

None of this would be possible without the leveraged income and time freedom created through digital products.

As you create your digital products, I encourage you to consider how your success can fuel meaningful impact beyond business growth:

1.  **Allocate Impact Percentages** Could you dedicate a percentage of each sale to causes you care about?
2.  **Create Opportunity Packages** Might you offer scholarships or reduced-cost access to those who couldn't otherwise afford your products?
3.  **Develop Community Initiatives** How could your expertise support non-profit organizations or community groups?
4.  **Build Impact Partnerships** Could you collaborate with mission-aligned organizations to create greater change?

When digital business success connects to meaningful impact, the entire entrepreneurial journey becomes more fulfilling and purpose-driven. Your products don't just create financial freedom—they create the foundation for significance beyond success.

## Chapter Summary: Key Takeaways

- The 80/20 principle helps focus on high-impact elements that deliver most of your product's value
- Digital products fall into four main categories, each with specific creation requirements
- Simple creation pathways exist for each product type, requiring minimal technical expertise

- The production mindset shift from perfectionism to completion is critical for success
- Rapid content creation techniques help extract and organize your knowledge efficiently
- AI tools can accelerate creation when used to enhance rather than replace your expertise
- Production quality should focus on clarity and results rather than unnecessary polish
- Basic equipment is sufficient for creating high-value digital products
- User-friendly platforms simplify the technical aspects of hosting and delivering products
- A structured launch timeline helps bring your product to market efficiently
- The post-launch improvement cycle transforms your initial product through customer feedback
- Digital product success creates opportunities for meaningful impact beyond business

## Action Steps:

1. Select the appropriate product type for your validated idea
2. Create a detailed content outline for your digital product
3. Choose one rapid content creation technique to begin development
4. Set up your minimum viable technical infrastructure
5. Establish a specific creation schedule with completion dates
6. Implement the 80/20 rule by identifying your product's core value elements

7. Determine how your digital product success will fund meaningful impact

8. Schedule your product launch date and work backward to create milestones

If you're passionate about **impact, purpose, and real results,** we want to hear from you. **Partner with Neo**. Visit PartnerWithNeo.com/apply to explore how we can collaborate.

# CHAPTER 8

# THE SEVEN-FIGURE FUNNEL FRAMEWORK

**"I** 've created my digital product, but nobody's buying it."

This is perhaps the most heartbreaking statement I hear from entrepreneurs. They've poured their expertise and effort into creating something valuable, only to launch it into a void of silence and minimal sales.

The painful truth is that creating an excellent digital product is only half the battle. The other half—often the more challenging half—is getting that product in front of the right people and convincing them to buy.

In previous chapters, we've covered the mindset foundations for success, identified your digital product, and walked through the creation process. Now we'll focus on the system that transforms your digital product from a hidden gem into a thriving business asset: the Seven-Figure Funnel Framework.

# Why Traditional Marketing Fails for Digital Products

Before we dive into the framework, let's address why traditional marketing approaches often fail with digital products:

## The Invisible Value Problem

Unlike physical products that customers can see, touch, and immediately understand, digital products sell invisible transformations. Their value isn't immediately apparent, making traditional "feature-focused" marketing ineffective.

## The Trust Barrier

Purchasing digital products requires significant trust. Customers must believe that invisible digital assets will deliver real-world results, creating a psychological barrier that traditional marketing rarely addresses.

## The Implementation Anxiety

Many potential customers worry they won't implement what they learn or that the product won't work for their specific situation. This creates resistance that feature-focused marketing doesn't overcome.

## The Information Overwhelm

In a world saturated with free content, potential customers often wonder why they should pay for information. Traditional marketing fails to adequately differentiate paid products from free alternatives.

The Seven-Figure Funnel Framework addresses these challenges directly, creating a systematic path that transforms strangers into enthusiastic customers.

# The Death of Websites and Birth of Funnels

Let me make a bold statement: For digital product businesses, traditional websites are largely obsolete.

This might sound extreme, but consider the typical website experience:

- Visitors arrive and see multiple navigation options
- They browse various pages with no clear direction
- They might read some content, get distracted, and leave
- No relationship is established, and no meaningful data is captured
- The visitor disappears, likely forever

This scattered approach might work for informational purposes but fails miserably for selling digital products. The alternative? Sales funnels.

A sales funnel is a strategic path that guides potential customers through a carefully designed experience—from their first interaction with your brand through the purchase decision and beyond.

Unlike websites, funnels:

- Have a single, clear objective for each page
- Capture visitor information early in the process
- Build relationship and trust systematically
- Address objections in a strategic sequence
- Guide visitors toward a specific conversion action

The difference in results is staggering. When I shifted from a traditional website to my first sales funnel, my conversion rate increased by 342%, and my average order value nearly doubled.

# The Seven-Figure Funnel Framework Overview

The Seven-Figure Funnel Framework is a comprehensive system I've developed and refined through years of testing across hundreds of digital products. It consists of seven interconnected elements that, when properly implemented, create a predictable flow of customers and revenue.

Here are the seven elements:

1. **Lead Generation Magnet**
2. **Value-Building Sequence**
3. **Core Offer Presentation**
4. **Objection Elimination System**

5. **Conversion Accelerators**
6. **Purchase Maximizers**
7. **Retention & Ascension Path**

Each element serves a specific purpose in transforming strangers into customers and customers into advocates. Let's explore each one in detail.

# 1. Lead Generation Magnet

The foundation of any successful funnel is an irresistible lead generation magnet—a free resource that solves a specific problem for your ideal customer in exchange for their contact information.

An effective lead magnet must be:

## Specific Rather Than Comprehensive

Focus on solving one clearly defined problem rather than offering general information. "The 5-Step Framework for Writing Emails That Sell" is more effective than "The Ultimate Guide to Email Marketing."

## Quick to Consume and Implement

Your lead magnet should deliver value in 5-15 minutes, not hours or days. The faster someone can experience a "win," the more likely they'll engage with your paid offerings.

## Directly Related to Your Paid Products

The lead magnet should demonstrate your approach to solving problems while naturally leading toward your paid solution. It should create an "aha moment" that makes your paid offer the logical next step.

## Genuinely Valuable on Its Own

The lead magnet must deliver real value, not just tease information that's only available in your paid products. It should stand alone as something people would happily pay for.

Some highly effective lead magnet formats include:

- **Frameworks or Checklists**: Structured approaches to solving specific problems
- **Templates or Swipe Files**: Ready-to-use resources that save time and effort
- **Assessments or Calculators**: Interactive tools that provide personalized insights
- **Video Trainings**: Concise lessons that deliver immediate value
- **Resource Compilations**: Carefully curated collections of valuable tools or information

My most successful lead magnet has been my "Instagram Profit Calculator," which helps entrepreneurs estimate how much revenue they could generate from their Instagram following. This simple tool has attracted over 50,000 leads and generated millions in downstream sales because it:

1. Addresses a specific curiosity (revenue potential)
2. Delivers immediate value (personalized calculation)

3. Naturally leads to my paid offerings (Instagram monetization strategies)
4. Provides genuine insight on its own

When designing your lead magnet, ask yourself: "What small win can I help my potential customers achieve that will create momentum toward the bigger transformation my paid product delivers?"

# 2. Value-Building Sequence

Once someone has downloaded your lead magnet, they enter the value-building sequence—a strategic series of communications that establish your authority, build relationship, provide additional value, and prepare them for your offer.

This sequence typically includes:

## Immediate Delivery Communication

The first message delivers your lead magnet and sets expectations for what's coming next. This is your first impression, so make it exceptional by:

- Delivering the promised resource immediately
- Providing clear instructions for implementation
- Setting expectations for future communications
- Including a personal touch that builds connection

## Authority-Establishing Content

The next 2-3 communications demonstrate your expertise and unique approach through valuable content such as:

- Case studies showcasing client results
- Behind-the-scenes insights into your methodology
- Myth-busting content that challenges conventional wisdom
- Transformative frameworks that organize complex topics

## Problem-Deepening Messages

These communications help potential customers fully understand the cost of not solving their problem and the value of finding the right solution. Effective approaches include:

- Future-pacing consequences of inaction
- Sharing stories of others who faced similar challenges
- Highlighting hidden obstacles they may not have considered
- Quantifying the true cost of the problem over time

## Solution-Revealing Communications

The final messages in your sequence begin introducing your approach to solving the problem while creating anticipation for your full solution. These might include:

- Partial frameworks that demonstrate your approach
- "One thing" messages that share a single powerful strategy
- Short trainings that create "aha moments"

- Success stories that build belief in possibility

This value-building sequence serves multiple crucial purposes:

1. It conditions potential customers to open and engage with your communications
2. It establishes your credibility through demonstrated expertise, not just claims
3. It builds genuine relationship through consistent value delivery
4. It creates anticipation for your offer before you make it

My standard value-building sequence includes seven messages delivered over 10-14 days. This timeline allows sufficient engagement without losing momentum. Each message is designed to move potential customers closer to the realization that my paid solution is the logical next step in their journey.

# 3. Core Offer Presentation

After building value and relationship, it's time to present your core offer—your primary digital product. This presentation must address the unique challenges of selling digital products we discussed earlier.

Effective core offer presentations include these key elements:

## The Transformation Story

Begin by telling the story of the transformation your product creates—not just what it contains, but how it changes your customers' lives. This narrative helps potential customers envision themselves experiencing similar results.

My Digital Business Accelerator presentation starts with the story of Carlos, who went from working 70-hour weeks in his service business to generating $267,000 in his first year with digital products. This narrative immediately helps potential customers see what's possible.

## The Unique Methodology

Clearly articulate your distinct approach to solving the problem. Name your methodology and explain why it works differently (and better) than other approaches.

In my presentation, I outline my "Profit Amplification Process"—a specific five-step methodology for creating and scaling digital products. Naming and explaining this process differentiates my approach from generic advice.

## The Implementation Pathway

Show potential customers exactly how they'll implement your solution. Break down the process into clear stages or modules that feel achievable rather than overwhelming.

I present my course structure as a 60-day implementation journey with specific outcomes for each phase, making the path to results concrete and manageable.

## Evidence and Validation

Provide substantial proof that your approach works through case studies, testimonials, screenshots, and specific results. The more varied and concrete your evidence, the more persuasive your presentation.

My presentations include diverse forms of evidence:

- Video testimonials from students
- Before-and-after screenshots of results
- Specific metrics and outcomes
- Transformation stories across different industries

## Objection Anticipation

Directly address the common concerns and objections your potential customers have. By raising and resolving these objections proactively, you build trust and remove purchase barriers.

I explicitly address objections like "I don't have time," "I'm not tech-savvy," and "I don't have an audience yet" by showing how my program accounts for these challenges.

## Clear Call to Action

End with a crystal-clear next step that makes the purchase decision simple and low-risk. This might be enrolling directly, scheduling a call, or taking advantage of a limited-time offer.

My presentations always end with a specific, time-sensitive invitation with clear benefits for immediate action.

Your core offer presentation can take many formats, including:

- Webinars or virtual workshops
- Video sales letters
- Text-based sales pages
- Automated presentation sequences
- Live challenge events

The format matters less than ensuring all key elements are present and aligned with your audience's preferences. My most successful presentations combine multiple formats, providing options for different learning and buying styles.

# 4. Objection Elimination System

Even the most compelling offer presentation won't convert all potential customers immediately. Many will hesitate due to specific concerns or objections. The objection elimination system addresses these barriers systematically.

First, identify the most common objections to purchasing your product. These typically fall into four categories:

## Value Objections

"Is this worth the investment?" "Will I get results that justify the cost?" "Could I find this information for free elsewhere?"

## Implementation Objections

"Do I have time to use this?" "Is it too complicated for someone like me?" "Will I actually follow through?"

## Timing Objections

"Is this the right time for me?" "Should I wait until X happens first?" "Can I put this off until later?"

## Trust Objections

"Is this person credible?" "Have others like me succeeded with this?" "What if it doesn't work for my specific situation?"

Once you've identified specific objections, create targeted content that addresses each one:

## Objection-Specific Case Studies

Share stories of past customers who had the same objection but moved forward and achieved success. For example, for the time objection, feature someone with a busy schedule who implemented your program successfully.

## Objection-Focused FAQs

Create detailed FAQ resources that specifically address common concerns with honest, thorough responses. These can be written, audio, or video format.

## Perspective-Shifting Content

Develop content that reframes objections by changing how potential customers think about the issue. For example, shifting from "Do I have time for this?" to "Can I afford not to make time for this?"

## Guarantee Structures

Create risk-reversal guarantees that directly address major objections. For instance, an implementation guarantee that promises support until the customer achieves specific results.

My objection elimination system includes:

- A decision-making framework that helps potential customers evaluate the true cost of inaction
- "Day in the life" content showing how busy people implement the program
- Technology walkthrough videos for those concerned about technical requirements
- Comparison guides that contrast my approach with alternatives
- A comprehensive money-back guarantee that eliminates financial risk

This system doesn't just overcome objections—it builds deeper trust and demonstrates that you truly understand your customers' concerns.

# 5. Conversion Accelerators

Conversion accelerators are strategic elements that create urgency and incentive to purchase now rather than "someday." Without these elements, even interested prospects often delay decisions indefinitely.

Effective and ethical conversion accelerators include:

## Genuine Scarcity

Legitimate limitations on availability create urgency to act. Examples include:

- Limited enrollment periods for cohort-based programs
- Capacity constraints for programs with personal support

- First-access opportunities for new products

I open enrollment for my Digital Business Accelerator only three times yearly, creating natural enrollment windows that drive decision-making.

## Time-Based Incentives

Special bonuses or pricing available for a limited time reward prompt action. These might include:

- Early-bird pricing for first enrollees
- Fast-action bonuses for 24-48 hour decisions
- Deadline-based incentives for enrollment periods

My launches typically include three time-sensitive bonuses that decrease in value as the enrollment period progresses.

## Social Momentum

Evidence of others taking action creates powerful social proof that accelerates decisions. This includes:

- Live enrollment counters
- "Who's in" announcements
- Community formation activities
- Public commitment opportunities

During launches, I share daily enrollment updates and stories of new members, creating momentum that drives additional sales.

## Decision-Simplifying Offers

Special offers that make the decision easier and more attractive, such as:

- Payment plans that reduce initial investment
- Bundle offers that increase perceived value
- Implementation support that addresses major concerns
- Bonus resources that enhance the core offering

My standard offer includes both full-pay and payment plan options, plus implementation support that specifically addresses concerns about follow-through.

The key to ethical conversion acceleration is ensuring that these elements are genuine, not artificial. Manufactured scarcity or false urgency damages trust, while authentic limits and incentives respect the customer's intelligence while encouraging timely decisions.

# 6. Purchase Maximizers

Once someone decides to purchase, purchase maximizers increase the value of each transaction through strategic offering of complementary products or enhanced versions of your core offer.

The most effective purchase maximizers include:

## Order Bumps

These are one-click additions offered during the checkout process that enhance the core purchase. Effective order bumps:

- Are low-priced ($27-97 typically)
- Directly enhance the main purchase
- Solve an immediate related problem
- Are easy to understand quickly

My standard order bump is a $47 "Implementation Accelerator" that helps customers get faster results from my main program. This simple addition increases average order value by 22%.

## One-Time Offers (OTOs)

These are special offers presented immediately after purchase that complement the initial product. Effective OTOs:

- Enhance but aren't required for the core product
- Solve the "next problem" customers will face
- Offer exceptional value compared to regular pricing
- Include fast-action incentives

After purchasing my Digital Business Accelerator, customers see a one-time offer for my "Traffic Amplifier" program at 50% off the regular price. This OTO has a 31% conversion rate and significantly increases customer lifetime value.

## Bundle Upgrades

These offer enhanced versions of the core product with valuable additions. Effective bundles:

- Include highly desirable bonuses that enhance results
- Offer clear value comparison to the standard option
- Often include implementation support or customization
- Present a compelling "value ratio" (e.g., "Get 3x the value for just 30% more")

My "implementation package" upgrade adds group coaching and personalized feedback to the standard course, doubling the average transaction value for those who select it.

## Fast-Start Options

These provide accelerated implementation through additional support. Effective fast-start options:

- Address the primary fear of slow implementation
- Include personalized elements like coaching or feedback
- Create accountability for early action
- Demonstrate special attention for serious customers

My "VIP Implementation" package includes a private onboarding call and two accountability check-ins, converting at 18% and adding significant revenue to each launch.

Purchase maximizers not only increase immediate revenue but often improve customer results by providing additional resources and support.

When thoughtfully designed, they create a win-win: more value for customers and more revenue for your business.

# 7. Retention & Ascension Path

The final element of the Seven-Figure Funnel Framework focuses on keeping customers engaged while providing opportunities for deeper investment in additional solutions.

Effective retention and ascension paths include:

## Onboarding Excellence

The customer journey immediately after purchase sets the tone for their entire experience. Effective onboarding:

- Welcomes customers and reinforces their decision
- Provides clear first steps for implementation
- Establishes usage patterns and expectations
- Identifies potential early obstacles and addresses them

My onboarding sequence includes a welcome video, a "start here" guide, and an implementation checklist that gets customers taking action within 24 hours of purchase.

## Success Milestones

Structured celebrations of progress keep customers engaged and building momentum. Effective milestone systems:

- Recognize small wins early in the process
- Provide clear indicators of progress
- Celebrate completion of key implementation steps
- Share customer achievements with the community

My programs include specific "win acknowledgments" at each module completion, from digital badges to community recognition, maintaining motivation throughout the implementation process.

## Community Integration

Connecting customers with peers creates accountability and increases product usage. Effective community integration:

- Introduces new members to the existing community
- Facilitates relationship-building between customers
- Creates engagement through community activities
- Provides peer support for implementation challenges

The private community for my Digital Business Accelerator includes weekly engagement activities, implementation partners, and showcase opportunities that significantly increase completion rates.

## Ascension Opportunities

Thoughtfully timed invitations to advanced or complementary offerings continue the customer journey. Effective ascension paths:

- Present logical next steps based on customer progress
- Offer solutions to new challenges that emerge after initial success
- Provide opportunities for deeper implementation or results
- Create exclusive options for your most engaged customers

My ascension path includes three distinct next steps based on customer goals and implementation success, from specialized implementation programs to my high-level mastermind.

The retention and ascension path transforms one-time transactions into ongoing relationships, increasing customer lifetime value while improving overall results and satisfaction.

# Implementing the Seven-Figure Funnel Framework

Now that you understand the seven elements, let's discuss implementation strategy for entrepreneurs at different stages:

## For Beginners (Under $10K Monthly Revenue)

If you're just starting your digital product business, focus on implementing these elements first:

1. **Create one high-converting lead magnet** that addresses a specific problem related to your core offer.
2. **Develop a simple 5-7 message value-building sequence** that establishes your expertise and relationship.
3. **Build a straightforward core offer presentation** focusing on transformation, methodology, and evidence.
4. **Implement one basic conversion accelerator** such as limited-time bonuses during launches.

This simplified approach allows you to start generating revenue while learning what resonates with your audience before adding more complex elements.

# For Growing Businesses ($10K-$50K Monthly Revenue)

As your business grows, expand your implementation to include:

1. **Develop 2-3 targeted lead magnets** for different segments of your audience.
2. **Create segment-specific value-building sequences** that address different entry points and pain points.
3. **Implement a comprehensive objection elimination system** based on actual customer feedback.
4. **Add 1-2 purchase maximizers** to increase average transaction value.
5. **Develop basic retention systems** focusing on onboarding and early success milestones.

This intermediate approach significantly increases conversion rates and customer value while still remaining manageable for small teams.

# For Scaling Businesses ($50K+ Monthly Revenue)

At the scaling stage, implement the full framework with sophistication:

1. **Develop a complete ecosystem of lead magnets** addressing various customer segments and entry points.
2. **Create advanced segmentation and personalization** in your value-building sequences.
3. **Implement multiple presentation formats** for different learning preferences.

4. **Develop a comprehensive suite of purchase maximizers** with sophisticated targeting.

5. **Build advanced retention and ascension systems** with multiple pathways based on customer behavior and goals.

This advanced implementation creates a highly efficient customer acquisition and development system that typically achieves 3-5x the revenue per visitor of simpler approaches.

# Funnel Technology Simplified

Many entrepreneurs get overwhelmed by the technical aspects of implementing sales funnels. Here's a simplified approach that works at any stage:

## Essential Tools for Beginners

1. **Landing Page Builder**: Platforms like ClickFunnels, Leadpages, or even Wix/Squarespace with funnel templates

2. **Email Service Provider**: Services like ConvertKit, ActiveCampaign, or Mailchimp

3. **Payment Processor**: Stripe, PayPal, or similar service

4. **Digital Product Delivery**: Teachable, Kajabi, or simple delivery through your email service provider

With just these four tools, you can implement the core elements of the Seven-Figure Funnel Framework without complex technical knowledge.

## Intermediate Tech Stack

As you grow, consider adding:

1. **Customer Relationship Management (CRM)**: For better tracking of customer interactions
2. **Webinar/Workshop Platform**: For live presentations and engagement
3. **Cart Abandonment Tools**: To recover potential lost sales
4. **Analytics Systems**: For more detailed funnel performance tracking

## Advanced Technology Considerations

At scale, explore:

1. **Marketing Automation Platforms**: For sophisticated segmentation and sequencing
2. **Custom Development**: For unique funnel elements specific to your business
3. **Split Testing Tools**: For continuous optimization of all funnel elements
4. **Integrated Customer Data Platforms**: For unified customer insights across touchpoints

Remember, technology should serve your strategy, not dictate it. Many entrepreneurs get distracted by complex tools before mastering the fundamentals of effective funnel strategy.

# Measuring Funnel Performance

To optimize your Seven-Figure Funnel Framework, track these key metrics for each element:

## Lead Generation Magnet

- Opt-in conversion rate (visitors to subscribers)
- Cost per lead (if using paid traffic)
- Lead quality score (engagement with follow-up content)

## Value-Building Sequence

- Open rates for each message
- Click-through rates on content links
- Engagement trends over the sequence length

## Core Offer Presentation

- Show-up rate (for live presentations)
- Engagement duration (how long people stay engaged)
- Conversion rate from presentation to sale

## Objection Elimination System

- Engagement with objection content
- Conversion rate after objection content consumption
- Most common remaining objections (from customer feedback)

## Conversion Accelerators

- Timing patterns of purchases during offer periods
- Conversion rates for different incentives
- Impact of social proof elements on conversion timing

## Purchase Maximizers

- Take-rate for each maximizer offered
- Average order value increase from maximizers
- Completion and satisfaction rates for maximizer elements

## Retention & Ascension Path

- Product consumption/completion rates
- Time to first ascension purchase
- Customer lifetime value progression

Start with the metrics most relevant to your current focus area rather than trying to track everything at once. As your funnel sophistication increases, your measurement approach can evolve accordingly.

# The Funnel and Foundation Connection

As we conclude this chapter, I want to emphasize how the Seven-Figure Funnel Framework connects to the greater purpose of creating impact beyond business success.

Effective funnels don't just generate more profit—they create better-served customers and expanded impact potential:

## Better-Qualified Customers

By thoroughly educating prospects before purchase, funnels create a customer base that's better prepared to implement and succeed with your offerings.

## More Valuable Transactions

Purchase maximizers don't just increase revenue—they provide customers with resources that enhance their results and experience.

## Greater Implementation Support

Retention elements improve customer completion and success rates, creating more transformational outcomes and testimonials.

## Expanded Impact Reach

The scalability of well-designed funnels allows you to serve many more people than traditional marketing approaches.

Through the Nehemiah Davis Foundation, we've seen how funnel-generated revenue can fund significant community initiatives. Our after-school programs, scholarship opportunities, and community events are all possible because of the leveraged business model that effective funnels create.

As you implement your own Seven-Figure Funnel Framework, consider:

- How might increased revenue allow you to serve those who can't afford your offerings?
- What community initiatives could your business success make possible?
- How could more efficient customer acquisition free your time for impact projects?
- What causes could benefit from a percentage of your growing revenue?

When business systems like the Seven-Figure Funnel Framework connect to purpose beyond profit, entrepreneurship becomes a powerful vehicle for meaningful change.

# Chapter Summary: Key Takeaways

- Traditional marketing approaches often fail for digital products due to unique challenges
- The Seven-Figure Funnel Framework provides a systematic approach to overcome these challenges
- Lead Generation Magnets attract ideal prospects by solving specific problems
- Value-Building Sequences establish authority and relationship before presenting offers
- Core Offer Presentations must focus on transformation, methodology, and evidence
- Objection Elimination Systems address specific concerns systematically

- Conversion Accelerators create ethical urgency for timely decisions
- Purchase Maximizers increase transaction value while enhancing customer experience
- Retention & Ascension Paths transform transactions into ongoing customer relationships
- Implementation should be staged based on business maturity and resources
- Basic technology is sufficient to begin implementing effective funnels
- Key metrics for each funnel element help optimize performance over time
- Effective funnels create both business success and expanded impact potential

# Action Steps:

1. Assess your current marketing approach against the Seven-Figure Funnel Framework
2. Identify which elements are missing or underperforming in your current system
3. Choose one element to implement or improve in the next 30 days
4. Set up basic tracking for key metrics related to your focus element
5. Create a 90-day implementation plan for the most critical funnel elements
6. Determine how increased revenue from your funnel could fund meaningful impact

7. Schedule weekly funnel optimization sessions to continually improve results
8. Consider what percentage of funnel revenue could support causes you care about

If you're passionate about **impact, purpose, and real results,** we want to hear from you. **Partner with Neo**. Visit PartnerWithNeo.com/apply to explore how we can collaborate.

# CHAPTER 9

# CONTENT THAT CONVERTS

**"I**'ve been creating content for months, but it's not leading to sales."

This frustration echoes across countless conversations I've had with entrepreneurs who diligently post on social media, write blog articles, and create videos without seeing meaningful business results.

The painful truth is that not all content is created equal. Many entrepreneurs exhaust themselves creating content that may attract likes and comments but fails to convert followers into customers. They confuse content that entertains with content that converts.

In previous chapters, we've covered creating digital products and building effective sales funnels. Now we'll focus on the critical bridge between audience building and sales: content that actually converts attention into revenue.

# The Content Disconnect

Before diving into specific strategies, let's understand why most content marketing efforts fail to generate sales:

## The Entertainment Trap

Many creators optimize for engagement metrics (likes, comments, shares) rather than conversion metrics (leads, sales, customers). While entertaining content may build an audience, it often attracts people interested in free value rather than paid solutions.

## The Missing Strategy

Random content creation without a clear conversion path leads nowhere. Each piece needs strategic intent—knowing exactly what action you want the consumer to take and how it advances them toward a purchase.

## The Authority Disconnect

Generic content that simply regurgitates common knowledge fails to position you as the go-to expert worth investing in. Without demonstrating unique expertise, your paid offerings won't seem necessary.

## The Value Confusion

When your free content tries to solve complete problems, potential customers don't understand why they should pay for your solutions. Strategic content illuminates problems and partial solutions while positioning your paid offerings as the complete answer.

The solution to these challenges isn't creating more content—it's creating strategic content with clear conversion intent. This is what I call Content That Converts.

# The Category King Strategy

One of the most powerful approaches to creating content that converts is becoming what I call a "Category King"—the recognized authority in a specific area of expertise.

Being a Category King means:

- You're the first person people think of for a specific topic
- Your approach or framework is distinctly recognizable
- You're known for concrete results in your area
- Other experts reference your work or approach

Becoming a Category King drives conversions because:

1. It eliminates comparison shopping (you're viewed as unique)
2. It justifies premium pricing (category leaders command higher rates)
3. It creates demand rather than just capturing it

4. It attracts the right prospects already aligned with your approach

Here's how to implement the Category King strategy:

# 1. Define Your Category

Identify a specific problem, approach, or outcome you can own. The narrower, the better. Instead of "business coach," you might be "the financial freedom coach for service-based entrepreneurs" or "the client attraction specialist for introverted consultants."

To define your category effectively:

- Identify what unique perspective or methodology you bring
- Determine which segment of your market is most underserved
- Consider your personal story or journey that creates authenticity
- Analyze where your results have been most impressive

My own category is clearly defined: I'm known specifically for helping service entrepreneurs transform their expertise into digital products and build wealth through online business models. This specificity makes my content immediately relevant to my ideal audience while being distinctly associated with me.

# 2. Create Your Signature Framework

Develop a unique framework or system that organizes your approach. This gives your audience a mental model to understand your methodology and differentiates you from generic advice.

Effective signature frameworks:

- Have a memorable name (ideally something you can trademark)
- Use a specific number of steps or elements (3, 5, 7, etc.)
- Create their own vocabulary or terminology
- Organize complex topics into understandable structures

My Seven-Figure Funnel Framework, which we explored in the previous chapter, serves this purpose. When people see content about this framework, they immediately associate it with me, even if my name isn't attached.

## 3. Document Concrete Results

Systematically collect and share specific, detailed results that your approach creates. This means going beyond generic testimonials to showcase measurable outcomes.

Effective result documentation includes:

- Before and after metrics (revenue, time saved, specific improvements)
- Process photos or videos showing transformation
- Detailed case studies with multiple data points
- Third-party verification when possible

My content regularly features specific client results with actual numbers: "Carlos increased his monthly revenue from $12,000 to $47,000 in 94 days using the Digital Product Accelerator system" rather than vague statements like "Carlos grew his business significantly."

## 4. Teach One Core Concept Consistently

Instead of covering random topics, focus relentlessly on teaching and reinforcing your core concept across all content. This repetition builds recognition and ownership of your category.

This doesn't mean creating repetitive content. Rather, you're approaching your core concept from different angles, diving deeper over time, and applying it to different situations—but always reinforcing your primary message.

My content consistently returns to the concept of transforming expertise into leveraged digital income, whether I'm discussing mindset, tactical implementation, or case studies. This repetition has made this concept synonymous with my brand.

## 5. Create Volume in Your Category

To truly own a category, you need to dominate the conversation with high-volume, high-quality content on your topic. This is where most entrepreneurs fall short—they don't create enough content to achieve "top of mind" status.

My recommendation: Create 50+ pieces of content focused on your category as quickly as possible. This might include:

- Social media posts
- Short-form videos
- Articles or blog posts
- Podcast episodes

- Email newsletters
- Live streams

When I committed to owning my category, I created 63 pieces of content in 45 days, all focused on digital product creation and online business models. This volume established me as the go-to voice in this space and dramatically increased my conversion rates.

# The Content Conversion Framework

Beyond the Category King strategy, specific content formats and approaches directly drive conversion. Here's my four-part Content Conversion Framework that transforms passive consumers into active customers:

## 1. Problem Illumination Content

This content helps your audience recognize and understand problems they may be experiencing but haven't fully acknowledged or understood. It creates awareness and urgency without immediately pushing solutions.

Effective formats include:

- Diagnostic quizzes or assessments
- "Signs you might be..." lists
- Cost calculation tools or articles
- Day-in-the-life scenarios showing pain points
- Myth-busting content that reveals hidden problems

Example: My "7 Signs Your Service Business Has Hit a Ceiling" post helps entrepreneurs recognize growth limitations they might be dismissing or normalizing. This recognition creates receptivity to my digital product solutions that remove these limitations.

## 2. Methodology Revelation Content

This content provides glimpses into your approach without giving away the complete system. It demonstrates your unique expertise and methodology while creating desire for the full solution.

Effective formats include:

- Framework overviews (without implementation details)
- Case study breakdowns showing your approach in action
- Before/after transformations with methodology highlights
- Process comparisons (conventional approach vs. your approach)
- "One thing" content that shares a single powerful technique

Example: My "Digital Product Ecosystem Overview" video explains the concept and structure of a complete digital product lineup without providing implementation details. It demonstrates my expertise while naturally leading viewers to want my comprehensive program.

## 3. Objection Elimination Content

This content proactively addresses common concerns or objections that prevent purchases. It removes mental barriers without being defensive or overly "salesy."

Effective formats include:

- Success stories of people who overcame specific obstacles
- "How to know if you're ready" content
- Resource requirement clarifications
- Mindset shift content that reframes limiting beliefs
- Expert perspective that challenges conventional wisdom

Example: My "Created My First Digital Product With No Tech Skills" interview series features successful clients who initially worried about technical limitations. These stories directly address a primary objection while building belief in possibility.

## 4. Opportunity Amplification Content

This content emphasizes the cost of inaction and the value of your solution without explicitly selling. It creates urgency by highlighting what's possible and what's at stake.

Effective formats include:

- Future-pacing content that envisions positive outcomes
- Opportunity window content that highlights timing advantages
- Contrast content that compares possible futures
- Investment perspective content (cost vs. value analysis)
- "What if" scenarios that expand possibility thinking

Example: My "Digital vs. Service Income: A Five-Year Projection" calculator helps entrepreneurs visualize the long-term impact of adding digital revenue streams compared to remaining solely in service delivery. This creates motivation to invest in my digital business programs.

When systematically created and strategically deployed, these four content types work together to move your audience from awareness to purchase without aggressive selling tactics.

# Content Repurposing Mastery

One of the most powerful efficiency strategies for creating content that converts is mastering the art of content repurposing—transforming one piece of content into multiple formats to reach different audience segments and platforms.

Here's my 1:10 repurposing system that creates ten content pieces from a single source:

## 1. Create One Core Content Piece

Start by creating one substantial piece of content that thoroughly addresses an important topic for your audience. This might be:

- A 30-60 minute video training
- A comprehensive podcast episode
- A detailed blog article or guide
- A live workshop or presentation

This core piece should be thorough enough to contain multiple valuable insights, examples, stories, and actionable advice.

## 2. Extract Short-Form Video Clips

Identify 3-5 powerful moments, insights, or explanations from your core content and extract them as standalone short-form video clips (30-90 seconds each) optimized for platforms like Instagram Reels, TikTok, or YouTube Shorts.

Each clip should:

- Make a single compelling point that stands alone
- Begin with a strong hook that stops scrollers
- End with a clear call to action
- Include captions for accessibility and sound-off viewing

## 3. Create Quote Graphics

Pull 2-3 powerful quotes or key statements from your content and transform them into visually appealing quote graphics for Instagram, Facebook, or LinkedIn.

These should:

- Feature your branding elements
- Use highly readable typography
- Include your handle or website
- Be designed for maximum shareability

## 4. Develop a Written Article

Transform the core content into a written article format that can be published on your blog, Medium, LinkedIn articles, or as a guest post on relevant sites.

For video or audio source content, this might require transcription and editing, but the result is valuable evergreen content that serves those who prefer reading to watching or listening.

## 5. Create an Email Sequence

Break your core content into a series of 2-3 emails that deliver the value in digestible segments while building relationship with your email subscribers.

This sequence can:

- Dive deeper into specific aspects of the topic
- Include additional examples not in the original content
- Feature subscriber-specific calls to action
- Invite direct responses and engagement

## 6. Design a Practical Worksheet

Create an implementation tool related to your content topic that helps people apply what they've learned, such as:

- A checklist for implementation
- A worksheet for personalized application
- A decision-making framework

- A resource compilation
- A planning template

This practical resource serves as both valuable content and a lead generation tool when offered in exchange for contact information.

## 7. Record an Audio Version

For written core content, record an audio version that serves podcast listeners or those who prefer to consume content while commuting, exercising, or completing other tasks.

This can be distributed through:

- Your podcast feed (if you have one)
- A "read aloud" feature on your blog
- Audio-specific platforms like Spotify or Apple Podcasts
- Social audio features like Twitter Spaces recordings

This repurposing strategy transforms one content creation session into multiple assets that work together to reinforce your message across platforms while respecting different content consumption preferences.

My team and I use this system weekly, creating one substantial piece of content that generates at least ten additional assets. This approach has allowed us to maintain high-volume output while actually reducing creation time by approximately 60%.

# The 30-Day Content Sprint

While consistent content creation is important for long-term success, I've found that concentrated "content sprints" are particularly effective for establishing category ownership and generating momentum.

Here's my 30-Day Content Sprint framework that rapidly produces a substantial body of conversion-focused content:

## Week 1: Foundation Development

During the first week, focus on creating cornerstone content pieces that establish your category position:

**Day 1-2:** Create your signature framework overview content

- A detailed explanation of your methodology
- Visual representations of your system
- Core principles and philosophy

**Day 3-4:** Develop three in-depth case studies

- Detailed transformation stories
- Specific implementation examples
- Concrete results and outcomes

**Day 5-7:** Produce your definitive guide

- Comprehensive overview of your approach
- Step-by-step implementation guidance
- Common challenges and solutions

These foundational pieces will provide rich material for repurposing throughout the rest of the sprint.

## Week 2: Problem-Focused Content

The second week focuses on illuminating problems and creating awareness:

**Day 8-10:** Create diagnostic content

- Assessment tools or quizzes
- "Signs you might have this problem" content
- Cost of inaction calculations

**Day 11-14:** Develop myth-busting content

- Common misconceptions in your field
- Why conventional approaches fail
- Hidden obstacles to success

This content helps your audience recognize and acknowledge problems that your offerings solve.

## Week 3: Solution Glimpses

The third week provides compelling glimpses of your solution approach:

**Day 15-17:** Share methodology elements

- Individual components of your system
- Key principles in action

- Before/after demonstrations

**Day 18-21:** Present expert perspective

- Your unique viewpoint on industry trends
- Contrarian positions with supporting evidence
- Predictions and insights

This content establishes your authority while creating desire for your complete solution.

## Week 4: Conversion Focus

The final week directly supports purchase decisions:

**Day 22-24:** Address common objections

- Success stories overcoming specific concerns
- Resource requirement clarifications
- Implementation support explanations

**Day 25-27:** Highlight opportunity windows

- Timing advantages
- First-mover benefits
- Limited availability realities

**Day 28-30:** Provide decision-making frameworks

- Investment perspectives
- Readiness assessments
- Next step clarity

This content systematically removes purchase barriers while creating motivation to act.

Throughout the 30-day sprint, each piece of content should include appropriate calls to action based on where it falls in the conversion sequence.

I use this sprint approach quarterly to inject fresh momentum into my marketing efforts while establishing deeper ownership of my category. The concentrated focus creates compound impact that sporadic content simply can't achieve.

# Content Distribution Strategy

Creating conversion-focused content is only effective if it reaches your target audience. Here's my three-tier distribution approach that ensures maximum impact:

## Tier 1: Owned Channels

These are platforms you control directly and should receive your primary focus:

**Email List** Your email subscribers represent your most valuable audience because:

- You own the communication channel
- Open rates typically exceed social media reach percentages
- You can segment and personalize messaging
- Sequential delivery allows for strategic education

I send at least two value-focused emails weekly plus specific campaign messages. Every piece of content we create is adapted for email delivery.

**Your Website/Blog** Your website serves as your content hub that you fully control:

- All significant content should live here permanently
- Optimize for search engine discovery
- Structure for easy navigation by topic
- Include clear conversion pathways from every piece

We publish 2-4 in-depth articles monthly on our website, each strategically aligned with our offers and optimized for both search and conversion.

**Your Podcast/Channel** If you maintain a podcast or dedicated channel:

- Publish on a consistent, predictable schedule
- Use episode descriptions strategically for conversion
- Create content series that build toward offers
- Include verbal calls to action within episodes

My weekly podcast specifically structures content to support our current focus areas and always includes clear next steps for listeners.

## Tier 2: Rented Land

These platforms provide audience access but operate under policies you don't control:

**Instagram/Facebook/TikTok** For social media platforms:

- Adapt content specifically for each platform's format

- Focus on native content rather than cross-posting
- Use platform-specific features (Stories, Reels, Lives)
- Always include a clear next step or call to action

We maintain active presences on Instagram and Facebook, posting 4-5 times weekly on each platform with content specifically formatted for optimal engagement.

**LinkedIn/Medium/Industry Platforms** For professional and publishing platforms:

- Share more in-depth, detailed content
- Engage in relevant conversations and comments
- Establish thought leadership positioning
- Connect discussions to your frameworks and approaches

I publish original content on LinkedIn weekly and repurpose key articles for Medium monthly, always with strategic bio links and calls to action.

**YouTube/Video Platforms** For video-centric platforms:

- Optimize titles and thumbnails for discovery
- Structure content with clear value propositions
- Use end screens and cards strategically
- Include verbal and visual calls to action

We publish two types of YouTube content: in-depth training videos biweekly and shorter tactical videos weekly, each designed to lead viewers to specific next steps.

## Tier 3: Borrowed Audiences

These opportunities leverage other people's audiences:

**Guest Podcast Appearances** When appearing on others' shows:

- Prepare platform-specific talking points
- Offer exclusive resources for listeners
- Share stories and examples not found in your content
- Focus on delivering exceptional value while naturally mentioning your offers

I aim for 2-4 guest podcast appearances monthly, each with a custom resource or offer for that specific audience.

**Guest Articles/Features** When publishing on others' platforms:

- Create original content specifically for their audience
- Include your signature frameworks when relevant
- Offer genuine value that stands alone
- Link to related resources on your platforms when appropriate

We publish 1-2 guest articles monthly on high-relevance industry sites, always with strategic bio links to specific resources.

**Partner Promotions** When collaborating with aligned partners:

- Create custom content specifically for their audience
- Offer exclusive resources or opportunities
- Respect the existing relationship with their audience
- Focus on exceptional value delivery

I participate in 3-4 strategic partner promotions annually, each with custom presentations and offers developed specifically for that opportunity.

This three-tier approach ensures your content reaches both existing audiences and new prospects while maintaining focus on the channels you control.

# Content That Builds Trust

Beyond direct conversion, your content strategy should include elements specifically designed to build deep trust. These trust-building content types create the foundation for long-term customer relationships:

## Behind-the-Scenes Content

Sharing your process, challenges, and real-world implementation builds authenticity and connection. Effective approaches include:

- Day-in-the-life content showing your actual work
- Process documentation revealing how you create results
- Challenge narratives showing how you overcome obstacles
- Team introductions humanizing your business

I regularly share our content creation process, business development challenges, and team collaboration through Instagram Stories and email segments. This transparency builds connection beyond transaction-focused content.

## Thought Leadership Content

Demonstrating advanced thinking and industry perspective establishes authority that drives premium positioning. Effective formats include:

- Industry trend analysis and predictions
- Research summaries with your expert interpretation
- Contrarian perspectives with supporting evidence
- Philosophical frameworks challenging conventional thinking

My quarterly "State of Digital Business" reports provide in-depth analysis that positions our team as forward-thinking experts rather than simply tactical implementers.

## Philosophy and Values Content

Sharing your deeper beliefs and principles attracts aligned customers while repelling poor fits. Effective approaches include:

- Origin stories explaining your motivations
- Value manifestos clarifying what you stand for
- Purpose narratives connecting business to impact
- Ethical frameworks guiding your decisions

I regularly share content about how our business supports the Nehemiah Davis Foundation and why we believe business success should create community impact. This attracts clients who share these values while repelling those solely focused on profit.

## Education-First Content

Prioritizing genuine learning over selling builds credibility and reciprocity. Effective formats include:

- Step-by-step tutorials providing complete processes
- Resource compilations offering genuine value
- Comparison guides providing objective analysis
- Fundamental concept explanations building foundations

Our monthly in-depth training workshops provide complete, actionable education without aggressive selling, building trust that ultimately drives higher conversion rates on our premium offerings.

## Long-Form Demonstration Content

Showing your expertise in action through extended content builds conviction in your capabilities. Effective approaches include:

- Live implementation sessions showing real-time problem-solving
- Extended case studies following complete transformations
- Detailed breakdowns of complex processes
- Multi-part series exploring topics with depth

My "Watch Me Build" live stream series shows real-time implementation of our methodologies, demonstrating both expertise and practical application in ways sales-focused content never could.

These trust-building content types complement direct conversion content, creating a balanced approach that both drives immediate sales and builds long-term business value through customer relationship development.

# Creating Content at Scale

As your business grows, maintaining high-quality content production requires systems and team support. Here's how to scale your content creation without sacrificing quality or authenticity:

## The Content Council Approach

Rather than trying to produce everything yourself, establish a content council composed of:

- You as the vision and strategy leader
- A content manager overseeing production
- Subject matter experts providing insights
- Production specialists handling formatting
- Distribution coordinators managing publishing

This team approach allows you to maintain strategic direction while delegating appropriate elements of execution.

## The Content Matrix System

Create a strategic content planning matrix that maps:

- Key topics aligned with your offers
- Primary content formats for each topic
- Distribution channels for each format

- Conversion goals for each piece
- Production responsibilities for team members

This system ensures all content serves strategic objectives rather than being created randomly.

## The Batch Production Method

Instead of creating content continuously, implement batch production:

- Schedule focused creation blocks (4-6 hours)
- Produce multiple pieces of similar content in one session
- Group similar production tasks for efficiency
- Process content in stages (outlining, creating, editing, formatting)

I use monthly content production days where we create 15-20 pieces of core content in a single intensive session, which are then adapted for various platforms throughout the month.

## The Content Template Library

Develop standardized templates for recurring content types:

- Social media frameworks with proven formats
- Email structures for different message types
- Video scripts with proven engagement patterns
- Article outlines for various content categories

These templates streamline creation while maintaining consistent quality and conversion effectiveness.

## The Feedback Loop Process

Implement systematic content performance review:

- Track key metrics for each content type
- Identify highest-performing formats and topics
- Analyze conversion patterns across channels
- Refine future content based on data insights

We conduct a monthly content performance review that directly informs the next month's content strategy, continuously improving conversion effectiveness.

These scaling systems have enabled us to increase our content production by 300% while reducing my personal time investment by 70%, all while maintaining consistent brand voice and strategic alignment.

# Content and Community Impact

As we conclude this chapter, I want to emphasize how content that converts can simultaneously serve business growth and community impact.

Through the Nehemiah Davis Foundation, we've seen how strategic content can:

1. **Raise Awareness for Important Causes** Content that highlights community needs and opportunities creates visibility for issues that might otherwise remain in the shadows.
2. **Educate About Impact Opportunities** Beyond selling products, content can educate audiences about ways to contribute to meaningful change through their purchasing decisions.

3. **Showcase Transformation Stories** Sharing stories of community impact inspires others to consider how their own success might create positive change.
4. **Build Community Support Networks** Content can connect like-minded individuals committed to both business success and social responsibility.

When developing your content strategy, consider how it might serve dual purposes:

- How could your expertise benefit underserved communities?
- What content could you create that serves both business and social goals?
- How might you feature impact stories alongside business transformation narratives?
- What educational resources could you provide for those unable to afford your paid offerings?

My own content increasingly integrates business strategy with impact opportunities. For example, our case study content often highlights how client success has enabled them to give back to their communities. This approach attracts customers aligned with our values while amplifying our impact message.

## Chapter Summary: Key Takeaways

- Not all content is created equal—strategic content that converts differs fundamentally from general content marketing

- The Category King strategy establishes your authority in a specific niche through framework development and results documentation
- The Content Conversion Framework uses four content types to systematically move audiences from awareness to purchase
- Content repurposing transforms one core piece into multiple assets across formats and platforms
- The 30-Day Content Sprint rapidly establishes category ownership through concentrated creation efforts
- A three-tier distribution strategy ensures content reaches both existing audiences and new prospects
- Trust-building content complements conversion content to create sustainable business relationships
- Scaling systems enable consistent content production without overwhelming your personal capacity
- Strategic content can simultaneously drive business growth and community impact

## Action Steps:

1. Define your specific category using the guidelines provided
2. Create your signature framework that organizes your approach
3. Implement the 1:10 content repurposing system with your next piece of content
4. Plan a 30-day content sprint focused on your primary offering
5. Audit your current distribution strategy and strengthen underutilized channels
6. Develop three pieces of trust-building content in formats you haven't used before

7. Identify one scaling system to implement in the next 30 days
8. Consider how your content strategy could incorporate community impact elements

If you're passionate about **impact, purpose, and real results,** we want to hear from you. **Partner with Neo**. Visit PartnerWithNeo.com/apply to explore how we can collaborate.

# CHAPTER 10

# SOCIAL MEDIA MASTERY

**"I**'ve been posting on social media every day for months but I'm not seeing any real business results."

This frustration is all too common among entrepreneurs who diligently create social media content without a strategic approach. They measure success by likes and followers rather than leads and sales, mistaking visibility for profitability.

The hard truth is that most entrepreneurs are using social media incorrectly. They treat these powerful platforms as digital billboards or personal diaries rather than sophisticated business development tools. The result is exhausting effort with minimal return.

In previous chapters, we've covered creating digital products, building effective sales funnels, and developing strategic content. Now we'll focus on transforming social media from a time-consuming distraction into a predictable business growth engine.

# The Social Media Success Triangle

Before diving into platform-specific strategies, let's understand the foundational framework that drives social media success regardless of which platforms you use. I call this the Social Media Success Triangle:

## 1. Strategic Positioning

The foundation of social media success isn't posting frequency but clear strategic positioning. This means:

- **Defining your social media persona**: The specific role you play for your audience (guide, catalyst, mentor, provocateur, etc.)
- **Establishing your content pillars**: 3-5 core topics that align with your expertise and offerings
- **Developing your unique voice**: The distinct communication style that makes your content recognizable
- **Creating your visual identity**: Consistent visual elements that reinforce your brand

Social media success begins with these strategic decisions, not tactics. Without clear positioning, even the most sophisticated posting strategies will fail to drive business results.

I spent my first two years on social media posting randomly without clear positioning. Despite daily consistency, my results were mediocre at best. When I finally defined my position as "the digital product specialist for service entrepreneurs" and established content pillars around mindset, methodology, and monetization, my conversion rates increased dramatically—even though my posting frequency actually decreased.

## 2. Engagement Engineering

The second element of the triangle is deliberately engineering engagement rather than hoping for it randomly. This means:

- **Creating content specifically designed to generate responses**
- **Strategically engaging with your ideal customers' content**
- **Building relationships through meaningful conversation**
- **Facilitating connections between community members**

Most entrepreneurs post and hope for engagement. Successful social media marketers engineer it deliberately through content formats and engagement practices specifically designed to create interaction.

When I implemented systematic engagement strategies, including my "Three Response Rule" (creating posts that require at least three back-and-forth exchanges), my content reach increased by 278% within 30 days, and—more importantly—my direct message conversations with potential customers increased five-fold.

## 3. Conversion Architecture

The final element of the triangle is creating clear pathways from social media engagement to business results. This includes:

- **Establishing clear calls to action in your content**
- **Developing direct message conversion systems**

- **Creating content-to-offer alignment**
- **Building retargeting systems for engaged audiences**

This is where most social media efforts fail. Without intentional conversion architecture, even highly engaged audiences rarely translate to revenue.

When I implemented my Direct Message Conversion System (which we'll explore later in this chapter), my conversion rate from social media engagement to sales calls increased from 3% to 21%—a 7x improvement with no increase in posting frequency.

The Social Media Success Triangle provides the foundation for everything else in this chapter. Without all three elements working together, social media becomes either a vanity project or an exhausting obligation rather than a powerful business development channel.

## Platform Selection Strategy

One of the most common social media mistakes is trying to maintain a presence on too many platforms simultaneously. This approach inevitably leads to mediocre results across all platforms rather than excellence on the ones most aligned with your business.

Here's a strategic approach to platform selection:

# 1. The Primary Platform Approach

Instead of diluting your efforts across multiple platforms, identify ONE primary platform where you'll focus 70-80% of your social media resources. This should be:

- Where your ideal customers naturally congregate
- Aligned with your content creation strengths
- Suitable for your industry and offerings
- A platform you personally enjoy using

For my business, Instagram became my primary platform because:

- My target audience (service entrepreneurs aged 25-45) actively uses it
- My teaching style works well in both feed posts and Stories formats
- The visual nature complements my framework-based teaching approach
- I personally enjoy the creative aspects of the platform

Selecting Instagram as my primary platform and dedicating 70% of my social media resources there allowed me to develop true platform mastery rather than platform mediocrity.

## 2. The Omnichannel Myth

Many "experts" advocate maintaining active presences across all major platforms. For most entrepreneurs, this advice is counterproductive. Here's why:

- Each platform has its own culture, content preferences, and algorithmic patterns
- Mastering a platform requires focused attention and experimentation
- Cross-posting the same content performs poorly due to platform-specific optimization requirements
- Your time and creative energy are limited resources

Unless you have a dedicated social media team, the omnichannel approach typically results in poor performance everywhere rather than excellence anywhere.

I initially tried maintaining active presences on Instagram, Facebook, LinkedIn, YouTube, and Twitter simultaneously. The result was mediocre engagement, minimal conversion, and personal burnout. When I shifted to focusing primarily on Instagram with secondary attention to LinkedIn, both platforms began performing significantly better.

## 3. The Strategic Expansion Approach

Once you've established mastery on your primary platform, consider adding ONE secondary platform that:

- Reaches a complementary audience segment
- Uses content types you're already creating

- Serves a specific business objective
- Can be maintained with 20-30% of your social media resources

For my business, LinkedIn became my strategic secondary platform because:

- It reached more corporate professionals interested in digital transformation
- I could adapt my teaching content with minimal modifications
- It specifically supported our higher-ticket consulting offers
- I could maintain a strong presence with just 2-3 posts weekly

This focused approach—mastery of one primary platform with strategic usage of one secondary platform—consistently outperforms the scattered approach of maintaining mediocre presences everywhere.

# Instagram Growth Strategy

Since Instagram is the primary platform for many coaches, consultants, and service entrepreneurs, let's explore a comprehensive strategy for this specific platform:

## 1. Profile Optimization for Conversion

Your Instagram profile should function as a micro-sales page, not just a biography. Optimize your:

**Profile Photo:** Use a clear, professional headshot with good lighting and a natural expression. This creates immediate trust through personal connection.

**Username:** Choose a handle that's:

- Easily searchable
- Professional and memorable
- Preferably your name or business name
- Free from unnecessary numbers or symbols

**Name Field:** Use your name plus a keyword phrase that describes what you do. This improves discoverability through search.

**Bio:** Structure your bio with:

- A clear statement of who you help and how
- Proof of credibility (results, experience, etc.)
- A specific promise or benefit
- A clear call to action

**Link:** Don't just link to your homepage. Use a dedicated landing page specifically designed for Instagram traffic, or a link management tool that offers multiple destination options.

My optimized Instagram profile generates 37% more link clicks than my previous generic profile, translating directly to more leads and customers.

## 2. Content Strategy That Converts

Instagram content should be strategically varied to serve different objectives in your marketing funnel:

**Attraction Content (30%)** Content designed to reach new audiences through shareability and algorithm-friendly formats:

- Carousel posts with valuable lists or frameworks
- Contrarian takes on industry topics
- Visually striking infographics or process maps
- Relatable statements about industry challenges

**Engagement Content (30%)** Content designed to generate meaningful interaction with your existing audience:

- Open-ended questions related to your topic
- "This or that" decision prompts
- Polls and interactive elements in Stories
- Genuine behind-the-scenes content

**Authority Content (20%)** Content designed to establish your expertise and unique approach:

- Teaching your signature frameworks
- Case study results and transformations
- Your perspective on industry developments
- Deep-dive educational content

**Conversion Content (20%)** Content designed to directly move people toward your offers:

- Offer announcements with clear benefits
- Client success stories related to specific offers
- Problem-solution content that aligns with your offerings
- Direct invitation content with calls to action

This balanced approach ensures your Instagram presence serves the entire marketing funnel rather than just building awareness without conversion.

# 3. The Instagram Growth Equation

Growing a quality Instagram following requires understanding the platform's fundamental growth equation:

**Reach × Conversion Rate × Retention = Growth**

**Reach** strategies include:

- Using 20-30 strategic hashtags per post
- Posting during high-engagement hours for your audience
- Creating shareable content formats (especially carousels)
- Engaging with trending topics in your industry
- Collaborating with complementary accounts

**Conversion Rate** (from viewer to follower) strategies include:

- Creating "pattern interrupt" first impressions
- Delivering unexpected value in content
- Using strong calls to action for profile visits
- Ensuring your profile promises specific benefits

**Retention** strategies include:

- Delivering consistent value aligned with follower expectations
- Varying content formats to maintain interest
- Creating serialized content that builds anticipation
- Acknowledging and interacting with engaged followers

When I optimized all three components of this equation rather than focusing solely on reach (as most do), my follower growth rate increased from approximately 500 to 2,500 monthly, while engagement rates doubled.

## 4. The Direct Message Conversion System

While public content builds visibility, direct message (DM) conversations drive conversion. Here's my systematic approach to DM conversion:

**Conversation Starters:** Create content specifically designed to generate DM conversations:

- "DM me for ___" offers in content
- "Comment ____ for my private resource on this topic"
- Instagram Story polls or questions that naturally lead to conversations
- Exclusive offer announcements for "first 10 people to message me"

**The CARE Conversation Framework:** Once conversations begin, follow this framework:

- **Connect:** Establish genuine rapport based on their situation
- **Assess:** Ask questions to understand their specific challenges

- **Recommend:** Provide genuine value and direction based on their needs
- **Elevate:** If appropriate, elevate the conversation to your offer

**The Value-First Approach:** Every DM interaction should provide standalone value regardless of whether it leads to a sale:

- Share a relevant resource or insight
- Provide a quick assessment of their situation
- Offer a specific recommendation they can implement
- Connect them with others who might help

**The Conversion Bridge:** When appropriate, transition from conversation to conversion:

- "Based on what you've shared, I think __ might be a perfect fit for you."
- "Would you like to explore how we might work together on this?"
- "I actually have a program specifically designed for this situation."

This system transformed my Instagram from a content platform to a sales platform, generating 35-50 qualified sales conversations monthly.

# LinkedIn Strategy for Authority Positioning

If LinkedIn is one of your chosen platforms, here's a focused strategy for establishing authority and generating high-ticket opportunities:

## 1. Profile Optimization for Credibility

Your LinkedIn profile should position you as a recognized authority in your field:

**Professional Photo:** Use a high-quality headshot with professional attire appropriate for your industry.

**Background Image:** Create a custom banner that communicates your core offering or upcoming opportunity.

**Headline:** Go beyond your job title to include your specialized expertise and the outcome you create.

**About Section:** Structure this as a mini-case study of your approach using:

- The problem you solve
- Your unique methodology
- Specific results you've achieved
- Clear next steps for engagement

**Featured Section:** Highlight your best content, media appearances, and credential proof to establish immediate credibility.

My optimized LinkedIn profile generates approximately 35% more inbound inquiries than my previous version, specifically from higher-value potential clients.

## 2. Content Strategy for Thought Leadership

LinkedIn rewards different content approaches than more casual platforms:

**Industry Insight Posts (40%)**

- Analysis of significant trends in your field
- Interpretation of news and developments
- Predictions about future industry direction
- Original research or data presentation

**Experience-Based Content (30%)**

- Lessons from client work (anonymized when necessary)
- Behind-the-scenes of your professional process
- Challenges and solutions from your experience
- Counterintuitive findings from your practice

**Value-Focused Teaching (20%)**

- Step-by-step processes from your methodology
- Decision frameworks for common challenges
- Resource recommendations with context
- Checklists and assessment tools

**Strategic Stories (10%)**

- Narrative content that illustrates key principles
- Transformation stories with clear lessons
- Personal journey elements that establish relatability
- Client success narratives that demonstrate results

This content mix positions you as a thoughtful industry leader rather than just a service provider.

# 3. The Strategic Engagement Approach

LinkedIn's algorithm heavily rewards engagement. Implement these practices:

**60-30-10 Rule**

- Spend 60% of your LinkedIn time engaging with others' content
- Spend 30% creating and publishing your own content
- Spend 10% on direct outreach and relationship development

**Power Player Strategy** Identify 20-30 "power players" in your industry whose audiences overlap with your ideal clients. Consistently engage with their content through:

- Thoughtful comments that add meaningful perspective
- Questions that stimulate further discussion
- Relevant insights from your experience
- Appreciation for valuable viewpoints

**Strategic Commenting** When commenting on others' posts:

- Be among the first 5 commenters for maximum visibility

- Write 3-5 sentence comments that add genuine value
- Include a perspective not mentioned in the original post
- Avoid self-promotion in comments

**Community Cultivation** Actively connect people within your network:

- Tag relevant connections in valuable discussions
- Facilitate introductions between complementary professionals
- Publicly acknowledge and highlight others' achievements
- Create discussion opportunities through thoughtful questions

These engagement practices have consistently generated more visibility and opportunity than content creation alone on LinkedIn.

# The Social Selling Methodology

Regardless of which platforms you choose, effective social selling requires a systematic approach to converting social media relationships into business opportunities:

## 1. The Value Ladder Approach

Create a clear progression of value offerings that move social connections toward becoming clients:

**Free Value:** Consistently provide content and insights that solve real problems without requiring any commitment.

**Low-Commitment Opportunities:** Offer ways for followers to experience your approach through low-risk engagements (free workshops, assessments, consultations).

**Initial Investment Offerings:** Create accessible entry-point products or services that demonstrate your value while requiring minimal financial commitment.

**Core Offerings:** Present your primary products or services to those who have experienced your value through previous steps.

**Premium Experiences:** Provide elevated options for your most committed clients who want deeper implementation or more personalized support.

This graduated approach respects the relationship-building process rather than rushing to high-ticket offers prematurely.

## 2. The Content-to-Conversation Method

Systematically convert content engagement to direct conversations:

**Engagement Trigger Content** Create posts specifically designed to identify qualified prospects through their responses:

- "Comment 'interested' if you're struggling with ___"
- "Which of these challenges is biggest for you? A, B, or C?"
- "Tag someone who needs help with ___"

**Strategic Response System** Develop standardized but personalized responses to engagement:

- Thank them for their engagement
- Provide immediate value related to their response
- Ask a follow-up question that deepens the conversation
- When appropriate, move the conversation to direct messaging

**Conversation Guidance Framework** Once in direct conversation, use a structured approach:

- Ask questions that reveal their specific situation
- Share relevant examples or case studies
- Provide customized recommendations
- Present appropriate next steps based on their needs

This systematic approach converted my social media from primarily a content platform to a business development channel generating 30-40 qualified opportunities monthly.

## 3. The Social Proof Amplification System

Strategically collect and deploy social proof to accelerate trust and conversion:

**Result Documentation Process** Create a systematic approach to capturing client results:

- Regular check-in points to identify progress
- Standardized questions to elicit specific outcomes
- Templates for clients to share their experiences

- Media capture guidance (screenshots, before/after images)

**Testimonial Optimization Framework** Transform raw feedback into compelling testimonials by ensuring they include:

- Specific, measurable results
- Initial skepticism overcome
- The specific element of your offering that created breakthrough
- Personal and emotional impact beyond just metrics

**Strategic Deployment Schedule** Share social proof consistently across touchpoints:

- Rotate testimonials through regular content
- Feature client results at specific objection points
- Use industry-specific success stories for different segments
- Present relevant proof in direct conversations based on prospect concerns

**Permission and Promotion System** Create mutual benefit from success stories:

- Obtain clear permission for all testimonial usage
- Promote your clients when featuring their results
- Create joint content highlighting their success
- Facilitate connections that benefit testimonial providers

This systematic approach to social proof has consistently improved conversion rates across all platforms and offers.

# Social Media Automation Without Losing Authenticity

The greatest challenge with social media marketing is balancing effectiveness with efficiency. Here's how to automate strategically without sacrificing the authentic connection that drives results:

## 1. The 70-20-10 Rule of Automation

- 70% of your content can be batch-created and scheduled
- 20% should be created in response to current events and conversations
- 10% must be real-time, authentic sharing

This balanced approach maintains authenticity while allowing for systematic content production.

## 2. The Batching and Scheduling System

**Content Batching** Create content in dedicated blocks rather than daily scrambles:

- Set aside 2-4 hours weekly for batch creation
- Prepare content in themed clusters for coherence
- Create multiple variations of key messages
- Develop content assets that can be reused (graphics, frameworks, etc.)

**Strategic Scheduling** Schedule content for maximum impact:

- Use platform analytics to identify high-engagement timeframes
- Vary content types throughout the week
- Create content patterns your audience can anticipate
- Leave strategic gaps for timely, responsive content

**Automation Tools** Leverage tools without surrendering the human element:

- Content scheduling platforms appropriate for your primary networks
- Template systems for consistent formatting
- Organization systems for content assets
- Analytics dashboards for performance tracking

I use a monthly content creation day to batch 70-80% of my social content, freeing daily bandwidth for responsive engagement and relationship building—the elements that truly drive conversion.

## 3. The Engagement Efficiency System

Even engagement can be systematized without losing authenticity:

**Timeblocking Approach**

- Schedule 2-3 dedicated 15-minute engagement sessions daily
- Focus exclusively on meaningful interaction during these blocks
- Prioritize responding to your content engagement first

- Use remaining time for proactive engagement with strategic accounts

**Prioritization Framework** Create clear priorities for limited engagement time:

1. Direct messages from potential customers
2. Comments on your conversion-focused content
3. Responses from strategic engagement targets
4. New connections within your ideal customer profile
5. General community engagement

**Response Templates** Develop flexible templates for common interactions:

- Appreciation responses for different engagement types
- Question frameworks that advance conversations
- Value-delivery responses for common inquiries
- Conversion bridge messages for sales opportunities

This systematic approach reduces social media management time by approximately 60% while maintaining authentic connection.

# Social Media for Social Impact

As we conclude this chapter, I want to highlight how mastering social media can amplify both business success and community impact.

Through the Nehemiah Davis Foundation, we've leveraged social media to:

1. **Increase Awareness of Community Needs** Strategic social content has highlighted specific needs in underserved communities, dramatically increasing volunteer participation and resource donations.
2. **Amplify Success Stories** Sharing transformation narratives from foundation participants has inspired others to both seek support and contribute to community initiatives.
3. **Create Support Communities** Social platforms have enabled us to build virtual support networks that extend the foundation's impact beyond physical events and programs.
4. **Mobilize Rapid Response** During crises and urgent needs, social media has enabled us to quickly mobilize resources and volunteers where they're most needed.

When developing your social media strategy, consider how it might serve dual purposes:

- How could your expertise benefit underserved communities through social content?
- What impact stories could you share alongside business content?
- How might your social platform amplify important causes?
- How could your business success enable social impact that you document and share?

My own social content increasingly integrates business strategy with foundation stories. For example, we regularly feature entrepreneurs who have used their business success to create community impact, aligning our social media with our core belief that success should create significance.

# Chapter Summary: Key Takeaways

- Social media success requires the balanced integration of positioning, engagement, and conversion systems
- Focus on mastering one primary platform rather than maintaining mediocre presences across many
- Platform-specific strategies (Instagram, LinkedIn) should align with both business objectives and platform cultures
- The social selling methodology creates a systematic path from connection to conversion
- Strategic automation and efficiency systems free bandwidth for authentic engagement
- Social media can simultaneously drive business growth and community impact

# Action Steps:

1. Evaluate your current social media approach against the Success Triangle framework
2. Select your primary platform using the criteria provided
3. Optimize your profile on your chosen platform for maximum conversion
4. Implement the balanced content strategy for your primary platform
5. Develop your direct message conversion system
6. Create a batching and scheduling system that works for your schedule
7. Consider how your social media could incorporate community impact elements

8.    Implement the 70-20-10 rule for authentic automation

If you're passionate about **impact, purpose, and real results,** we want to hear from you. **Partner with Neo**. Visit PartnerWithNeo.com/apply to explore how we can collaborate.

# CHAPTER 11

## THE CHALLENGE FORMULA

After spending years studying the most effective ways to rapidly grow digital businesses, I've come to a powerful conclusion: nothing converts better than a well-executed challenge.

When I look at the watershed moments in my business—the explosive growth periods that took us to new levels—they all center around challenges. My first six-figure month came immediately after running my first challenge. We crossed the seven-figure mark through challenge-based launches. And our clients consistently see their highest conversion rates when implementing the Challenge Formula I'm about to share with you.

In previous chapters, we've covered creating digital products, building effective funnels, developing strategic content, and mastering social media. Now we'll focus on the most powerful conversion vehicle I've ever encountered: the Challenge Formula that transforms strangers into customers in as little as 5-7 days.

# What Is a Challenge and Why Does It Work?

A challenge is a structured, time-limited experience that guides participants through a series of actions toward a specific outcome or transformation. Unlike webinars or workshops that primarily deliver information, challenges focus on implementation and results.

Challenges work because they leverage powerful psychological principles:

## 1. Commitment and Consistency

When someone commits to a challenge, they activate what psychologists call the "consistency principle"—the desire to remain consistent with previous actions. This initial commitment creates momentum that carries into offer consideration.

## 2. Reciprocity

By delivering genuine value and helping participants achieve meaningful wins before presenting an offer, you create a natural reciprocity response that increases conversion rates.

## 3. Community and Social Proof

Challenges create temporary communities where participants experience the power of collective energy and witness others' success, building confidence in the process and the offer.

## 4. Transformation Experience

Participants don't just learn about your approach—they experience it directly, creating trust that no marketing claim could establish.

## 5. Urgency and Scarcity

The time-limited nature of challenges creates natural urgency without artificial pressure tactics.

My 5-Day Digital Business Challenge consistently converts at 12-18% to our core offer—compared to 3-5% for webinars and 7-9% for traditional launches. The difference is so significant that challenges have become our primary conversion mechanism across all our offers.

# The Three Challenge Frameworks

Before diving into implementation, let's examine the three primary challenge frameworks and when to use each:

## 1. The Outcome Challenge

This framework focuses on helping participants achieve a specific, tangible result by the end of the challenge period.

**Structure:**

- Days 1-2: Foundation setting and initial actions
- Days 3-4: Implementation and refinement
- Day 5: Completion and celebration of results

**Best For:**

- Concrete, achievable outcomes (create a sales page, write an email sequence, design a logo)
- Offers that solve specific problems rather than comprehensive transformations
- Audiences that need proof of concept before investing further

**Example:** My "5-Day Sales Page Challenge" helps participants create a complete high-converting sales page in five days. This tangible outcome demonstrates capability and builds confidence for our more comprehensive Digital Business Accelerator program.

## 2. The Foundation Challenge

This framework focuses on establishing the critical foundational elements necessary for long-term success in a particular area.

**Structure:**

- Day 1: Mindset and vision clarification
- Day 2: Strategy and approach alignment
- Day 3: System and process development
- Day 4: Implementation preparation
- Day 5: Initial execution and feedback

**Best For:**

- Complex transformations requiring proper foundations
- High-ticket offers that solve multi-faceted problems

- Audiences needing to unlearn incorrect approaches before succeeding

**Example:** Our "Digital Product Foundation Challenge" helps participants identify their most valuable digital product opportunity and create the strategic foundation for successful development. This naturally leads to our comprehensive Digital Product Mastery program for full implementation.

## 3. The Transformation Challenge

This framework focuses on initiating personal or professional transformation through a structured shift in thinking and behaving.

**Structure:**

- Day 1: Awareness and pattern recognition
- Day 2: Possibility expansion and vision
- Day 3: Strategy development and planning
- Day 4: Initial implementation and feedback
- Day 5: Reinforcement and next steps

**Best For:**

- Mindset or identity-based transformations
- Premium coaching or mentorship programs
- Audiences requiring perspective shifts before tactical implementation

**Example:** The "Expert to Authority Challenge" helps service providers transition from trading time for money to building authority-based businesses. This mindset and strategy shift perfectly positions participants for our Expert Authority Accelerator program.

Each framework has its place depending on your offer, audience, and objectives. Throughout this chapter, I'll primarily reference the Foundation Challenge as it's the most versatile, but the principles apply to all three frameworks.

# The 5-Day Challenge Structure

The most effective challenge duration for most businesses is five days—long enough to create meaningful transformation but short enough to maintain high engagement throughout. Here's the day-by-day structure I've found most effective:

## Day 1: Vision and Mindset

**Purpose:** Break limiting patterns, expand possibility thinking, and establish clear direction

**Key Components:**

- Pattern Interrupt: Challenge existing assumptions and approaches
- Possibility Expansion: Showcase what's truly possible with examples and stories
- Vision Crystallization: Guide participants to define their specific desired outcome
- Micro-Win: Provide an immediate, achievable success

- Community Building: Establish connection among participants

**Engagement Activities:**

- Completion declarations in comments
- Vision sharing in community
- Quick implementation exercise
- Mindset commitment exercise

Day 1 focuses more on mindset than tactics because without addressing limiting beliefs first, tactical guidance often goes unimplemented. My Digital Product Challenge Day 1 spends 70% of the time addressing "can I really do this?" concerns before introducing strategic content.

# Day 2: Strategic Framework

**Purpose:** Provide the strategic foundation for success with your unique methodology

**Key Components:**

- Problem Magnification: Deepen understanding of the problem's impact
- Methodology Introduction: Present your signature approach or framework
- Strategy Personalization: Guide participants to apply the framework to their situation
- Common Mistakes Illumination: Highlight pitfalls to avoid
- Success Path Clarification: Map the journey from current state to desired outcome

**Engagement Activities:**

- Framework application exercise
- Strategy declaration in community
- Question and answer session
- Peer feedback opportunities

Day 2 positions your methodology as the solution to the magnified problem, establishing your unique approach while providing immediately applicable value. In our Digital Business Challenge, Day 2 introduces our "Authority Asset Framework," which becomes the foundation for both challenge success and our paid offerings.

# Day 3: Implementation Foundations

**Purpose:** Start the transition from knowledge to action with foundational implementation

**Key Components:**

- First Implementation Step: Guide completion of the first critical action
- Obstacle Navigation: Address common implementation challenges
- Resource Identification: Help participants gather what they'll need for success
- Progress Measurement: Establish metrics and tracking mechanisms
- Quick Win Creation: Design and celebrate an achievable milestone

**Engagement Activities:**

- Implementation checkpoint sharing
- Resource list creation
- Progress tracker development
- Challenge question submission

Day 3 marks the critical transition from learning to doing. It's where many challenges lose momentum, so we focus heavily on creating achievable implementation steps that build confidence. In our challenges, we deliberately design Day 3 actions to be 80% easier than participants expect, creating momentum through exceeded expectations.

# Day 4: Acceleration and Refinement

**Purpose:** Accelerate results and refine approach based on initial implementation

**Key Components:**

- Implementation Acceleration: Provide advanced strategies to speed progress
- Feedback Integration: Help participants refine based on initial results
- Common Obstacle Navigation: Address challenges emerging from implementation
- Advanced Strategy Introduction: Share next-level approaches for those progressing quickly
- Progress Celebration: Acknowledge and reinforce progress made

**Engagement Activities:**

- Implementation showcase
- Refinement questions
- Peer collaboration opportunities
- Progress visualization exercise

Day 4 addresses the natural variation in participant progress by providing options for both those who are succeeding quickly and those facing challenges. This personalization dramatically increases engagement compared to one-size-fits-all approaches. In our challenges, we typically offer "track selection" on Day 4, allowing participants to choose between acceleration content or additional support content.

# Day 5: Completion and Continuation

**Purpose:** Complete the challenge promise and present the natural next step

**Key Components:**

- Challenge Completion: Guide participants to finish the promised outcome
- Results Celebration: Acknowledge achievements and progress
- Limitation Identification: Honestly address the limitations of what can be accomplished in five days
- Next Level Introduction: Present your offer as the natural continuation path
- Decision Support: Provide frameworks for making the right investment decision

**Engagement Activities:**

- Results sharing in community
- Celebration and acknowledgment
- Success story highlights
- Next step declaration

Day 5 focuses on delivering on your challenge promise while naturally bridging to your offer. The key is genuine celebration of what's been accomplished alongside honest recognition of what would require further support. In our Digital Business Challenge, Day 5 includes substantial implementation content alongside our offer presentation, maintaining value delivery throughout.

# The VIP Experience Strategy

One of the most powerful enhancements to the standard challenge format is adding a VIP experience option. This approach creates multiple benefits:

1. **Pre-Selling Opportunity:** VIP upgrades allow monetization before your main offer
2. **Higher Engagement:** VIP participants consistently show 3-4x higher challenge completion rates
3. **Self-Identification:** VIP participants self-identify as serious action-takers
4. **Increased Conversion:** VIP participants convert to your main offer at 2-3x the rate of standard participants

Here's the VIP Experience framework we've found most effective:

## VIP Component 1: Exclusive Pre-Challenge Session

Host a special session 1-2 days before the main challenge begins that:

- Provides advanced preparation for success
- Offers VIP-only frameworks or resources
- Creates connection among VIP participants
- Sets expectations for the challenge experience

This session creates immediate value for VIP participants while helping them begin with momentum.

## VIP Component 2: Daily Implementation Support

Provide additional support throughout the challenge:

- Daily Q&A sessions following the main challenge content
- Implementation review opportunities
- More detailed explanation of challenge concepts
- Personalized feedback on progress

This additional support dramatically increases implementation rates and results.

## VIP Component 3: Private Community

Create a separate, exclusive community experience:

- Private community space (Facebook group, Circle community, etc.)
- More direct access to you and your team
- Peer collaboration opportunities
- Recognition of VIP status and progress

This exclusivity enhances commitment and creates stronger community bonds.

## VIP Component 4: Exclusive Resources

Provide VIP-only resources that enhance the challenge experience:

- Advanced implementation templates
- Detailed guides or swipe files
- Done-for-you elements that accelerate progress
- Bonus trainings on complementary topics

These resources both justify the VIP investment and increase success rates.

## VIP Component 5: Special Offer Access

Provide preferred access to your main offer:

- Early access before standard participants
- Special bonuses not available to others
- Preferred pricing or payment terms

- Implementation support guarantees

This preferential treatment rewards VIP commitment while creating natural momentum for your main offer.

Our standard VIP upgrade price ranges from $97-297 depending on the challenge topic and main offer price point. We typically see 15-20% of challenge registrants choose the VIP option, creating significant revenue before the main offer presentation.

More importantly, VIP participants convert to our core offers at 30-35% compared to 8-12% for standard participants—making the VIP experience valuable far beyond its direct revenue.

# Challenge Promotion Strategy

Creating an excellent challenge is only effective if you can attract participants. Here's the promotion framework I've found most effective:

## 1. Challenge Positioning

Position your challenge to highlight three key elements:

- The specific outcome or transformation it delivers
- The time-limited nature of the experience
- The zero or low financial risk of participation

Effective challenge positioning statements follow this format: "Join the [CHALLENGE NAME] and [SPECIFIC OUTCOME] in just [TIMEFRAME], even if [COMMON OBJECTION]."

Examples: "Join the 5-Day Sales Page Challenge and create a high-converting sales page in just 5 days, even if you're not a writer or designer."

"Join the Digital Product Foundation Challenge and identify your perfect digital product in just 5 days, even if you've struggled with digital product ideas before."

This positioning focuses on the transformation rather than the educational content, attracting action-takers rather than information collectors.

## 2. Promotion Timeline

For optimal results, follow this promotion timeline:

**2 Weeks Before Launch:** Announcement content

- Teaser posts about the upcoming challenge
- Problem-focused content related to challenge topic
- Behind-the-scenes preparation content
- Early interest sign-up opportunity

**10 Days Before Launch:** Registration opening

- Official announcement with challenge details
- Early registration incentives
- Clear outcome promises
- FAQ content addressing common questions

**7-1 Days Before Launch:** Registration push

- Social proof from previous challenge participants
- Specific outcome highlighting content

- Urgency-building content as start date approaches
- Final call content in last 48 hours

**During Challenge:** Attraction through results

- Participant win spotlights
- Behind-the-scenes glimpses
- Last chance to join messaging (first 1-2 days only)
- Community energy highlighting

This timeframe creates sufficient awareness without dragging the promotion period too long.

## 3. Multi-Channel Promotion

Effective challenge promotion utilizes multiple channels:

**Email Sequence**

- Initial announcement (10 days before)
- Detail explanation (7 days before)
- Social proof focus (5 days before)
- Objection handling (3 days before)
- Final call (1 day before)

**Social Media Content**

- Announcement posts on all platforms
- Daily themed content addressing different aspects
- Story/Reel content showing preparation
- Live sessions answering questions
- Countdown content as launch approaches

**Partner Promotion**

- Affiliate partnership opportunities
- Guest content on aligned platforms
- Collaboration announcements
- Joint live sessions with partners

**Paid Advertising**

- Targeted ads to warm audiences
- Retargeting to website visitors
- Lookalike audiences based on previous participants
- Engagement-focused ad objectives

The most effective promotion combines these channels rather than relying on any single approach.

# 4. Registration Conversion Optimization

Optimize your registration process for maximum conversion:

**Registration Page Elements**

- Clear outcome promise in headline
- Day-by-day challenge breakdown
- Specific dates and time commitments
- Social proof from previous participants
- FAQ section addressing common concerns
- Low friction registration form

### Registration Confirmation Process

- Immediate confirmation page with next steps
- Confirmation email with access instructions
- Text message confirmation (if using SMS)
- Calendar invitations for all challenge sessions
- Preparation guidance to ensure readiness

### Community Access Guidance

- Clear instructions for joining community
- Community guidelines and expectations
- Introduction prompt to encourage engagement
- Initial engagement opportunities before challenge begins

Our challenge registration page conversion rates typically range from 35-50% for warm traffic and 15-25% for cold traffic—significantly higher than webinar or lead magnet conversion rates.

# Challenge Delivery Excellence

The difference between average and exceptional challenges often comes down to delivery execution. Here's how to deliver a challenge that converts:

## 1. Technical Setup

Ensure reliable technical infrastructure:

### Delivery Platform Options

- Zoom for live sessions
- Facebook Group for community
- Email for daily communication
- Website member area for resources

**Content Delivery Checklist**

- Pre-recorded components ready in advance
- Backup recording setups for live elements
- Automated email sequences scheduled
- Resource access systems tested

**Team Roles and Responsibilities**

- Host/presenter role (primary content delivery)
- Community manager (engagement facilitation)
- Technical support (troubleshooting assistance)
- Question monitor (gathering and organizing questions)

A seamless technical experience allows participants to focus entirely on the content rather than struggling with access or technical issues.

## 2. Engagement Maximization

Create systems that maximize active participation:

**Daily Accountability Systems**

- Check-in posts or forms
- Implementation verification processes
- Progress tracking mechanisms
- Completion celebrations

## Community Facilitation Strategies

- Strategic question prompts
- Peer connection opportunities
- Win sharing frameworks
- Implementation showcases

## Gamification Elements

- Points or recognition for completion
- Special acknowledgment for top implementers
- Daily challenge "champions" highlighting
- Progress visualization tools

Challenges with structured engagement systems show 70-80% higher completion rates than those relying solely on content delivery.

# 3. The Challenge Energy Curve

Manage the natural energy flow of challenges:

## Day 1: Excitement and Possibility (100% Energy)

- Leverage initial enthusiasm
- Create immediate momentum
- Establish strong community connection
- Set clear expectations

## Day 2: Strong Engagement (90% Energy)

- Build on Day 1 momentum
- Deepen methodology understanding

- Strengthen community bonds
- Create early wins

**Day 3: The Valley (60% Energy)**

- Combat the natural mid-challenge dip
- Focus heavily on quick wins
- Increase encouragement and recognition
- Simplify implementation steps

**Day 4: Resurgence (75% Energy)**

- Build momentum toward completion
- Highlight progress already made
- Increase community celebration
- Foreshadow final day breakthroughs

**Day 5: Peak and Anticipation (95% Energy)**

- Celebrate challenge completion
- Create closure on challenge promise
- Build excitement for next steps
- Transition energy toward your offer

Understanding and proactively managing this energy curve dramatically improves completion rates and participant satisfaction.

# 4. Support Systems

Create multi-layered support to ensure participant success:

## Question Management System

- Daily Q&A sessions
- Question collection mechanisms
- Common question resources
- Individual response protocols

## Implementation Support

- Templates and frameworks
- Examples and models
- Troubleshooting guides
- Personalized feedback opportunities

## Technical Assistance

- Access troubleshooting resources
- Platform navigation guidance
- Alternative access methods
- Dedicated technical support

## Mindset and Motivation Support

- Daily encouragement messages
- Obstacle navigation guidance
- Perspective-shifting content
- Recommitment opportunities

Comprehensive support systems ensure participants can overcome the inevitable obstacles that arise during implementation.

# The Challenge-to-Offer Bridge

The culmination of your challenge is the transition to your paid offer. This critical bridge must be constructed thoughtfully:

## 1. Preselling Throughout the Challenge

Create organic anticipation for your offer through:

**Future-Pacing References**

- Subtle mentions of "what comes next"
- References to the complete journey beyond the challenge
- Stories featuring past participants' post-challenge journeys
- Glimpses of the full methodology

**Natural Limitation Acknowledgment**

- Honest discussion of what can realistically be accomplished in the challenge timeframe
- Transparency about where additional support accelerates results
- Clarification of the difference between foundation and complete implementation
- Recognition of varying implementation speeds and support needs

### Results Comparison Illustrations

- Showcasing results differences between challenge-only participants and program participants
- Timeline comparisons for self-implementation versus supported implementation
- Resource investment comparisons (time, energy, learning curve)
- Risk and probability of success comparisons

These elements create natural curiosity about your offer without explicit selling during the challenge content.

## 2. The Bridge Session Framework

The offer presentation should follow this proven framework:

### Results Celebration (10-15 minutes)

- Acknowledge specific achievements during the challenge
- Celebrate participant implementation and wins
- Recognize the community that has formed
- Express genuine appreciation for participation

### Limitation Honesty (5-10 minutes)

- Discuss what wasn't possible within the challenge timeframe
- Address the reality of continuing the journey solo
- Acknowledge the obstacles that typically arise next
- Share statistics on self-implementation success rates

**Complete Journey Revelation (15-20 minutes)**

- Present the complete transformation path beyond the challenge
- Explain your comprehensive methodology
- Share the full results possible with complete implementation
- Contrast the challenge foundation with the complete journey

**Offer Presentation (20-30 minutes)**

- Present your program as the natural next step
- Detail the specific components and support
- Explain implementation mechanisms
- Share the investment details clearly

**Decision Facilitation (10-15 minutes)**

- Provide decision-making frameworks
- Address common questions and concerns
- Explain enrollment process and next steps
- Create appropriate urgency for decision-making

This structured approach maintains focus on participant success while creating a natural transition to your offer.

# 3. Offer Optimization for Challenge Audiences

Tailor your offer specifically for challenge participants:

**Challenge-Specific Bonuses**

- Resources that directly build on challenge work
- Implementation acceleration tools

- Challenge work integration assistance
- Extended support for challenge-specific outcomes

**Social Proof Selection**

- Testimonials from previous challenge participants
- Before-and-after stories that begin with challenge participation
- Results comparisons between challenge-only and program participants
- Progress timelines showing the post-challenge journey

**Challenge-Conscious Pricing**

- Acknowledge the investment already made in challenge participation
- Consider challenge completion bonuses or discounts
- Offer challenge-specific payment plans
- Provide implementation guarantees related to challenge foundation

These tailored elements create higher relevance and conversion compared to standard offer presentations.

# The Data-Driven Challenge Improvement System

The true power of challenges emerges when you implement a systematic improvement process based on data rather than assumptions:

## 1. Challenge Metrics Dashboard

Track these essential metrics for every challenge:

**Registration Metrics**

- Registration conversion rate by traffic source
- VIP upgrade percentage
- Cost per registration (for paid traffic)
- Registration timing patterns

**Engagement Metrics**

- Daily participation percentages
- Challenge completion rate
- Community engagement statistics
- Question submission patterns

**Conversion Metrics**

- Overall offer conversion rate
- VIP vs. standard conversion comparison
- Conversion by engagement level correlation
- Post-challenge conversion timeline

## Satisfaction Metrics

- Net Promoter Score from participants
- Testimonial submission rate
- Positive/negative feedback ratio
- Referral generation statistics

This comprehensive data collection enables continuous improvement rather than relying on subjective impressions.

# 2. Post-Challenge Analysis Process

After each challenge, conduct a structured analysis:

## Participant Journey Mapping

- Identify where engagement dropped
- Recognize peak engagement points
- Track conversion correlations with specific activities
- Note variation patterns among participant segments

## Content Effectiveness Evaluation

- Determine highest value content based on engagement and feedback
- Identify content that created confusion or resistance
- Assess delivery methods effectiveness
- Evaluate support resource utilization

## Conversion Pathway Analysis

- Map the journey of converted vs. non-converted participants

- Identify key decision inflection points
- Analyze objection patterns in non-converted participants
- Evaluate timing patterns in conversion decisions

**ROI and Efficiency Assessment**

- Calculate total revenue (VIP upgrades + offer sales)
- Determine profit margin after delivery costs
- Assess team time investment efficiency
- Evaluate long-term customer value from challenge participants

This methodical analysis creates a continuous improvement cycle that enhances results with each challenge iteration.

# Challenge Integration with Your Business Model

Beyond standalone challenge events, here's how to integrate challenges into your broader business ecosystem:

## 1. The Perpetual Challenge Model

Create an evergreen challenge that runs continuously:

**Automated Delivery System**

- Pre-recorded content delivered on a set schedule
- Automated email sequences
- Self-guided community engagement
- Scheduled offer presentation

## Rolling Cohort Structure

- Weekly or monthly new participant groups
- Combined community with continuous fresh energy
- Regular live engagement sessions
- Ongoing enrollment opportunities

## Scaling Support Systems

- Templated response systems for common questions
- Community-based peer support mechanisms
- Designated support team roles
- Tiered support options based on investment level

This approach creates consistent lead generation and sales without the intensity of live challenge delivery.

# 2. The Challenge Ecosystem Strategy

Deploy multiple challenges for different business objectives:

## Front-End Challenges

- Low-pressure introductory experiences
- Broad appeal to wider audiences
- Focus on immediate small wins
- Bridge to core offer challenges

## Core Offer Challenges

- Directly aligned with primary programs
- Deeper transformation experiences

- Higher-touch delivery approach
- Primary revenue generation focus

**Ascension Challenges**

- Designed for existing customers
- Focus on next-level results
- Community-strengthening emphasis
- Higher-tier offer conversion

**Reactivation Challenges**

- Targeted to past participants and customers
- Fresh content on evolving methodologies
- Reconnection with your brand and community
- Re-engagement with current offers

This diversified approach serves multiple business objectives simultaneously.

# 3. The Challenge Calendar Strategy

Strategically schedule challenges throughout your annual business cycle:

**Quarterly Flagship Challenges**

- Major live-delivered events
- Full team support allocation
- Primary revenue generation focus
- Comprehensive promotion campaigns

## Monthly Micro-Challenges

- Shorter duration (1-3 days)
- Narrower outcome focus
- Lighter delivery requirements
- Targeted audience segments

## Annual Summit Challenge

- Premium experience once yearly
- Higher investment VIP components
- Industry or affiliate partner integration
- Multiple offer integration opportunities

This structured approach creates predictable revenue patterns while maintaining sustainable delivery capacity.

# Challenge Impact Amplification

As we conclude this chapter, I want to highlight how challenges can serve both business growth and community impact simultaneously.

Through the Nehemiah Davis Foundation, we've incorporated challenge methodologies to:

1. **Skill Development in Underserved Communities** We've adapted our challenge framework to create free skill-building challenges for underserved youth, teaching digital skills, entrepreneurship fundamentals, and financial literacy.

2. **Resource Mobilization** Challenge structures have proven remarkably effective for mobilizing volunteers, donations, and community support for foundation initiatives.

3. **Mentorship Programs** The challenge framework provides excellent structure for short-term mentorship programs that create meaningful impact within sustainable time commitments.

When developing your challenge strategy, consider how it might serve dual purposes:

- Could your challenge model be adapted to serve those who can't afford your paid offerings?
- Might a "give one, get one" model work for your challenges?
- How could your business challenge success fund impact-focused challenges?
- Could challenge participants contribute to community initiatives as part of their experience?

My own business now funds a complete "shadow program" of free challenges through the foundation for every paid challenge we run. This has dramatically expanded our impact while creating deeper meaning for our team and participants.

## Chapter Summary: Key Takeaways

- Challenges represent the most effective conversion vehicle for digital products and services
- The 5-Day Challenge Framework creates transformation that naturally leads to offer consideration

- VIP experiences increase both monetization and main offer conversion rates
- Effective promotion requires multi-channel strategies and clear outcome positioning
- Delivery excellence depends on technical setup, engagement systems, and energy management
- The challenge-to-offer bridge should feel like a natural continuation of the participant journey
- Data-driven improvement systems create continuously enhancing results
- Challenges can be integrated into your business model through various deployment strategies
- Challenge methodologies can simultaneously serve business growth and community impact

## Action Steps:

1. Select the appropriate challenge framework for your primary offer
2. Design your 5-day challenge structure using the guidelines provided
3. Create your VIP experience components and pricing
4. Develop your challenge promotion plan using the multi-channel approach
5. Establish your technical delivery infrastructure
6. Script your challenge-to-offer bridge session
7. Create your metrics dashboard for performance tracking
8. Consider how your challenge could incorporate community impact elements

If you're passionate about **impact, purpose, and real results,** we want to hear from you. **Partner with Neo**. Visit PartnerWithNeo.com/apply to explore how we can collaborate.

# CHAPTER 12

# PRE-CHALLENGE PREPARATION

In the previous chapter, we explored the transformative power of challenges as a conversion vehicle for your digital products. Now we'll focus on a critical element that many entrepreneurs overlook: the extensive preparation required before your challenge even begins.

My team and I have a saying: "Challenges are won or lost before Day 1." The groundwork you lay in the weeks leading up to your challenge often determines its success more than the actual challenge content itself. This pre-challenge period creates the foundation for everything that follows.

After running hundreds of challenges and helping our clients generate millions in revenue through this approach, I've identified specific pre-challenge systems that dramatically increase both participation and conversion. In this chapter, I'll share the exact preparation framework that has consistently produced exceptional results.

# The Pre-Challenge Timeline

Effective challenge preparation follows a specific timeline. Here's the framework I recommend:

## 4 Weeks Before Launch: Strategic Foundation

- Clarify challenge positioning and outcomes
- Develop challenge structure and content outline
- Create preliminary marketing assets
- Set up technical infrastructure

## 3 Weeks Before Launch: Content Development

- Record any pre-challenge content
- Create challenge workbooks and resources
- Develop email sequences
- Prepare community guidelines and structure

## 2 Weeks Before Launch: Marketing Initiation

- Begin teaser and anticipation content
- Activate early registration for existing audience
- Prepare team and support systems
- Finalize all challenge delivery components

## 1 Week Before Launch: Full Promotion

- Launch primary registration campaign

- Activate partner and affiliate promotions
- Conduct pre-challenge audience engagement
- Implement final technical checks

## 3 Days Before Launch: Final Preparation

- Send participant preparation materials
- Conduct system and delivery tests
- Brief team on roles and responsibilities
- Prepare day-by-day facilitation plans

This structured timeline prevents the last-minute scramble that often undermines challenge effectiveness. Let's explore each phase in detail.

# Creating Anticipation Through Strategic Marketing

The most successful challenges begin building momentum weeks before the official start date. Here's how to create powerful anticipation:

## 1. The Problem Amplification Sequence

Before announcing your challenge, strategically amplify awareness of the problem your challenge solves through:

**Content Series Approach** Create a themed content series highlighting:

- The cost of the problem your challenge addresses
- Common misconceptions about solving this problem

- Why conventional approaches often fail
- Stories of transformation when the problem is solved correctly

This content prepares your audience psychologically to seek a solution, positioning your challenge as the answer they've been looking for.

**Strategic Questioning** Use questions in your content that help your audience recognize their need:

- "Are you struggling with _____?"
- "What if you could finally _____?"
- "What's preventing you from achieving _____?"
- "How would your life/business change if you could _____?"

These questions create self-recognition of the problem, making your challenge announcement more impactful.

**Future Pacing** Help your audience envision a future after solving this problem:

- Paint a vivid picture of life/business after transformation
- Create contrast between current struggles and future possibilities
- Share stories of others who have experienced this transformation
- Use "imagine if..." scenarios to expand possibility thinking

This approach creates emotional investment in finding a solution before you ever mention your challenge.

## 2. The Teaser Campaign Strategy

Once you've amplified problem awareness, implement a strategic teaser campaign:

**The Coming Soon Announcement** Create curiosity without full revelation:

- "Something game-changing is coming on [date]..."
- "I've been working on something that will transform how you _____..."
- "The solution to _____ is coming sooner than you think..."
- "After helping X people achieve _____, I'm about to share exactly how..."

This creates initial curiosity and attention without specific details.

**The Behind-the-Scenes Approach** Share glimpses of challenge preparation:

- Snapshots of content creation process
- Brief videos explaining why you're creating this challenge
- Testimonials from past participants or beta testers
- Insights into your development process

This creates connection and authenticity while building anticipation.

**The Waitlist Strategy** Create perceived exclusivity through early access:

- "Limited spots will be available..."
- "Early access for the first X people who join the waitlist..."
- "Special bonuses for waitlist members only..."

- "Be the first to know when registration opens..."

This creates action before official registration opens and builds your challenge prospect list.

## 3. The Challenge Announcement Framework

When officially announcing your challenge, use this high-conversion framework:

**The Problem-Solution-Invitation Structure**

- Begin by clearly articulating the problem and its impact
- Introduce your challenge as the specific solution
- Present the invitation to participate with clear benefits
- Create appropriate urgency for quick registration

This structure creates clear context for why your challenge matters now.

**The Outcome-Focused Approach** Focus on transformation rather than features:

- Emphasize specific results participants will achieve
- Highlight the timeframe for these results (5 days, etc.)
- Address who the challenge is specifically designed for
- Contrast with alternative approaches that take longer or cost more

This positions your challenge based on outcomes rather than process.

**The Accessibility Emphasis** Remove barriers to participation:

- Highlight the free or low-cost nature of the challenge
- Emphasize the reasonable time commitment required
- Address common objections to participation
- Provide clear technological requirements and support

This increases registration by addressing hesitations proactively.

Our clients who implement this strategic marketing approach consistently see 40-60% higher registration rates compared to those who simply announce their challenge without preparation.

# Registration Optimization Systems

Getting people to register for your challenge requires more than just compelling marketing. These systems significantly increase registration conversion:

## 1. The High-Conversion Registration Page

Create a registration page specifically designed to convert interest into sign-ups:

**Essential Page Elements**

- Benefit-focused headline emphasizing transformation
- Brief video explaining the challenge and outcomes
- Clear day-by-day breakdown of the challenge
- Specific dates, times, and commitment expectations

- Social proof from previous participants
- FAQ section addressing common concerns
- Simple registration form requesting only essential information

**Psychological Triggers** Incorporate key conversion elements:

- Loss aversion ("Don't miss this opportunity...")
- Social proof ("Join X others who have already registered...")
- Scarcity where authentic ("Limited spots available...")
- Reciprocity ("Access these free resources when you register...")
- Commitment cues ("Say yes to your transformation...")

**Mobile Optimization** Ensure seamless mobile experience:

- Fast-loading page elements
- Large, easily tappable buttons
- Minimal form fields
- Auto-filling capabilities where possible
- Single-screen view of key benefits

Our optimized registration pages typically convert at 40-50% for warm traffic and 20-30% for cold traffic—significantly higher than industry averages.

# 2. The Registration Follow-Up Sequence

What happens immediately after registration dramatically impacts show-up rates:

**Immediate Confirmation Experience**

- Thank you page with clear next steps
- Immediate confirmation email with access details
- SMS confirmation if phone number was collected
- Calendar invitations for all challenge sessions
- Quick-start guide or preparation instructions

**Engagement Bridge Activities** Provide pre-challenge activities to maintain momentum:

- Simple preparation exercises
- Community introduction prompts
- Pre-challenge assessment or quiz
- Resource access to build commitment

**Reminder Systems** Implement multi-channel reminder strategy:

- Email sequence with increasing frequency as challenge approaches
- SMS reminders for critical moments (if permission granted)
- Calendar notifications with accurate details
- Community announcements and excitement-building

Effective registration follow-up can increase challenge show-up rates by 30-40%, dramatically improving your ultimate conversion rates.

# 3. The VIP Conversion System

If offering a VIP experience (as recommended in Chapter 11), implement these conversion strategies:

**Clear Value Articulation**

- Specific additional outcomes for VIP participants
- Tangible benefits that justify the investment
- Concrete examples of enhanced experience
- Direct comparison between standard and VIP experiences

**Strategic Timing Options**

- Immediate upsell during initial registration
- Follow-up opportunity after standard registration
- Limited-time special pricing for early decision
- Last-chance upgrade before challenge begins

**Social Proof Emphasis**

- Testimonials specifically from previous VIP participants
- Results comparison between standard and VIP experiences
- Community recognition elements for VIP members
- Behind-the-scenes glimpses of VIP experience

**Scarcity Implementation** When authentically applicable:

- Limited VIP spots with real constraints
- Deadline-based decisions with actual timing requirements
- Special bonuses for first X upgrades
- One-time opportunities that won't be repeated

Proper VIP conversion implementation typically results in 15-25% of registrants choosing the premium option, creating significant pre-challenge revenue while identifying your most committed participants.

# Building Your Challenge Community

The community experience often determines challenge success more than content alone. Here's how to build a vibrant community before your challenge begins:

## 1. Community Platform Selection

Choose the right environment for your challenge community:

**Platform Options Comparison**

- Facebook Groups: Highest familiarity and engagement frequency
- Circle: More professional environment with superior organization
- Discord: Excellent for tech-savvy audiences and multiple discussion threads
- Mighty Networks: Strong community-building features with course integration

**Selection Criteria** Base your decision on:

- Your audience's existing platform comfort
- The complexity of your challenge content and discussions
- Your team's familiarity with moderation tools

- Integration requirements with your other systems

**Setup Optimization** Regardless of platform, implement:

- Clear navigation and organization structure
- Consistent branding and professional appearance
- Explicit guidelines and expectations
- Streamlined access process with minimal friction

The right platform creates the foundation for meaningful community engagement throughout your challenge.

## 2. Pre-Challenge Community Activation

Don't wait until the challenge begins to activate your community:

**Welcome Experience** Create a structured welcome process:

- Personalized welcome for each new member
- Introduction thread with specific prompts
- Community orientation guidance
- Initial connection activities

**Relationship Facilitation** Actively facilitate connections:

- Common interest identification
- Geographical or industry groupings
- Experience level matching
- Goal similarity recognition

**Pre-Challenge Engagement Activities** Implement specific engagement strategies:

- Daily discussion prompts related to the challenge topic
- Simple implementation activities that build confidence
- Resource sharing opportunities
- Success vision declarations

**Expectation Setting** Clearly establish community culture:

- Explicit community values and guidelines
- Participation expectations and norms
- Support request protocols
- Celebration and recognition practices

Communities that establish engagement patterns before the challenge begins show 50-70% higher active participation during the actual challenge.

# 3. Team Roles and Responsibilities

Effective community management requires clear role definition:

**Host/Facilitator Role**

- Delivers primary challenge content
- Sets overall energy and tone
- Recognizes achievements and progress
- Makes key announcements and transitions

## Community Manager Role

- Welcomes new members
- Facilitates discussions and connections
- Answers general questions
- Maintains engagement momentum

## Support Specialist Role

- Addresses technical issues
- Provides access assistance
- Resolves platform-specific challenges
- Ensures resource availability

## Content Engagement Role

- Identifies and elevates success stories
- Responds to implementation questions
- Provides additional resources as needed
- Gathers feedback for improvements

Even if you're a solo entrepreneur, consider how to distribute these functions or simplify them appropriately for your capacity. Clear role definition prevents critical gaps in the community experience.

# Technical Preparation for Seamless Delivery

Technical issues can derail even the most brilliant challenge content. These systems ensure smooth delivery:

## 1. Content Delivery Infrastructure

Establish reliable systems for delivering your challenge content:

**Live Session Setup** For synchronous delivery:

- Professional video streaming platform (Zoom, Stream-Yard, etc.)
- Backup recording mechanisms
- Moderator and technical support roles
- Engagement tools (polls, chat, Q&A)

**Automated Delivery Systems** For asynchronous elements:

- Scheduled email delivery
- Learning management system access
- Resource distribution automation
- Progress tracking mechanisms

**Hybrid Approach Optimization** For combined synchronous/ asynchronous:

- Clear communication about delivery methods
- Consistent access protocols across platforms

- Unified scheduling system
- Integrated experience design

This infrastructure prevents the technical failures that often undermine challenge effectiveness.

## 2. Resource Organization and Access

Create systems for organized resource delivery:

**Resource Hub Structure**

- Central location for all challenge materials
- Logical organization by challenge day/topic
- Clear naming conventions
- Progressive access as appropriate

**Access Simplification**

- Single sign-on where possible
- Bookmark/shortcut guidance
- Mobile-friendly access options
- Alternative access methods when needed

**Technical Support Framework**

- Written troubleshooting guides
- Video tutorials for complex processes
- Live support availability during critical periods
- Peer support facilitation in community

Proper resource organization eliminates the friction that often prevents full participation and implementation.

## 3. Testing and Quality Assurance

Implement thorough testing before your challenge begins:

**Complete Participant Journey Testing**

- Registration process testing across devices
- Email delivery verification across providers
- Community access testing with various scenarios
- Content access and functionality verification

**Technical Integration Validation**

- Payment processing systems (for VIP or paid challenges)
- Automation sequence testing
- Platform integrations and data flow
- Notification and reminder systems

**Load Testing for Scale**

- Simultaneous access capacity verification
- Video streaming performance with expected attendance
- Community platform performance with anticipated activity
- Support system capacity for expected volume

**Backup System Preparation**

- Alternative delivery options if primary systems fail
- Content backup processes

- Communication protocols for technical issues
- Recovery procedures for various scenarios

Thorough testing prevents the technical issues that can derail challenge momentum and participant experience.

# Team Preparation and Coordination

Even with excellent content and systems, your team's preparation significantly impacts challenge success:

## 1. Team Training and Readiness

Prepare everyone involved for effective execution:

**Challenge Familiarization**

- Complete content review for all team members
- Clear understanding of challenge objectives and structure
- Familiarity with participant journey and experience
- Alignment on key messaging and positioning

**Role-Specific Training**

- Detailed responsibility review for each function
- Technical system training as needed
- Communication protocols and standards
- Problem-solving authorities and boundaries

**Scenario Planning**

- Common challenge scenario response planning
- Objection handling preparation
- Technical issue resolution procedures
- Difficult situation management protocols

Well-prepared teams create coherent experiences that build participant confidence and trust.

## 2. Communication and Coordination Systems

Establish clear team communication processes:

**Daily Briefing Structure**

- Pre-challenge day preparation meeting
- Mid-day check-in process
- End-of-day review and adjustment planning
- Next-day preparation protocol

**Real-Time Communication Channels**

- Dedicated team messaging platform
- Priority notification protocols
- Decision escalation processes
- Quick response mechanisms

**Documentation Systems**

- Participant question and issue tracking
- Common response templates and resources

- Feedback collection and organization
- Improvement opportunity identification

These systems ensure consistent experience delivery while enabling rapid adaptation to emerging needs.

# 3. Energy and Enthusiasm Cultivation

Prepare your team to bring authentic energy to the challenge:

**Purpose Connection**

- Remind team of challenge impact and importance
- Share participant stories and transformations
- Connect daily activities to larger mission
- Celebrate team contribution to outcomes

**Personal Preparation Practices**

- Rest and renewal planning before challenge
- Energy management strategies during intensive periods
- Support and encouragement among team members
- Celebration and acknowledgment practices

**Engagement Modeling**

- Authentic enthusiasm demonstration
- Consistent positivity and solution focus
- Proactive engagement with participants
- Visible implementation of challenge principles

Team energy dramatically influences participant experience and implementation. Deliberate energy cultivation creates a more powerful challenge atmosphere.

# Participant Preparation for Maximum Success

Beyond your own preparation, setting participants up for success is critical:

## 1. Pre-Challenge Resource Provision

Provide resources that prepare participants for successful implementation:

**Welcome Package**

- Challenge overview and expectations
- Day-by-day schedule with time commitments
- Required materials or preparation list
- Technology setup guidance

**Mindset Preparation Materials**

- Common obstacle anticipation guidance
- Commitment reinforcement resources
- Success visualization exercises
- Implementation preparation frameworks

### Technical Readiness Resources

- Platform access instructions
- Application or tool setup guidance
- Testing opportunities for critical systems
- Troubleshooting and support information

Proper participant preparation dramatically increases implementation rates and ultimately improves conversion to your paid offerings.

## 2. Expectation Setting and Management

Set clear, realistic expectations that support successful experiences:

### Time Commitment Clarity

- Specific daily time requirements
- Implementation time recommendations
- Live session duration and scheduling
- Flexible participation options for different situations

### Results Expectation Framework

- Realistic outcome expectations for challenge timeframe
- Progress indicators and milestones
- Success definition across different scenarios
- Long-term versus short-term results contextualization

### Participation Guidance

- Optimal engagement recommendations
- Minimum effective participation guidelines

- Recovery options for missed components
- Personalization guidance for different situations

Clear expectations prevent disappointment while maximizing satisfaction and implementation.

## 3. Early Win Engineering

Design pre-challenge experiences that create immediate confidence:

**Quick Implementation Activities**

- Simple preparatory exercises with immediate results
- Low-barrier starting points for building momentum
- Small-scale versions of challenge methodology
- Confidence-building preliminary steps

**Community Connection Facilitation**

- Structured introduction activities
- Accountability partner matching
- Interest or goal-based grouping
- Early support system development

**Preliminary Resource Utilization**

- Immediate-access tools or templates
- Pre-challenge assessment with personalized insights
- Orientation guides with implementation planning
- Reference materials for confidence building

Early wins create momentum and belief that significantly impact challenge implementation and completion rates.

# Financial Preparation and Monetization Strategy

While challenges often begin as free or low-cost experiences, thoughtful financial preparation maximizes revenue outcomes:

## 1. Challenge Business Model Clarity

Be strategic about your challenge's business model:

**Revenue Source Identification**

- VIP upgrade opportunities
- Affiliate product integration
- Main offer conversion expectations
- Recurring revenue components

**Investment Return Projection**

- Cost analysis for challenge delivery
- Expected conversion metrics at each stage
- Lifetime value considerations for challenge participants
- Indirect benefits (testimonials, case studies, content creation)

**Financial Success Metrics**

- Primary revenue objectives
- Secondary value creation goals

- Long-term business impact expectations
- Future monetization opportunities

Clear business model understanding guides appropriate investment and focus throughout the challenge process.

# 2. Offer Preparation and Integration

Prepare your post-challenge offer for maximum conversion:

### Offer Alignment with Challenge Experience

- Natural progression from challenge content
- Clear solution to limitations encountered during challenge
- Expanded implementation of challenge methodology
- Enhanced results beyond challenge capabilities

### Offer Presentation Development

- Compelling presentation materials
- Case studies and social proof
- Objection handling preparation
- Clear value articulation

### Purchase Process Optimization

- Streamlined checkout experience
- Payment options and accessibility
- Immediate access and onboarding process
- Post-purchase communication sequence

Thoughtfully prepared offers that align perfectly with the challenge experience significantly outperform hastily assembled promotions.

## 3. Alternative Monetization Planning

Develop multiple revenue opportunities beyond your core offer:

**Strategic Partner Opportunities**

- Complementary service provider partnerships
- Affiliate product integration
- Joint venture possibilities
- Ongoing referral relationships

**Resource Monetization Options**

- Challenge resource package upgrades
- Implementation tool access
- Template or system licenses
- Specialized application opportunities

**Extended Support Models**

- Post-challenge implementation groups
- One-on-one support options
- Specialized implementation assistance
- Accountability continuation programs

Diversified monetization creates more resilient challenge economics while serving participants at various investment levels.

# Challenge Impact Alignment

As we conclude this chapter, I want to emphasize how your pre-challenge preparation can strengthen the connection between business success and meaningful impact:

## 1. Purpose Integration Throughout Experience

Weave your impact mission into the challenge structure:

**Purpose Communication**

- Share your impact vision in challenge materials
- Connect challenge topics to broader significance
- Highlight how participant success contributes to greater good
- Demonstrate your own implementation of impact principles

**Participant Contribution Opportunities**

- Challenge-related donation or support options
- Implementation that includes impact components
- Community contribution activities
- Shared purpose celebrations

**Impact Story Integration**

- Share transformation stories beyond business success
- Highlight community or social outcomes of your work
- Demonstrate the ripple effect of participant implementation
- Connect challenge principles to broader change

This purpose integration attracts aligned participants while creating deeper meaning and commitment.

## 2. Scholarship and Access Programs

Create opportunities for those who couldn't otherwise participate:

**Needs-Based Access Models**

- Scholarship application processes
- Pay-what-you-can options for certain components
- Sponsored participation opportunities
- Community-funded access programs

**Impact-Organization Partnerships**

- Free access for nonprofit staff or volunteers
- Specialized implementation for impact organizations
- Collaborative delivery with aligned causes
- Resource sharing with complementary initiatives

**Tiered Support Structures**

- Core value available to all participants
- Enhanced support based on need and capacity
- Peer-based assistance programs
- Mentorship matching across experience levels

These programs expand your impact while creating more diverse, vibrant challenge communities.

Through the Nehemiah Davis Foundation, we've implemented these approaches across our challenges, offering scholarship access to under-served entrepreneurs while integrating community service components into implementation exercises. This not only expands our impact but creates deeper meaning for all participants.

When developing your challenge preparation, consider:

- How might your challenge support those who couldn't otherwise access it?
- What impact elements could be integrated into the participant experience?
- How could challenge success fund meaningful community initiatives?
- What purpose beyond profit could unite your challenge community?

These considerations transform challenges from mere marketing vehicles to meaningful impact opportunities.

## Chapter Summary: Key Takeaways

- Thorough pre-challenge preparation often determines challenge success more than the actual content
- The preparation timeline should begin at least 4 weeks before your challenge launch
- Strategic marketing creates anticipation through problem amplification and teaser campaigns
- Registration optimization systems significantly increase participation rates

- Community building should begin before the challenge starts to establish engagement patterns
- Technical preparation ensures seamless delivery and prevents momentum-killing issues
- Team coordination and energy management create consistent, enthusiastic experiences
- Participant preparation resources increase implementation and completion rates
- Financial preparation clarifies monetization strategy and maximizes conversion
- Purpose and impact integration creates deeper meaning and attracts aligned participants

## Action Steps:

1. Create your challenge preparation timeline with specific milestones
2. Develop your pre-challenge content strategy using the problem amplification approach
3. Design your registration page and follow-up sequence for maximum conversion
4. Select and set up your community platform with pre-challenge activation plan
5. Establish your technical infrastructure and testing protocols
6. Create participant preparation resources and early win opportunities
7. Clarify your challenge business model and monetization strategy

8. Identify how your challenge can incorporate purpose and impact elements

If you're passionate about **impact, purpose, and real results,** we want to hear from you. **Partner with Neo**. Visit PartnerWithNeo.com/apply to explore how we can collaborate.

# CHAPTER 13

## DURING THE CHALLENGE

In the previous chapters, we explored the power of the Challenge Formula and the critical importance of pre-challenge preparation. Now we turn our attention to perhaps the most crucial phase: what happens during the actual challenge.

The execution phase is where your preparation meets reality. It's where participant experience is directly shaped, engagement is cultivated, and the foundation for conversion is established. Even with flawless preparation, poor execution can undermine your results. Conversely, masterful execution can elevate even a modestly prepared challenge into a transformational experience.

After running hundreds of challenges and generating millions in revenue, I've identified specific execution strategies that dramatically increase both participant results and conversion rates. In this chapter, I'll share the execution framework that has consistently produced exceptional outcomes across diverse topics and industries.

# The Daily Execution Rhythm

Successful challenges follow a consistent daily rhythm that provides structure while maintaining engagement. Here's the framework I recommend:

## 1. The Morning Energy Ignition

*Purpose: Set the tone and energy for the day's experience*

**Key Components:**

- Quick-start announcement 15-30 minutes before main content
- Enthusiasm and energy injection
- Clear expectations for the day
- Acknowledgment of previous day's implementation
- Excitement building for today's content

**Implementation Methods:**

- Brief live stream in community
- Energetic email/message delivery
- Short voice or video message
- Community engagement prompt

This morning energy ignition dramatically increases participation rates by creating anticipation and structure. My challenges typically see 30-40% higher attendance when implementing this simple practice.

## 2. The Core Content Delivery

*Purpose: Deliver primary value and implementation guidance*

**Key Components:**

- Context setting and connection to overall journey
- Main teaching or framework presentation
- Step-by-step implementation guidance
- Common obstacle navigation
- Immediate application opportunity

**Optimal Timing:** Schedule your core content delivery when your audience is most likely to engage fully:

- Predictable time each day (consistency builds habit)
- Aligned with typical availability for your audience
- Sufficient duration for complete delivery (30-90 minutes typical)
- Buffer time for questions and clarification

**Delivery Approaches:**

- Live video workshop with interaction
- Pre-recorded video with live Q&A
- Live audio with visual supplements
- Text-based delivery with multimedia support

The core content delivery should represent approximately 40% of your daily engagement with participants—sufficient to provide value without overwhelming implementation time.

## 3. The Implementation Acceleration

*Purpose: Move participants from knowledge to action*

**Key Components:**

- Structured implementation time allocation
- Step-by-step action guidance
- Resource provision for application
- Progress tracking mechanisms
- Immediate feedback opportunities

**Implementation Methods:**

- Timed implementation sprints (25-45 minutes)
- Guided worksheet completion
- Technical demonstration and practice
- Breakout implementation groups
- Co-working sessions with expert support

This deliberate focus on implementation—not just content consumption—is what separates high-converting challenges from information-only events. When we added structured implementation acceleration to our challenges, completion rates doubled and conversion rates increased by approximately 35%.

# 4. The Community Reinforcement

*Purpose: Harness the power of collective energy and social proof*

**Key Components:**

- Progress sharing opportunities
- Implementation feedback exchanges
- Question and solution threads

- Win celebration and acknowledgment
- Peer support activation

**Facilitation Approaches:**

- Structured sharing prompts
- Recognition and highlighting systems
- Discussion facilitation techniques
- Expert response frameworks
- Connection opportunities creation

Community reinforcement provides the social accountability and support that dramatically increases completion. Our data shows that participants who actively engage in the community are 3-4 times more likely to complete challenge tasks and convert to paid offers.

# 5. The Day Closure and Bridge

*Purpose: Solidify the day's progress and create anticipation for tomorrow*

**Key Components:**

- Day summary and key takeaway reinforcement
- Implementation acknowledgment and celebration
- Common question addressing
- Preview of tomorrow's content
- Clear next steps before next session

**Delivery Methods:**

- Brief live wrap-up session
- End-of-day message or email

- Voice note or short video
- Community closing thread

This intentional closure prevents the feeling of incompletion that often leads to challenge abandonment. It also builds anticipation for the next day's content, maintaining momentum throughout the challenge.

The daily rhythm creates a predictable structure that guides participants through the transformation process while maintaining engagement and energy. Like a heartbeat for your challenge, this consistent rhythm prevents the energy drops that often plague multi-day events.

# Engagement Maximization Strategies

Beyond the daily rhythm, specific engagement strategies significantly impact participant experience and results:

## 1. The 80/20 Engagement Framework

Focus your engagement efforts where they create maximum impact:

**The 20% of Participants Who Drive 80% of Energy** Identify and nurture your most engaged participants:

- Provide special recognition for active implementation
- Highlight their questions and contributions
- Create visibility for their progress and results
- Leverage their energy to inspire others

**The 20% of Engagement Opportunities That Create 80% of Results** Focus on high-leverage engagement moments:

- Implementation declaration points
- Question and obstacle sharing opportunities
- Win celebration moments
- Breakthrough acknowledgments
- Community contribution opportunities

**The 20% of Content That Generates 80% of Implementation** Emphasize and reinforce your most actionable content:

- Highlight key implementation steps
- Create additional support around critical concepts
- Develop supplementary resources for crucial applications
- Provide extra clarification for foundational elements

This focused approach prevents spreading engagement efforts too thin while maximizing impact on overall challenge success.

## 2. The Active Participation Acceleration System

Proactively increase participation through systematic engagement:

**Multiple Modality Engagement** Create diverse participation opportunities for different preferences:

- Written reflection and sharing
- Audio or video contribution options
- Live interaction opportunities
- Private reflection alternatives
- Visual sharing possibilities

**Progressive Commitment Escalation** Start with low-barrier participation and gradually increase investment:

- Simple one-click or one-word initial engagements
- Short response opportunities building to deeper sharing
- Private reflection progressing to public sharing
- Individual work advancing to collaborative activities
- Basic implementation expanding to comprehensive application

**Strategic Recognition Deployment** Use recognition to reinforce desired participation:

- Immediate acknowledgment of contributions
- Public highlighting of implementation examples
- Specific praise for vulnerability and breakthroughs
- Recognition evolution throughout challenge progression
- Connection between participation and results

When we implemented these systematic engagement strategies, our average daily participation rates increased from 30-40% to 60-70% of registered participants—dramatically improving overall results and conversion.

# 3. The Energy Management System

Proactively address the natural energy fluctuations during multi-day challenges:

**Day 1: Enthusiasm Maximization (100% Energy)**

- Capitalize on initial excitement
- Create immediate wins for momentum

- Establish strong community connection
- Set clear expectations and structure

## Day 2: Continuation Momentum (80-90% Energy)

- Build on Day 1 success
- Deepen methodology understanding
- Strengthen community bonds
- Address early implementation questions

## Day 3: The Valley Navigation (60-70% Energy)

- Acknowledge the mid-challenge dip as normal
- Simplify implementation requirements
- Increase encouragement and support
- Focus on tangible progress visualization
- Inject new energy through pattern interrupts

## Day 4: Breakthrough Facilitation (70-80% Energy)

- Highlight emerging results and patterns
- Connect current implementation to ultimate outcomes
- Increase peer support activation
- Build anticipation for challenge completion

## Day 5: Completion and Continuation (90-95% Energy)

- Celebrate challenge journey and achievements
- Connect challenge experience to longer-term transformation
- Create closure on challenge promises
- Build excitement for next steps and opportunities

This proactive energy management prevents the abandonment that often occurs during multi-day experiences, particularly at the critical Day 3 valley where most challenges lose 40-60% of their active participants.

# Content Delivery Excellence

The way you deliver your content significantly impacts both engagement and results:

## 1. The Transformational Teaching Framework

Structure your content delivery for maximum impact:

**Context Before Content** Always establish why before what:

- Connect to participant goals and challenges
- Explain the significance of today's topic
- Relate to the overall transformation journey
- Create relevance before delivering information

**Concept Before Detail** Provide the big picture before specifics:

- Explain the overall framework or approach
- Clarify the intended outcome
- Share the high-level methodology
- Then dive into step-by-step implementation

**Concrete After Conceptual** Move from understanding to application:

- Start with concept explanation
- Transition to specific examples

- Follow with implementation demonstrations
- Conclude with personalized application guidance

**Confirmation Through Application** Solidify learning through immediate implementation:

- Provide structured application opportunities
- Guide real-time implementation where possible
- Create feedback mechanisms for verification
- Connect application to expected outcomes

This teaching structure creates both intellectual understanding and practical implementation ability—a combination that dramatically improves results.

## 2. The Engagement Escalation Method

Design your delivery to progressively deepen engagement:

**The 3-Minute Hook** Capture attention immediately through:

- Powerful outcome statement
- Unexpected insight or perspective
- Compelling problem articulation
- Intriguing question or scenario

**The 7-Minute Context** Establish relevance and importance through:

- Clear problem-solution framing
- Personal connection to the topic
- Significance explanation
- Implementation preview

**The Core Content Blocks (10-15 Minutes Each)** Deliver primary teaching in digestible segments:

- Single concept focus per block
- Concept-example-application pattern
- Interaction or reflection opportunity
- Bridge to next content block

**The Implementation Transition** Move from learning to action through:

- Clear action step articulation
- Resource introduction and explanation
- Common obstacle anticipation
- Success visualization

This structured delivery maintains engagement throughout longer content sessions while maximizing both understanding and implementation.

# 3. The Multi-Learning Style Approach

Accommodate diverse learning preferences within your delivery:

**Visual Learners** Include elements specifically for visual processors:

- Frameworks and models
- Process visualizations
- Example demonstrations
- Screen sharing where appropriate

**Auditory Learners** Support those who learn best through hearing:

- Clear verbal explanations

- Storytelling and examples
- Analogies and metaphors
- Conceptual relationships

**Kinesthetic Learners** Engage those who learn through doing:

- Real-time implementation opportunities
- Physical engagement prompts
- Application exercises
- Tangible practice opportunities

**Reading/Writing Learners** Support those who process through text:

- Written summaries or guides
- Note-taking prompts and structures
- Text-based resources
- Written reflection opportunities

This comprehensive approach ensures all participants can engage with your content through their preferred learning channels, dramatically improving both retention and implementation.

# Support System Optimization

The support you provide during your challenge often determines participant success more than the content itself:

## 1. The Tiered Support Framework

Create a multi-level support system that serves all participants:

**Level 1: Self-Service Support** Resources that empower independent problem-solving:

- Comprehensive FAQ resources
- Step-by-step implementation guides
- Troubleshooting checklists
- Example libraries and swipe files

**Level 2: Community Support** Leverage collective wisdom through facilitated peer assistance:

- Question thread structures
- Implementation feedback exchanges
- Peer review opportunities
- Problem-solving discussions

**Level 3: Team Support** Provide scalable team assistance for common needs:

- Daily Q&A sessions
- Implementation feedback mechanisms
- Technical assistance channels
- Progress review opportunities

**Level 4: Expert Support** Reserve your direct involvement for maximum leverage:

- Strategic direction guidance
- Complex situation navigation
- Specialized application assistance
- Breakthrough facilitation

This tiered approach ensures everyone receives appropriate support while preserving your highest-value input for where it creates the greatest impact.

## 2. The Question Management System

Develop systematic approaches to handling participant questions:

**Question Collection Methods**

- Dedicated question threads or forms
- Question submission opportunities during content
- Email or message submission options
- Voice or video question capabilities

**Question Categorization Process** Organize questions for efficient handling:

- Content clarification questions
- Implementation challenges
- Technical issues
- Strategic application questions
- Mindset or approach questions

**Response Prioritization Framework** Determine which questions receive what type of attention:

- High-leverage questions benefiting many participants
- Clarification needs blocking implementation
- Strategic questions revealing teaching opportunities
- Pattern-indicating questions showing common challenges

**Response Format Options** Provide answers through appropriate channels:

- Live Q&A addressing for widespread relevance
- Written responses for reference value
- Video or audio explanations for complex topics
- Resource provision for comprehensive needs

An effective question management system ensures participants receive the guidance they need while maximizing your team's support capacity.

## 3. The Implementation Support Matrix

Provide structured assistance for the application phase:

**Implementation Guidance Documentation** Create comprehensive resources for independent application:

- Step-by-step implementation guides
- Example libraries showing diverse applications
- Common obstacle navigation guides
- Decision-making frameworks for personalization

**Progress Tracking Systems** Help participants monitor their advancement:

- Implementation checklists
- Progress visualization tools
- Milestone tracking mechanisms
- Completion acknowledgment processes

**Feedback Mechanisms** Provide input on participant implementation:

- Peer review structures
- Team feedback opportunities
- Self-assessment frameworks
- Example comparison resources

**Course Correction Support** Help participants navigate when implementation doesn't go as planned:

- Troubleshooting guides
- Alternative approach resources
- Adaptation frameworks for different situations
- Recovery guidance for implementation challenges

Comprehensive implementation support dramatically increases completion rates and results, directly impacting your conversion potential.

# The Challenge Momentum Maintenance System

Maintaining momentum throughout your challenge requires deliberate strategies:

## 1. The Win Acceleration Framework

Create structured opportunities for participants to experience success:

**Day 1 Immediate Win Engineering** Design an achievable first-day victory:

- Simple but meaningful implementation task
- Quick completion capability (15-30 minutes)
- Clear evidence of progress
- Connection to broader challenge goals

**Daily Victory Milestones** Incorporate achievable wins into each day's experience:

- Completion acknowledgment mechanisms
- Progress visualization opportunities
- Implementation evidence sharing
- Specific accomplishment recognition

**Cumulative Achievement Visualization** Help participants see their progress over time:

- Challenge journey mapping
- Progress tracking visualizations

- Before-and-during comparisons
- Transformation documentation opportunities

**Community Celebration Rituals** Create cultural practices around achievement recognition:

- Dedicated win sharing threads or sessions
- Peer acknowledgment practices
- Implementation showcase opportunities
- Community recognition rituals

These structured win opportunities create the motivation and momentum that sustains participation throughout the challenge journey.

## 2. The Obstacle Navigation System

Proactively address the challenges that typically derail participants:

**Common Obstacle Anticipation** Identify and prepare for predictable challenges:

- Time constraints and competing priorities
- Technical difficulties or limitations
- Knowledge or skill gaps
- Confidence or mindset barriers
- Application confusion or uncertainty

**Preemptive Solution Provision** Provide resources before obstacles arise:

- Time management and productivity guidance
- Technical tutorials and support resources

- Simplified application alternatives
- Mindset and confidence-building tools
- Clarification resources and examples

**Real-Time Challenge Response** Create systems for addressing emerging obstacles:

- Daily problem-solving threads or sessions
- Rapid response protocols for critical barriers
- Peer solution-sharing mechanisms
- Alternative path provisions when needed

**Recovery Pathway Development** Help participants get back on track after disruptions:

- "Getting back on track" guides
- Simplified catch-up options
- Key component focus for limited time
- Community re-engagement opportunities

This proactive obstacle management prevents the abandonment that typically occurs when participants encounter inevitable challenges.

## 3. The Accountability Architecture

Create multi-layered accountability that sustains implementation:

**Personal Accountability Structures** Help participants commit to themselves:

- Public declaration opportunities
- Daily commitment mechanisms

- Progress tracking systems
- Completion documentation processes

**Peer Accountability Systems** Leverage the power of social commitments:

- Implementation partner matching
- Small group formation for accountability
- Progress sharing expectations
- Peer check-in structures

**Community Accountability Culture** Establish implementation as a community norm:

- Regular implementation check-in rituals
- Community-wide progress tracking
- Culture of celebration for action-taking
- Visible implementation highlighting

**Leadership Accountability Touch Points** Provide direct accountability at key moments:

- Strategic check-in opportunities
- Implementation acknowledgment practices
- Completion recognition systems
- Progress celebration from leadership

This comprehensive accountability architecture significantly increases completion rates by providing the external structure many participants need for consistent implementation.

# The Conversion Path Integration

While your challenge focuses primarily on delivering transformation, strategic elements throughout the experience set the stage for offer conversion:

## 1. The Value Escalation Approach

Demonstrate increasing value throughout the challenge journey:

**Value Demonstration Sequence** Create a progressive value experience:

- Day 1: Immediate but modest value delivery
- Day 2: Expanded methodology value
- Day 3: Personalized application value
- Day 4: Advanced strategy value
- Day 5: Complete transformation glimpse

**Limitation Transparency** Honestly acknowledge the constraints of the challenge format:

- Time limitations and their impact
- Depth restrictions in a group format
- Personalization boundaries in free or low-cost experiences
- Implementation support constraints

**Extended Journey Glimpses** Provide organic visibility into further transformation:

- References to additional methodology components
- Examples of extended implementation results

- Stories featuring complete journey outcomes
- Mentions of related areas beyond challenge scope

This approach creates natural interest in your extended offerings without explicit selling during the challenge itself.

## 2. The Problem Evolution Framework

Help participants recognize the evolving nature of their challenges:

**Initial Problem Clarification** Begin with the presenting problem:

- Acknowledge the challenge that brought them to you
- Validate their recognition of this need
- Provide immediate value addressing this concern
- Create initial wins related to this problem

**Root Cause Illumination** Progressively reveal deeper issues:

- Help identify underlying factors
- Connect surface challenges to core issues
- Demonstrate the impact of these deeper elements
- Provide initial guidance on addressing roots

**Solution Expansion Recognition** Expand awareness of the complete solution landscape:

- Illuminate the full transformation pathway
- Clarify the comprehensive approach needed
- Contrast partial versus complete resolution
- Share examples of full journey implementation

This evolution creates natural recognition that the challenge represents a starting point rather than a complete solution—setting the stage for offer consideration without pushy selling.

## 3. The Social Proof Integration Strategy

Strategically incorporate evidence throughout the challenge experience:

**Participant Success Spotlighting** Highlight emerging wins within the current challenge:

- Daily implementation showcases
- Progress acknowledgment and amplification
- Breakthrough celebration and sharing
- Result documentation and recognition

**Previous Participant Journey Sharing** Incorporate stories from past challenge participants:

- Challenge transformation examples
- "Where are they now" updates
- Challenge-to-program transition stories
- Long-term result documentation

**Program Participant Showcasing** Strategically feature results from your paid offerings:

- Brief program participant spotlights
- Result comparisons across different journeys
- Specific transformation examples
- Implementation depth demonstrations

This integrated approach builds credibility and desire through authentic examples rather than marketing claims, creating natural interest in your complete solution.

# Challenge Impact Expansion

As we conclude this chapter, I want to highlight how excellence in challenge execution can amplify both business success and community impact:

## 1. The Accessibility Enhancement Approach

Create multiple access paths to your challenge value:

**Learning Style Accommodation** Ensure content is accessible across preferences:

- Visual elements for visual learners
- Audio options for auditory processors
- Text-based alternatives for readers
- Implementation support for kinesthetic learners

**Technology Flexibility** Provide alternative participation methods:

- Mobile-friendly access options
- Low-bandwidth alternatives
- Non-video participation paths
- Alternative platform options when possible

**Schedule Accommodation** Support diverse life situations:

- Replay availability for live components
- Alternative implementation timeframes
- Catch-up resources and guidance
- Flexible engagement options

These accommodations expand who can benefit from your challenge beyond those with ideal circumstances.

## 2. The Pay-It-Forward Framework

Integrate contribution opportunities throughout your challenge:

**Knowledge Sharing Culture** Encourage participant-to-participant support:

- Peer teaching opportunities
- Experience sharing invitations
- Solution contribution structures
- Resource sharing mechanisms

**Challenge Expansion Opportunities** Invite participants to extend impact:

- Sponsored access for others
- Resource contribution for community benefit
- Mentorship or support volunteering
- Expertise sharing in community

**Community Contribution Integration** Connect challenge implementation to broader impact:

- Implementation exercises that include giving components
- Application projects with community benefit
- Skill development that supports causes
- Knowledge application for those in need

This framework transforms your challenge from purely individual transformation to collective elevation—creating deeper meaning while expanding impact.

Through the Nehemiah Davis Foundation, we've integrated these approaches across our challenges, creating sponsored access programs while incorporating community service components into implementation exercises. This not only expands our impact but creates deeper meaning for all participants.

When executing your challenge, consider:

- How might you accommodate diverse circumstances and needs?
- What pay-it-forward opportunities could enhance the experience?
- How could implementation include meaningful contribution?
- What community-building practices would amplify collective benefit?

These considerations transform challenge execution from mere content delivery to meaningful community impact.

# Chapter Summary: Key Takeaways

- The daily execution rhythm creates structure and predictability that sustains engagement
- Engagement maximization strategies focus efforts where they create maximum impact
- Content delivery excellence combines transformational teaching with diverse learning styles
- Support system optimization ensures participants receive appropriate guidance at every stage
- Momentum maintenance systems prevent the abandonment common in multi-day experiences
- Conversion path integration creates natural interest in your offers without explicit selling
- Challenge impact expansion transforms individual transformation into collective elevation

# Action Steps:

1. Design your daily challenge rhythm with all five key components
2. Implement the 80/20 engagement framework for maximum leverage
3. Structure your content delivery using the transformational teaching model
4. Develop your tiered support system for comprehensive assistance
5. Create your win acceleration framework for sustained momentum

6. Implement the problem evolution approach for natural offer interest
7. Design your accessibility enhancement strategy for broader impact
8. Integrate pay-it-forward opportunities throughout your challenge

If you're passionate about **impact, purpose, and real results,** we want to hear from you. **Partner with Neo**. Visit PartnerWithNeo.com/apply to explore how we can collaborate.

# CHAPTER 14

---

# THE CHALLENGE CLOSE

The final day of your challenge represents a critical turning point. It's where participant transformation meets business opportunity— where the value you've delivered creates the foundation for offering your premium solution.

Many entrepreneurs approach this moment with anxiety, abruptly shifting from value-provider to salesperson. This sudden change in energy often creates disconnect and diminishes both the participant experience and conversion rates.

After helping entrepreneurs generate millions through challenge-based conversions, I've developed a systematic approach to the challenge close that feels natural, authentic, and highly effective. This approach transforms the sales process from a disconnected pitch into the natural next step in your participant's journey.

In this chapter, I'll share the exact close framework that has consistently produced exceptional conversion rates while maintaining relationship integrity and participant satisfaction.

# The Bridge Session Framework

The transition from challenge to offer requires a carefully structured approach that I call the Bridge Session. This framework creates a seamless path between free value and premium opportunity:

## 1. Celebration and Acknowledgment (10-15 minutes)

Begin by celebrating what participants have accomplished:

Transformation Recognition

- Acknowledge specific steps completed
- Highlight visible progress made
- Celebrate breakthroughs achieved
- Express genuine appreciation for participation

Community Acknowledgment

- Recognize the collective journey
- Appreciate vulnerable sharing
- Highlight support provided between participants
- Honor the community formed during the challenge

Your Gratitude Expression

- Share what the experience has meant to you
- Express appreciation for participant trust
- Acknowledge what you've learned from them
- Thank them for their commitment and implementation

This celebration phase creates positive energy while reinforcing the value already received—establishing that whatever comes next is a bonus, not the sole purpose of the challenge.

## 2. Challenge Journey Integration (5-10 minutes)

Connect all challenge components into a coherent framework:

Journey Recap

- Summarize the path traveled during the challenge
- Connect daily themes into a unified progression
- Highlight key concepts and frameworks covered
- Remind participants of resources and tools provided

Methodology Reinforcement

- Emphasize your unique approach or system
- Connect challenge elements to your overall methodology
- Illustrate how each piece contributes to transformation
- Clarify how the challenge fits within larger transformation

Progress Acknowledgment

- Recognize the foundation now established
- Clarify what's been accomplished during the challenge
- Connect current position to starting point
- Establish the groundwork created for further progress

This integration phase helps participants recognize the cohesive journey they've experienced rather than seeing the challenge as disconnected pieces, creating context for what follows.

# 3. Reality and Limitation Transparency (7-10 minutes)

Honestly address the limitations of the challenge format:

Time Constraint Acknowledgment

- Recognize the limited duration of the challenge
- Acknowledge what wasn't possible within this timeframe
- Validate that complete transformation requires more time
- Appreciate progress despite these constraints

Implementation Reality Check

- Address the challenges of self-implementation
- Acknowledge the obstacles on the solo journey
- Share statistics on self-implementation success rates
- Validate the difficulty of maintaining momentum alone

Common Next Steps Challenges

- Identify typical obstacles that arise after challenges
- Share patterns observed in previous participants
- Acknowledge the complexity of continued progress
- Recognize the reality of competing priorities and demands

This transparency phase creates honest recognition of challenges without creating artificial problems. It acknowledges reality without diminishing what's been accomplished.

# 4. Complete Solution Revelation (15-20 minutes)

Present your comprehensive offering as the natural next step:

Full Methodology Unveiling

- Reveal your complete transformation system
- Explain components beyond the challenge scope
- Illustrate the comprehensive pathway to desired outcomes
- Connect challenge experience to complete methodology

Support Structure Explanation

- Detail the support systems in your program
- Clarify implementation assistance available
- Explain accountability mechanisms
- Highlight community and connection components

Transformation Timeline Illustration

- Show the realistic timeframe for complete results
- Compare self-implementation versus supported journey
- Illustrate progress patterns with and without support
- Share examples of actual client journeys and timelines

Result Possibility Expansion

- Expand vision of what's truly possible
- Share specific client transformation stories
- Present concrete outcomes and achievements
- Connect aspirations to tangible possibilities

This revelation phase presents your offer as the logical continuation of the journey already begun—not a separate sales pitch but the next step on the same path.

# 5. Offer Presentation (10-15 minutes)

Clearly articulate your program specifics:

Program Structure Overview

- Explain the format and delivery approach
- Detail the timeline and duration
- Clarify the specific components included
- Outline the implementation process

Investment and Access Clarification

- Present the investment required
- Explain payment options and terms
- Clarify enrollment process
- Detail access and onboarding procedures

Guarantee and Risk Reversal

- Explain your confidence guarantee
- Detail the risk reversal approach
- Clarify the commitment expectations
- Address potential hesitations directly

Decision Timeline

- Explain when decisions need to be made

- Clarify any limited availability
- Detail any early decision bonuses
- Outline the exact next steps for interested participants

This presentation phase provides complete clarity without pressure tactics, empowering informed decisions rather than emotional reactions.

# 6. Participant Success Path (10-15 minutes)

Share the journey successful participants will experience:

Immediate Next Steps

- Detail the enrollment and welcome process
- Explain the first implementation actions
- Clarify how challenge work integrates
- Share the initial experience timeline

30-Day Transformation Vision

- Paint the picture of the first month
- Share typical early results and wins
- Illustrate the support and guidance provided
- Explain the momentum-building process

Complete Journey Illustration

- Show the full transformation arc
- Share specific milestone achievements
- Illustrate the complete implementation path
- Connect final outcomes to initial aspirations

Beyond-Program Vision

- Explain ongoing support and community
- Share alumni success patterns
- Illustrate long-term transformation impact
- Connect program completion to larger life/business changes

This success path phase creates vivid imagination of the journey, allowing participants to emotionally experience the transformation before deciding.

## 7. Decision Facilitation (10-15 minutes)

Help participants make the right decision for their situation:

Ideal Participant Clarification

- Clearly describe who the program is perfect for
- Explain specific situations where it creates most value
- Detail the readiness indicators that signal fit
- Share characteristics of your most successful clients

Not-Right-Now Recognition

- Acknowledge valid reasons for waiting
- Provide alternative resources for those not ready
- Express support regardless of decision
- Keep the door open for future participation

Decision Framework Provision

- Offer structured approach to making the decision

- Provide questions to consider when evaluating
- Suggest reflection process before deciding
- Recommend consultation with appropriate supporters

Questions and Clarification Invitation

- Open space for genuine questions
- Address concerns with honesty and transparency
- Provide additional information where needed
- Create safety for vulnerable inquiries

This facilitation phase respects participant autonomy while providing guidance for aligned decisions, creating trust through transparent support rather than pressure.

The Bridge Session framework transforms what could be an awkward sales pitch into a natural continuation of the value journey, connecting challenge experience to premium opportunity through logical progression rather than emotional manipulation.

# The Energetic Integrity Approach

Beyond structure, how you show up energetically during the close makes a profound difference in both conversion and relationship:

## 1. The Authentic Alignment State

Maintain complete congruence between your words, energy, and belief:

Personal Conviction Embodiment

- Connect deeply to your belief in your offering
- Align with the transformation you know is possible
- Center in the service of your work
- Release attachment to specific outcomes

Value Recognition Clarity

- Hold clear awareness of your offering's true value
- Maintain perspective on the transformation provided
- Connect to concrete client results and outcomes
- Recognize the fair exchange represented by your pricing

Service Orientation

- Maintain focus on participant benefit, not your gain
- See yourself as a guide to the right decision
- Hold commitment to the highest good for each person
- Trust the natural alignment of right decisions

Confidence Cultivation

- Release desperation or neediness energy
- Maintain certainty about your ability to deliver
- Stand firmly in your expertise and methodology
- Trust the value you've already demonstrated

This energetic alignment creates a foundation of authenticity that participants can feel—dramatically different from the typical "sales energy" that creates resistance.

## 2. The Energetic Generosity Principle

Give more than expected during the close itself:

Continuous Value Delivery

- Continue teaching throughout the presentation
- Provide insights even during offer components
- Offer implementation guidance within the close
- Share advanced concepts as part of the process

Unexpected Bonus Revelation

- Include surprise elements not previously mentioned
- Add value components beyond expectations
- Create genuine excitement through generosity
- Demonstrate abundance mindset through giving

Complete Transparency Approach

- Share more behind-the-scenes than typical
- Be radically honest about both benefits and challenges
- Reveal aspects typically hidden in sales processes
- Demonstrate trust through vulnerability

Above-and-Beyond Moments

- Provide unexpected personal touches
- Create memorable moments of connection
- Demonstrate care through attention to detail
- Show up fully present beyond normal boundaries

This energetic generosity creates reciprocity naturally without manipulation—participants feel genuinely served rather than sold to.

## 3. The Personal Connection Balance

Maintain authentic relationship during the business transition:

Individual Recognition Practice

- Acknowledge specific participants by name
- Reference personal shares or implementations
- Connect offer elements to individual situations
- Demonstrate that you see them as people, not prospects

Shared Journey Acknowledgment

- Position yourself as co-traveler, not distant guru
- Share appropriate personal experiences and challenges
- Connect through common aspirations and values
- Maintain warmth and accessibility throughout

Professional Boundaries Maintenance

- Balance personal connection with appropriate distance
- Maintain ethical clarity about the relationship
- Respect both intimacy and professional responsibility
- Create safety through clear role definition

Authentic Imperfection Comfort

- Allow natural humanity rather than polished perfection
- Recover gracefully from inevitable mistakes

- Demonstrate comfort with technology issues or interruptions
- Model resilience and presence through challenges

This balanced connection creates the relational foundation for authentic conversion without crossing into inappropriate familiarity or distance.

When I transformed my close approach from standard sales techniques to this energetic integrity method, my conversion rates increased from 7-9% to 15-20%—while simultaneously receiving feedback about how "non-salesy" and authentic the experience felt.

# Objection Response Mastery

Even with excellent challenge delivery and a strong close, participants will naturally have questions and concerns. How you address these dramatically impacts conversion:

## 1. The Preemptive Address Method

Proactively address common concerns before they arise:

Common Objection Identification
Recognize the typical concerns for your offer:
- Time availability concerns
- Financial investment hesitations
- Confidence and readiness doubts
- Implementation ability questions
- Result certainty hesitations

Authentic Integration Approach
Address these naturally within your presentation:

- "You might be wondering about..."
- "A question that often comes up is..."
- "Something I'd be thinking if I were you is..."
- "Let me address something important..."

Complete Transparency Response
Provide honest, thorough addressing:

- Acknowledge the legitimacy of the concern
- Provide perspective that may not be considered
- Share how the concern relates to your offering
- Offer genuine guidance for consideration

Solution Without Pressure
Present resolutions without pushing:

- Explain how your offer addresses the concern
- Share examples of others with similar situations
- Provide alternative perspectives to consider
- Trust participants to make their own connections

This preemptive approach demonstrates understanding and builds trust while reducing the perceived risk of the decision.

## 2. The Live Response Framework

When questions arise during or after your presentation, follow this approach:

Deep Listening Foundation
Begin with complete presence:

- Listen to understand, not to respond
- Avoid formulating answers while listening
- Seek the question behind the question
- Acknowledge the emotion beneath the words

Validation Before Response
Always validate before addressing:

- "That's a really important question…"
- "I appreciate you asking that…"
- "Many people wonder about that…"
- "That's something worth considering carefully…"

Holistic Response Structure
Provide comprehensive but concise answers:

- Direct answer to the specific question
- Relevant context for proper understanding
- Personal or client example for illustration
- Connection to their specific situation when possible

Empowered Choice Conclusion
End with autonomy reinforcement:

- "Does that help with your question?"
- "What are your thoughts about that?"
- "Would you like me to elaborate further?"
- "Is there a specific aspect of that I can clarify?"

This structured response creates satisfaction and trust while demonstrating your expertise and understanding.

## 3. The Decision Support Framework

For participants actively considering your offer, provide structured decision guidance:

Decision Clarity Questions
Offer reflective questions such as:

- "What would make this a clear yes for you?"
- "What specific concerns are you weighing?"
- "How does this align with your current priorities?"
- "What would need to be true for this to make sense?"

Personalized Guidance Provision
Offer individualized support:

- One-on-one decision consultation opportunities
- Specific resource recommendations for consideration
- Customized implementation vision for their situation
- Personal assessment of fit based on their circumstances

Pressure-Free Timeframe

Create appropriate space for decisions:

- Clear but reasonable decision windows
- Structured reflection guidance
- Alternative pathways if timing isn't right
- Support regardless of decision direction

Thank You Regardless Approach

Maintain relationship whatever the decision:

- Express gratitude for their consideration
- Acknowledge the thought they're putting in
- Respect their wisdom about their own situation
- Maintain connection beyond the immediate offer

This support framework helps participants make confident decisions while maintaining relationship integrity regardless of outcome.

# The Follow-Up Conversion System

The close session itself is just the beginning of the conversion process. A strategic follow-up system dramatically increases overall results:

## 1. The Immediate Integration Approach

Provide immediate value following your offer presentation:

Session Recording Access
Make the presentation available promptly:

- Send recording within 24 hours
- Include key timestamps for reference
- Provide accompaniment resources
- Add reflection questions for consideration

Clarity Resource Provision
Address common questions comprehensively:

- Detailed FAQ document addressing concerns
- Expanded explanation of program elements
- Specific examples and case studies
- Implementation illustrations and timelines

Decision Support Materials
Provide structured decision guidance:

- Decision consideration worksheet
- Program fit self-assessment
- Investment planning resources

- Implementation readiness evaluation

Additional Value Resources
Continue the value delivery relationship:

- Bonus training on related topic
- Implementation resource for challenge content
- Community continuation opportunity
- Unexpected gift or resource provision

This immediate follow-up maintains connection while providing resources that both support decisions and continue the value relationship.

## 2. The Segmented Follow-Up Sequence

Customize communication based on participant engagement:
High-Interest Segment

For those showing clear interest:

- Personal outreach offering decision support
- Specific addressing of their unique situation
- Implementation vision for their circumstances
- Direct invitation to enrollment conversation

Considering Segment
For those actively weighing the decision:

- Additional information addressing common concerns
- Client success stories relevant to their situation
- Alternative investment options if appropriate
- Decision timeline reminders with support

Low-Engagement Segment
For those with minimal engagement:

- Value continuation without pressure
- Alternative resource recommendations
- Future opportunity information
- Relationship maintenance focus

Already-Enrolled Segment
For those who have already joined:

- Immediate welcome and celebration
- Early implementation guidance
- Connection with current clients or community
- Excitement building for the journey ahead

This segmented approach provides appropriate support for each person's situation, dramatically increasing conversion through relevance.

## 3. The Final Opportunity Framework

Create appropriate urgency without manipulation:

Authentic Limitation Communication
Clearly explain genuine constraints:

- True capacity limits if applicable
- Honest program start date requirements
- Actual bonuses with expiration timing
- Genuine price increase plans if relevant

Value Focus (Not Fear)

Emphasize opportunity rather than loss:

- Benefits of prompt decision
- Advantages of immediate implementation
- Value of the complete package
- Support available for early commitment

Alternative Path Provision
Offer options for those not ready:

- Future program dates if applicable
- Alternative starting points
- Continued relationship opportunities
- Resources for self-implementation

Gratitude and Connection
Close with appreciation regardless of decision:

- Thank you for their participation
- Acknowledgment of their engagement
- Appreciation for their consideration
- Commitment to ongoing support

This framework creates appropriate decision motivation while maintaining relationship integrity through honest communication.

# Advanced Conversion Strategies

Beyond the fundamental frameworks, these advanced approaches can significantly enhance your results:

## 1. The Social Momentum Approach

Leverage the power of collective energy to support decisions:

Enrollment Celebration System
Create visibility for those joining:

- Public welcome for new participants (with permission)
- Excitement expressions for growing community
- Specific acknowledgment of diverse participants
- Selective sharing of implementation plans

Community Formation Initiation
Begin building community before program starts:

- Early access community for enrolled participants
- Connection opportunities between new members
- Shared vision building for the journey ahead
- Collective enthusiasm generation

Success Story Integration
Strategically share relevant transformations:

- Recent success highlights from current participants
- Specific outcome illustrations from past clients
- Diverse example selection for broad relatability

- Behind-the-scenes glimpses of transformation journeys

Social Proof Amplification
Ethically leverage testimonial evidence:

- Video testimonials from satisfied clients
- Before-and-after documentation
- Specific result verification and evidence
- Diverse experience representation

This social momentum creates a positive decision environment without manipulative pressure tactics.

# 2. The Multi-Modality Conversion System

Provide various decision and enrollment pathways:

Self-Service Enrollment Path
For independent decision-makers:

- Comprehensive information provision
- Clear digital enrollment process
- Immediate access and welcome
- Self-guided orientation systems

Conversation-Based Enrollment Path
For those needing personal guidance:

- Decision consultation opportunities
- Individualized question addressing
- Customized program vision creation
- Personal enrollment assistance

Small Group Decision Path
For those preferring collective consideration:

- Q&A session opportunities
- Small group decision workshops
- Peer discussion facilitation
- Collective enrollment opportunities

Payment Flexibility Options
For financial accessibility:

- Multiple investment structures
- Appropriate payment plans
- Scholarship or assistance programs where possible
- Value-aligned accessibility approaches

This multi-path approach honors different decision styles while creating maximum accessibility for your offer.

## 3. The Ascension and Descent Strategy

Create multiple entry points aligned with readiness:

Premium Offer Presentation
Lead with your comprehensive solution:

- Present complete transformation path
- Explain full support and implementation system
- Share comprehensive result possibilities
- Offer maximum value opportunity

Core Offer Alternative

Provide primary program option:

- Standard implementation pathway
- Essential support and guidance
- Complete methodology access
- Primary transformation focus

Starter Option Development

Create accessible beginning point:

- Foundational implementation focus
- Streamlined support approach
- Essential methodology components
- Initial transformation emphasis

Self-Implementation Resources

For those not ready for programs:

- Continued free content access
- Low-cost implementation tools
- Self-guided resource recommendations
- Future opportunity awareness

This multi-level approach creates appropriate entry points for various readiness levels, allowing relationship continuation regardless of current decision.

# The Ethical Conversion Philosophy

As we conclude this chapter, I want to address the deeper philosophy behind this approach to challenge conversion:

## The Three Conversion Principles

These fundamentals guide ethical, effective conversion:

1. True Value Exchange
Ensure genuine benefit alignment:

- Your offer provides greater value than its cost
- Participants genuinely benefit from enrollment
- The transformation justifies the investment
- You can deliver with integrity on all promises

2. Empowered Choice Facilitation
Support autonomous decisions:

- Provide complete information for informed choices
- Respect individual timing and readiness
- Honor the wisdom of hesitation when present
- Support non-enrollment decisions with grace

3. Relationship Beyond Transaction
Maintain connection regardless of purchase:

- Value participants as people, not just prospects
- Continue serving regardless of enrollment
- Appreciate contribution beyond purchase
- Recognize relationship value independent of revenue

These principles transform conversion from manipulation to service—creating sustainable business growth through integrity rather than pressure.

# Challenge Conversion for Community Impact

Through the Nehemiah Davis Foundation, we've discovered that challenge conversion can simultaneously serve both business growth and community impact:

## The Scholarship Model

For each challenge we run, we incorporate scholarship access:

- One paid enrollment sponsors one scholarship participant
- Challenge participants can contribute to scholarship fund
- Corporate partners underwrite community access
- Successful graduates sponsor future participants

This approach has allowed us to serve thousands who couldn't otherwise access our programs while creating meaningful connection between paying clients and scholarship recipients.

## The Community Contribution Integration

Our enrollment process includes impact opportunities:

- Option to contribute to community programs

- Implementation projects with community benefit
- Mentorship opportunities for scholarship participants
- Expertise sharing with nonprofit partners

This integration transforms the enrollment decision from purely personal advancement to meaningful contribution—deepening the significance of participation.

When developing your challenge conversion strategy, consider:

- How might your business success directly enable community access?
- What contribution elements could be integrated into your offer?
- How could paying clients connect with impact recipients?
- What structures would create sustainable community benefit?

These considerations transform challenge conversion from mere business transaction to meaningful impact vehicle.

## Chapter Summary: Key Takeaways

- The Bridge Session framework creates a seamless transition from challenge to offer
- Energetic integrity during your close significantly impacts both conversion and relationships
- Proactive objection addressing creates trust while reducing perceived risk
- Strategic follow-up systems continue the conversion process beyond the presentation

- Advanced strategies create multiple pathways for aligned decisions
- Ethical conversion principles transform sales from manipulation to service
- Challenge conversion can simultaneously drive business growth and community impact

## Action Steps:

1. Design your Bridge Session using the seven-component framework
2. Develop your energetic preparation practice for authentic alignment
3. Identify and create preemptive addressing for common objections
4. Create your segmented follow-up sequence for different engagement levels
5. Select appropriate advanced strategies for your specific audience
6. Review your approach for alignment with ethical conversion principles
7. Identify how your conversion process could incorporate community impact

If you're passionate about **impact, purpose, and real results,** we want to hear from you. **Partner with Neo**. Visit PartnerWithNeo.com/apply to explore how we can collaborate.

# CHAPTER 15

---

# THE POWER OF PRESENTATION

There's a moment in nearly every entrepreneur's journey when they realize a powerful truth: your ability to articulate your value determines your success more than the value itself. The most transformative expertise, locked behind ineffective communication, rarely reaches its potential impact or revenue.

Throughout the previous chapters, we've explored creating digital products, building marketing systems, and developing challenges. Now we turn to perhaps the most fundamental skill underlying all business success: the ability to present your ideas in a way that inspires action.

Whether you're delivering a webinar, speaking on stage, facilitating a challenge, or presenting an offer, your presentation skills directly impact your conversion rates, customer satisfaction, and ultimate impact. In this chapter, I'll share the presentation system that has helped me generate millions on stages and webinars while transforming countless lives through effective communication.

# The Presentation Preparation System

Extraordinary presentations begin long before you step on stage or go live on camera. This preparation system creates the foundation for powerful delivery:

## 1. The Outcome Clarity Process

Before developing any content, get absolutely clear on your desired outcomes:

**Transformation Objective** Define the specific change you want to create:

- Knowledge transformation (what they'll understand)
- Belief transformation (what they'll believe)
- Action transformation (what they'll do)
- Identity transformation (who they'll become)

**Audience Journey Mapping** Clarify where your audience starts and ends:

- Current understanding, beliefs, and feelings
- Primary questions, concerns, and objections
- Desired post-presentation state and mindset
- Specific intended actions following presentation

**Success Metrics Definition** Establish how you'll measure effectiveness:

- Engagement indicators during presentation
- Action metrics following presentation
- Conversion objectives if applicable
- Long-term implementation indicators

This outcome clarity prevents the common mistake of creating content based on what you want to say rather than the transformation you want to create.

## 2. The Presentation Structure Framework

With clear outcomes established, design your presentation structure:

**The 7-Part Presentation Framework**

- Attention-Grabbing Opening (3-5 minutes)
- Problem and Possibility Framing (5-7 minutes)
- Your Story and Credibility (3-5 minutes)
- Core Teaching/Content (15-20 minutes)
- Transformation Illustration (5-7 minutes)
- Implementation Guidance (5-10 minutes)
- Clear Call to Action (3-5 minutes)

**The Content Organization System** For each section, develop:

- Big idea or core message
- Supporting evidence or examples
- Stories that illustrate the concept
- Engagement elements for interaction
- Transition to the next section

**The Visual Support Structure** Design visual aids that enhance rather than distract:

- Simple, visually consistent slides
- One main idea per visual

- Minimal text (3-7 words per slide ideal)
- High-impact images or graphics
- Clear data visualization when needed

This structured approach creates a cohesive journey rather than disconnected information, guiding your audience to your intended outcome naturally.

## 3. The Delivery Preparation Process

Once your content is structured, prepare for actual delivery:

**Environmental Optimization** Set up your physical or virtual environment:

- Appropriate lighting and visibility
- Clear, quality audio capture
- Minimal background distractions
- Technical equipment testing
- Backup systems for potential failures

**Personal Energy Management** Develop pre-presentation rituals:

- Physical practices for energy and presence
- Mental techniques for focus and clarity
- Emotional preparation for authentic connection
- Spiritual/purpose alignment for deeper meaning

**Practice Methodology** Implement effective rehearsal techniques:

- Full run-through with timing
- Section-by-section refinement

- Challenging portions identification and extra practice
- Recorded practice for self-assessment
- Live feedback from trusted advisors

This preparation creates the confidence and presence that allows your content to shine without technical or personal distractions.

# The Engagement Maximization System

Even the best-structured content falls flat without active audience engagement. This system creates powerful connection throughout your presentation:

## 1. The Opening Connection Formula

Begin with immediate engagement rather than traditional introductions:

**Pattern Interrupt Opening** Start with something unexpected:

- Provocative question or statement
- Surprising statistic or fact
- Counterintuitive insight
- Compelling story opening

**Audience-Centered Framing** Make it immediately about them:

- Acknowledge their current situation
- Validate their challenges or desires
- Demonstrate understanding of their experience
- Create recognition moments ("That's me!")

**Early Engagement Activation** Get participation within the first 2-3 minutes:

- Simple yes/no questions with raised hands
- Brief written reflection prompts
- Low-risk sharing opportunities
- Quick pulse-check questions

**Clear Journey Preview** Set expectations for the experience:

- Outline what they'll learn/receive
- Address time commitment and format
- Explain participation expectations
- Create anticipation for key moments

This opening formula immediately establishes connection and engagement rather than beginning with the traditional "about me" introduction that delays audience investment.

## 2. The Continuous Engagement Rhythm

Maintain active participation throughout your presentation:

**The 5-Minute Engagement Rule** Create participation at least every 5 minutes:

- Direct questions requiring response
- Brief partner or self-reflection moments
- Quick application exercises
- Virtual or physical movements
- Chat or comment prompts

**Engagement Variety Approach** Use diverse engagement modalities:

- Physical (stand, raise hand, move)
- Verbal (speak, respond, share)
- Written (note, chat, comment)
- Mental (reflect, consider, evaluate)
- Emotional (feel, connect, relate)

**Escalating Involvement Pattern** Progressively deepen engagement:

- Begin with low-risk, simple participation
- Build to moderate sharing and application
- Advance to deeper reflection and consideration
- Culminate in substantive implementation commitments

This rhythm prevents the passive consumption that undermines both learning and conversion, creating an active experience that increases both retention and action.

## 3. The Virtual Engagement Mastery System

For online presentations, implement specific digital engagement strategies:

**Technical Engagement Optimization** Leverage platform-specific capabilities:

- Polls and surveys for data collection
- Chat prompts for written engagement
- Breakout rooms for small group interaction
- Reaction buttons for quick feedback

- Q&A features for question management

**Energy Transmission Techniques** Overcome the digital energy barrier:

- Increased vocal variety and expression
- More dynamic physical movement
- Enhanced facial expressiveness
- Shorter content segments with more interaction
- Direct camera eye contact for connection

**Attention Recapture Methods** Address the digital distraction challenge:

- Pattern interrupts every 3-5 minutes
- Clear signposting of important moments
- Unexpected elements that create focus
- Direct acknowledgment of potential distractions
- Periodic reorientation to key outcomes

These virtual-specific strategies address the unique challenges of online presentations, creating engagement despite the distance barrier.

# The Persuasive Presentation Framework

Beyond structure and engagement, specific persuasion principles dramatically increase the impact of your presentations:

## 1. The Story-Driven Persuasion System

Use strategic storytelling to create connection and conviction:

**The Personal Transformation Story** Share your relevant journey:

- Relatable starting point (similar to audience)
- Catalytic moment that initiated change
- Obstacle navigation and learning process
- Transformation results and new reality
- Connection to audience opportunity

**The Client Journey Narrative** Illustrate results through others' experiences:

- Selection of relatable case examples
- Specific situation details for authenticity
- Challenge and obstacle recognition
- Implementation and process illustration
- Concrete result documentation

**The Possibility Story** Paint the picture of potential transformation:

- Vivid "day in the life" future scenario
- Multi-sensory experience description
- Emotional and practical impact illustration

- Contrast with current limitations
- Bridge between vision and immediate next steps

These story frameworks create emotional connection and belief in possibilities more effectively than abstract concepts or data alone.

## 2. The Objection Integration Method

Address resistance proactively throughout your presentation:

**Common Objection Identification** Determine primary hesitations:

- Financial investment concerns
- Time and implementation doubts
- Confidence and ability questions
- Result certainty hesitations
- Timing and readiness concerns

**Strategic Objection Placement** Address concerns at optimal moments:

- Acknowledge natural questions when they arise
- Integrate objection resolution within content
- Address mindset concerns before tactical teaching
- Resolve implementation doubts before calls to action

**The "You Might Be Thinking" Framework** Introduce objections naturally:

- "You might be wondering…"
- "A question that often comes up…"
- "Something I would be asking at this point…"
- "I know what some of you are thinking…"

**Complete Resolution Approach** Provide thorough but concise addressing:

- Validate the legitimacy of the concern
- Share relevant perspective or context
- Provide evidence-based reassurance
- Connect to examples or case studies
- Offer alternative viewpoint consideration

This proactive objection handling prevents unaddressed concerns from blocking engagement or conversion later.

# 3. The Ethical Influence Framework

Implement persuasion principles with integrity:

**Reciprocity Activation** Give genuine value before requesting action:

- Deliver immediately applicable insights
- Provide useful tools or frameworks
- Offer unexpected additional resources
- Create meaningful "aha" moments
- Solve real problems during presentation

**Social Proof Integration** Demonstrate others' experience appropriately:

- Diverse example selection for relatability
- Specific, concrete result documentation
- Authentic challenge acknowledgment
- Implementation process illustration
- Various formats (stories, data, testimonials)

**Authority Establishment** Build credibility through demonstration:

- Expertise shown rather than claimed
- Relevant experience illustration
- Third-party validation when appropriate
- Documented results and case studies
- Vulnerable authenticity balancing competence

**Scarcity and Opportunity Framing** Create appropriate urgency without manipulation:

- Honest limitation explanation when real
- Opportunity focus rather than fear emphasis
- Benefit orientation versus loss framing
- Authentic timing considerations
- Alternative options for different situations

This ethical approach creates genuine influence through integrity rather than manipulation, building relationship rather than just driving transactions.

# The Presentation Delivery Excellence System

Beyond content and structure, how you actually deliver your presentation significantly impacts results:

## 1. The Authentic Presence Approach

Develop genuine connection through authentic presence:

**Personal Congruence Practice** Align your inner and outer experience:

- Connect to your genuine purpose and meaning
- Identify and release performance anxiety
- Access authentic enthusiasm and conviction
- Find personal connection to your material
- Center in service rather than self-focus

**Vulnerability Calibration** Share appropriately to build connection:

- Select relevant personal examples
- Acknowledge authentic challenges
- Share appropriate learning moments
- Demonstrate growth through difficulty
- Maintain appropriate professional boundaries

**Energy Management Mastery** Cultivate and direct your energy intentionally:

- Physical practices for presence and vitality
- Emotional regulation techniques
- Focus and attention management

- Recovery methods for maintaining stamina
- State shifts for different presentation segments

This authentic presence creates the connection foundation that enables influence beyond your actual content.

## 2. The Vocal and Physical Delivery System

Optimize the non-verbal elements of your presentation:

**Vocal Variety Mastery** Use your voice as an instrument:

- Strategic pace variation (faster for energy, slower for importance)
- Volume modulation for emphasis and attention
- Tone shifts to convey emotion and meaning
- Strategic pausing for impact and processing
- Articulation clarity for understanding

**Intentional Movement Patterns** Use physical movement purposefully:

- Stage positioning for different content segments
- Gesture amplification for emphasis
- Physical anchoring for key concepts
- Movement variation for energy management
- Stillness for powerful moments

**Facial Expression Consciousness** Leverage facial communication intentionally:

- Expanded expressiveness beyond normal conversation
- Authentic emotional congruence

- Eye contact patterns for connection
- Smile authenticity and appropriate timing
- Expression alignment with content

These delivery elements often impact audience perception and response more than your actual words, creating subconscious connection and credibility.

## 3. The Flexible Adaptation System

Respond effectively to real-time audience feedback:

**Engagement Monitoring Techniques** Continuously assess audience response:

- Body language and facial expression reading
- Participation level observation
- Chat or comment energy assessment
- Question patterns recognition
- Energy and attention pulse checks

**Real-Time Adjustment Strategies** Adapt based on audience feedback:

- Content pace modification
- Engagement approach shifts
- Example or story selection changes
- Explanation depth adjustment
- Format or structure flexibility

**Recovery Method Implementation** Address challenges effectively:

- Low-energy intervention techniques
- Distraction redirection strategies
- Confusion clarification approaches
- Technical problem navigation
- Difficult situation management

This flexibility prevents the "stick to the script regardless" approach that creates disconnect between presenter and audience.

# The Call to Action Mastery System

The culmination of your presentation—the invitation to next steps—requires specific strategies for maximum effectiveness:

## 1. The Action Bridge Framework

Create a seamless transition from content to invitation:

**Value Integration Summary** Consolidate the transformation journey:

- Recap key insights and learning moments
- Acknowledge progress and shifts already made
- Connect content elements into cohesive framework
- Remind of core transformation principles

**Implementation Reality Check** Address the self-implementation challenge:

- Acknowledge common obstacles to application
- Discuss the limitation of information without support
- Share typical implementation patterns honestly
- Recognize the challenge of isolated application

**Natural Next Step Framing** Position your offer as the logical continuation:

- Connect to the journey already begun
- Illustrate the complete path beyond presentation
- Show the gap between current and desired state
- Present your solution as the bridge to implementation

This bridge creates context for your invitation, making it feel like a natural continuation rather than an abrupt shift to selling.

## 2. The Clear Invitation Formula

Present your offer with clarity and confidence:

**Solution-Focused Presentation** Emphasize transformation over features:

- Lead with outcome and results
- Connect to specific audience desires
- Illustrate the transformation journey
- Show the before-and-after contrast

**Complete Clarity Approach** Provide comprehensive information:

- Specific components and elements
- Implementation process and timeline
- Support and accountability systems
- Expected results and milestones

**Value-Centric Investment Framing** Present pricing in context of value:

- Investment connected to outcomes
- Value comparison illustration
- Return on investment clarification
- Worth versus cost distinction

**Decision Simplification** Make the next step crystal clear:

- Exactly what to do next
- Precisely how to take action
- When the opportunity is available
- What happens immediately after decision

This clarity eliminates confusion that often prevents action, making the decision process straightforward and accessible.

## 3. The Decision Acceleration System

Create appropriate momentum toward commitment:

**Genuine Incentive Creation** Develop meaningful action motivators:

- Authentic bonuses that enhance experience
- Early decision benefits with real value

- Implementation support advantages
- Community or connection opportunities

**Social Proof Amplification** Share others' decision experiences:

- Diverse decision journey examples
- Initial hesitation acknowledgment
- Decision rationale illustration
- Post-decision experience sharing

**Risk Reversal Framework** Address fear and uncertainty directly:

- Guarantee or assurance explanation
- Risk-shifting from customer to you
- Confidence demonstration through policy
- Fair and clear terms articulation

**Immediate Action Emphasis** Create momentum toward prompt decision:

- Clear benefit for immediate action
- Simple, frictionless decision process
- Immediate access and implementation
- Quick-start support and orientation

This system creates appropriate urgency without manipulation, helping interested participants move forward without unnecessary delay.

# Presentation Technology Mastery

The technical aspects of presentation often determine whether your content can shine or gets undermined by distractions:

## 1. The In-Person Presentation Environment

For physical presentations, optimize these elements:

**Room Setup Optimization** Create an ideal physical environment:

- Seating arrangement for engagement
- Temperature and comfort considerations
- Lighting for visibility and energy
- Sound quality for all participants
- Visual line of sight optimization

**Technical Equipment Mastery** Ensure reliable technical function:

- Microphone selection and testing
- Presentation display systems
- Remote advancement devices
- Backup systems for critical components
- Support team coordination

**Physical Material Integration** Incorporate tangible elements effectively:

- Handout design and distribution
- Workbook or guide utilization
- Physical props or demonstrations

- Activity materials and tools
- Product or service examples

These environmental elements prevent the technical distractions that can undermine even excellent content.

## 2. The Virtual Presentation Technology System

For online presentations, master these technical considerations:

**Platform Selection and Optimization** Choose and configure appropriate technology:

- Platform features alignment with needs
- Technical requirement understanding
- Engagement tool availability
- Recording and distribution capabilities
- Integration with other systems

**Personal Technical Setup** Create a professional virtual environment:

- Camera positioning and quality
- Lighting arrangement for visibility
- Audio clarity and background noise elimination
- Internet connection stability
- Background presentation and distraction removal

**Technical Support Systems** Implement backup and assistance measures:

- Co-host or technical support person
- Multiple device login contingency

- Backup internet connection
- Alternative presentation access methods
- Technical issue response protocols

These virtual-specific considerations address the unique challenges of online presentation, preventing the technical issues that often plague digital events.

## 3. The Hybrid Presentation Approach

For presentations with both in-person and online audiences:

**Dual Audience Engagement** Create connection with both groups:

- Balanced attention distribution
- Virtual audience acknowledgment
- In-room participation without excluding online
- Technology for integrating both experiences
- Shared activities that work in both formats

**Technical Integration Solutions** Connect the physical and virtual seamlessly:

- Camera angles showing in-room experience
- Audio capture for room interactions
- Display systems for virtual participants
- Engagement tools that work for both audiences
- Team roles for managing dual experience

**Energy Balancing Techniques** Maintain connection across formats:

- Increased energy projection for virtual audience
- Direct address to both participant groups
- Intentional inclusion of both experiences
- Format-appropriate engagement activities
- Connection creation between audience types

This hybrid approach creates an equitable experience regardless of participation method, addressing the increasing prevalence of mixed-format presentations.

# Presentation as a Vehicle for Impact

As we conclude this chapter, I want to highlight how presentation excellence can serve both business growth and meaningful impact:

## 1. The Purpose Integration Approach

Weave impact mission throughout your presentation:

**Purpose Communication** Share your deeper why authentically:

- Connect your work to meaningful change
- Share impact stories alongside business ones
- Illustrate the ripple effect of transformation
- Link participant success to broader contribution

**Contribution Opportunity Integration** Incorporate giving elements:

- Impact metrics alongside business results
- Giving components of your business model
- Participant contribution opportunities
- Community impact initiatives

**Value Beyond Transaction Emphasis** Highlight the greater meaning:

- Industry or community advancement
- Collective wisdom expansion
- Legacy and long-term impact
- Transformation beyond immediate results

This purpose integration creates deeper connection while attracting aligned participants who value impact alongside results.

## 2. The Inclusive Presentation Framework

Make your presentation accessible to diverse audiences:

**Multiple Learning Style Accommodation** Support various processing preferences:

- Visual elements for visual learners
- Verbal explanation for auditory processors
- Interactive components for kinesthetic learners
- Conceptual and practical balance for different processors

**Inclusive Language and Examples** Create broad relatability:

- Diverse story selection and representation
- Varied industry and application examples
- Inclusive language and terminology
- Multiple implementation scenarios

**Accessibility Consciousness** Remove unnecessary barriers:

- Caption provision for hearing impaired
- Description of visual elements
- Transcript or alternative format availability
- Technology alternatives when needed
- Financial accessibility considerations

This inclusive approach expands who can benefit from your expertise, creating broader impact while building a more diverse community.

Through the Nehemiah Davis Foundation, we've implemented these presentation approaches across our educational initiatives, creating accessible learning experiences while incorporating our impact mission throughout. This has allowed us to serve diverse audiences effectively while maintaining the connection between business success and community contribution.

When developing your presentation approach, consider:

- How might your deeper purpose enhance rather than distract from results?
- What inclusive elements would expand your reach and impact?
- How could your presentation model the change you wish to create?

- What community-building elements would create connection beyond content?

These considerations transform presentations from mere information delivery or sales vehicles to meaningful experiences that create both business success and positive change.

## Chapter Summary: Key Takeaways

- Presentation preparation creates the foundation for effective delivery
- Engagement strategies transform passive listening into active participation
- Persuasive frameworks inspire action through ethical influence
- Delivery excellence creates connection beyond your actual content
- Effective calls to action create natural conversion opportunities
- Technical mastery prevents distractions from undermining your message
- Purpose integration creates deeper meaning and aligned attraction
- Inclusive approaches expand your impact while building diverse community

## Action Steps:

1. Develop your presentation preparation system for your next event

2. Implement the engagement maximization strategies appropriate for your format

3. Create your persuasive presentation framework with ethical influence principles

4. Practice the authentic presence approach for more effective delivery

5. Design your action bridge and clear invitation formula

6. Optimize your technical environment for distraction-free delivery

7. Integrate purpose elements throughout your presentation

8. Implement inclusive practices to expand your reach and impact

If you're passionate about **impact, purpose, and real results,** we want to hear from you. **Partner with Neo**. Visit PartnerWithNeo.com/apply to explore how we can collaborate.

# CHAPTER 16

# SCALING TO SEVEN FIGURES AND BEYOND

Throughout this book, we've explored the foundational elements of a successful digital business—from creating products and building funnels to mastering challenges and presentations. Now we turn our attention to scaling: the systematic expansion of your business beyond your personal capacity to create true freedom and impact.

Scaling is where most entrepreneurs struggle. They build successful six-figure businesses based on their personal expertise but hit a ceiling when their time, energy, and capacity reach their limits. The difference between a six-figure business and a seven-figure business isn't just more of the same—it's a fundamental shift in systems, structure, and leadership.

In this chapter, I'll share the scaling framework that has helped me build multiple seven-figure businesses while creating impact through the Nehemiah Davis Foundation. These principles apply whether you're currently at $100,000 or $900,000—providing the roadmap to break through your current ceiling.

# The Seven-Figure Mindset Shift

Before addressing tactical systems, we must address the essential mindset shifts that enable scaling:

## 1. From Doer to Leader

The most fundamental shift required for scaling is in your self-concept:

**The Expertise Trap Recognition** Acknowledge how personal implementation limits growth:

- Technical expertise that keeps you in delivery
- Perfectionism that prevents delegation
- Identity attachment to specific roles
- Fear of quality decline with expansion

**The Leadership Identity Development** Redefine your primary value to the business:

- Vision and direction setting
- Strategic decision-making
- Team development and culture creation
- Systems oversight and improvement
- Opportunity identification and evaluation

**The Impact Amplification Perspective** Recognize how leadership expands your contribution:

- Leveraging others' talents multiplies your impact
- System creation extends your reach beyond personal capacity

- Team development creates opportunity for others
- Scalable models serve more people than direct service

This mindset shift from primary implementer to leader is the foundation for everything that follows. Without it, the tactical systems will inevitably falter as you become the bottleneck to your own growth.

## 2. From Income to Asset Building

Scaling requires a longer-term perspective on business value:

**Business Value Orientation** Shift focus from monthly revenue to business asset:

- Building intellectual property and methodology
- Creating systems independent of founder
- Developing team capability and culture
- Establishing predictable, recurring revenue models
- Creating transferable or sellable business assets

**Reinvestment Perspective** View profits strategically rather than personally:

- Appropriate founder compensation but not maximization
- Strategic profit reinvestment for growth
- Balance between current lifestyle and future value
- Investment in assets rather than just expenses
- Long-term wealth creation vs. income generation

**Legacy Development Framework** Consider the multi-year and multi-generational impact:

- Business longevity beyond founder involvement
- Impact potential at scale over time
- Value creation for multiple stakeholders
- Contribution beyond immediate customer base
- Lasting change in industry or community

This expanded perspective creates decisions aligned with sustainable growth rather than short-term income maximization, enabling the patience and strategic thinking required for scaling.

## 3. From Scarcity to Abundance

Perhaps the most subtle but crucial mindset shift involves your relationship with resources:

**Resource Abundance Recognition** Expand your view of available resources:

- Talent abundance beyond your personal capacity
- Capital availability for valuable opportunities
- Time expansion through leverage and systems
- Knowledge accessibility through networks and teams
- Creative solutions beyond obvious constraints

**Collaboration Over Competition** Shift from competitive to collaborative perspective:

- Partnership opportunities with "competitors"

- Shared resource models for mutual benefit
- Ecosystem participation and contribution
- Industry elevation rather than domination
- Win-win approach to business relationships

**Generosity as Strategy** Recognize the strategic value of giving:

- Counter-intuitive advantages of generosity
- Relationship development through contribution
- Network expansion through support
- Reputation enhancement through sharing
- Karmic business returns through giving

This abundance mindset opens possibilities invisible through a scarcity lens, creating the psychological space for expansion beyond apparent resource limitations.

# The Scalable Business Model Framework

With the right mindset foundation, specific business model adjustments enable true scaling:

## 1. The Leverage Optimization System

Systematically increase your impact per unit of effort:

**Time Leverage Analysis** Identify opportunities for time multiplication:

- Activities with highest revenue per hour
- Tasks requiring your unique expertise vs. delegable ones

- Strategic vs. tactical responsibilities
- Highest leverage points in customer journey
- Energy-enhancing vs. energy-depleting activities

**Team Leverage Development** Create multiplication through others:

- Role design around leverage points
- Capability building and training systems
- Autonomy and decision authority frameworks
- Performance measurement and feedback loops
- Culture and value alignment mechanisms

**Technology Leverage Implementation** Use systems to extend human capacity:

- Automation of repetitive processes
- Integration between key systems
- Data capture and analysis capabilities
- Customer experience enhancement tools
- Team productivity amplification technologies

This systematic leverage approach creates the capacity for growth beyond personal bandwidth limitations.

## 2. The Recurring Revenue Architecture

Shift from transactional to recurring business models:

**Subscription Model Development** Create ongoing value delivery systems:

- Membership or continuity programs

- Access-based service models
- Content subscription platforms
- Software-as-a-service offerings
- Ongoing support and implementation programs

**Long-Term Program Design** Extend customer value timeline:

- 6-12 month implementation journeys
- Multi-stage transformation programs
- Progressive development pathways
- Tiered advancement systems
- Graduate and alumni programs

**Ecosystem Integration Approach** Connect offerings into cohesive journey:

- Logical progression between products/services
- Complementary offering development
- Cross-utilization of resources
- Integrated customer experience
- Lifetime value maximization strategy

This revenue architecture creates predictability and stability that enables confident investment in growth while reducing the constant pressure of new customer acquisition.

# 3. The Scalable Delivery Framework

Create systems for consistent value delivery beyond personal implementation:

**Methodology Systematization** Transform expertise into repeatable systems:

- Core methodology documentation
- Process mapping and standardization
- Implementation templating
- Quality assurance frameworks
- Continuous improvement mechanisms

**Team Capability Development** Build delivery capacity beyond yourself:

- Comprehensive training systems
- Certification and quality validation
- Mentorship and development pathways
- Culture and values integration
- Performance monitoring and improvement

**Client Success Systematization** Create consistent client experience:

- Customer journey mapping and optimization
- Touchpoint standardization and enhancement
- Progress tracking and celebration systems
- Obstacle identification and intervention protocols
- Outcome documentation and amplification

This delivery framework enables consistent quality at scale, addressing the common fear that growth will dilute excellence.

# The Team Development System

Perhaps no element impacts scaling potential more than your ability to build and lead an exceptional team:

## 1. The Role Design Framework

Create positions aligned with scaling objectives:

**Strategic Role Identification** Determine key leverage points requiring dedicated focus:

- Highest impact areas for specialized attention
- Customer journey critical moments
- Founder bottlenecks requiring delegation
- Essential functions for quality maintenance
- Growth opportunities needing dedicated resources

**Role Architecture Development** Design positions for maximum effectiveness:

- Clear outcomes and success metrics
- Decision authority and boundaries
- Primary responsibilities and priorities
- Essential capabilities and characteristics
- Development and growth pathways

**Compensation and Incentive Alignment** Create motivational structures that drive results:

- Base compensation appropriate to market and value
- Performance-based incentives aligned with outcomes

- Long-term retention and commitment incentives
- Non-financial motivation and recognition systems
- Culture-aligned reward structures

This intentional role design prevents the common scaling mistake of simply hiring replicas of yourself or adding headcount without strategic purpose.

## 2. The Talent Acquisition and Development System

Build your team with intention and effectiveness:

**Attraction Strategy Implementation** Develop proactive talent pipelines:

- Employer brand development
- Culture and vision communication
- Network and relationship cultivation
- Presence in talent communities
- Value proposition for ideal team members

**Selection Process Optimization** Design rigorous but efficient hiring processes:

- Clear capability and characteristic requirements
- Multi-stage evaluation procedures
- Cultural alignment assessment
- Practical skill and implementation evaluation
- Reference and background validation

**Onboarding and Integration Approach** Create strong foundations for new team members:

- Comprehensive orientation processes
- Initial wins and confidence building
- Culture immersion and value integration
- Relationship and connection development
- Clear expectations and feedback loops

**Continuous Development Framework** Build capabilities beyond initial hiring:

- Personalized growth planning
- Skill development resources and opportunities
- Leadership pathway creation
- Performance feedback and coaching
- Career progression transparency

This talent system ensures you attract, select, and develop the team members who will enable rather than limit your scaling journey.

## 3. The Leadership and Culture Framework

Create the environment that enables sustainable scaling:

**Vision and Direction Clarity** Establish the north star that guides decisions:

- Compelling purpose and mission
- Clear values and principles
- Inspiring future vision

- Strategic priorities and focus
- Key performance indicators and metrics

**Communication System Development** Create information flow that enables alignment:

- Regular rhythm of communication
- Transparency appropriate to roles
- Feedback channels in all directions
- Conflict resolution processes
- Celebration and recognition mechanisms

**Decision-Making Framework Implementation** Establish how choices are made at all levels:

- Authority and autonomy parameters
- Consultation requirements and boundaries
- Decision quality standards
- Responsibility and accountability clarity
- Learning and adjustment processes

**Culture Cultivation Approach** Intentionally develop your desired environment:

- Value demonstration and reinforcement
- Behavior standards and expectations
- Recognition and correction systems
- Story and narrative cultivation
- Ritual and tradition development

This leadership foundation creates the cohesion and alignment that prevents the fragmentation common in rapidly scaling organizations.

# The Growth Acceleration System

With the right foundation in place, specific growth strategies dramatically accelerate your scaling journey:

## 1. The Acquisition Channel Diversification Approach

Expand beyond founder-dependent marketing:

**Channel Portfolio Development** Build multiple sustainable lead sources:

- Paid advertising systems (social, search, display)
- Content marketing engines (blog, podcast, video)
- SEO and organic traffic generation
- Strategic partnership and affiliate programs
- Community and referral systems

**Channel Optimization Framework** Continuously improve channel performance:

- Testing and experimentation systems
- Data collection and analysis processes
- Key metric identification and tracking
- Conversion rate optimization approaches
- ROI-based investment decisions

**Channel Integration Strategy** Create synergy between acquisition methods:

- Cross-channel customer journeys
- Sequential exposure planning
- Attribution and influence modeling
- Complementary messaging and positioning
- Resource allocation based on integrated performance

This diversified approach prevents the common scaling vulnerability of single-channel dependency while creating predictable, sustainable growth.

## 2. The Strategic Partnership Framework

Leverage relationships for exponential growth:

**Partnership Opportunity Identification** Systematically discover collaboration potential:

- Complementary audience relationships
- Capability and resource complementarity
- Shared vision and value alignment
- Mutually beneficial opportunity structures
- Low-competition, high-synergy potential

**Partnership Development Process** Create successful collaborative relationships:

- Thoughtful outreach and connection
- Value-first relationship building
- Clear opportunity articulation

- Mutual benefit establishment
- Structured agreement development

**Partnership Optimization System** Maximize value from strategic relationships:

- Performance tracking and measurement
- Communication and coordination processes
- Continuous improvement mechanisms
- Relationship nurturing practices
- Expansion and evolution planning

This partnership approach creates growth leverage beyond your direct marketing investment, accelerating scaling through relationship rather than just resource deployment.

## 3. The New Market Expansion Strategy

Systematically enter new customer segments and opportunities:

**Market Opportunity Analysis** Identify promising expansion directions:

- Adjacent customer segment potential
- Geographical expansion opportunities
- Vertical market possibilities
- Complementary offering potential
- New application of existing methodology

**Minimum Viable Expansion Approach** Test new markets efficiently before full commitment:

- Limited feature or offering adaptation
- Controlled customer acquisition testing
- Rapid feedback collection and analysis
- Iterative improvement cycles
- Return-based expansion decisions

**Scaling Sequence Implementation** Expand methodically rather than simultaneously:

- Sequential rather than parallel market entry
- Success establishment before new expansion
- Learning integration between markets
- Resource allocation based on proven potential
- Capacity development aligned with expansion

This disciplined expansion prevents the dilution of focus and resources that often derails scaling attempts, creating sustainable growth rather than premature diversification.

# The Systems and Process Optimization Framework

As you scale, intentional systematization becomes increasingly critical:

## 1. The Business System Architecture

Create the operational backbone that enables scaling:

**Core Process Identification** Determine essential operational components:

- Customer acquisition systems
- Service delivery processes
- Team management and development
- Financial management and reporting
- Strategic planning and execution

**Process Documentation and Standardization** Transform implicit knowledge into explicit systems:

- Standard operating procedure development
- Process mapping and visualization
- Role and responsibility definition
- Quality standard establishment
- Exception handling protocols

**Continuous Improvement Integration** Build evolution capability into systems:

- Performance measurement mechanisms
- Feedback collection processes
- Regular review and reflection cycles

- Innovation and optimization incentives
- Adaptation and evolution protocols

This systematization creates consistency and scalability while reducing founder dependency for operational excellence.

## 2. The Technology Stack Integration

Leverage tools to enable and accelerate scaling:

**Technology Needs Assessment** Identify critical system requirements:

- Customer relationship management
- Marketing automation and measurement
- Team communication and collaboration
- Project and task management
- Financial tracking and reporting
- Knowledge management and training

**Stack Selection and Integration** Create a cohesive technology ecosystem:

- Tool selection based on requirements
- Integration between key systems
- Data flow and accessibility planning
- User adoption and training processes
- Security and compliance considerations

**Optimization and Evolution Approach** Continuously improve your technology foundation:

- Usage analysis and optimization
- Regular capability review
- Update and upgrade planning
- New technology evaluation
- Legacy system transition management

This technology foundation creates the infrastructure that supports rather than hinders growth, enabling the information flow and operational efficiency scaling requires.

## 3. The Financial Management System

Establish the fiscal foundation for sustainable growth:

**Financial Intelligence Framework** Create visibility into business performance:

- Key performance indicator identification
- Reporting automation and dashboarding
- Regular review and analysis cadence
- Forecasting and planning processes
- Cash flow management systems

**Investment Strategy Development** Make resource allocation decisions strategically:

- Return on investment analysis processes
- Growth opportunity evaluation criteria

- Risk assessment and management approach
- Capital allocation decision framework
- Resource optimization methodology

**Profitability and Sustainability Focus** Balance growth with financial health:

- Margin analysis and management
- Fixed and variable cost optimization
- Pricing strategy and value capture
- Revenue diversification planning
- Reserves and contingency development

This financial foundation prevents the cash flow challenges and unsustainable economics that often derail scaling businesses despite apparent success.

# Scaling for Impact

As we conclude this chapter, I want to emphasize how scaling your business enables expanded impact beyond profit:

## 1. The Impact Integration Model

Weave purpose throughout your scaling journey:

**Purpose-Aligned Scaling** Ensure growth advances mission:

- Impact metrics alongside business ones
- Purpose integration in strategic planning

- Value-aligned partnership development
- Mission-driven product/service expansion
- Purpose communication in growth narratives

**Resource Allocation for Impact** Dedicate growing resources to purpose:

- Percentage of profit for cause alignment
- Team time allocation for impact initiatives
- Capability application to social challenges
- Asset utilization for community benefit
- Platform leverage for awareness and education

**Stakeholder Benefit Expansion** Create value beyond shareholders:

- Team member thriving and development
- Customer transformation emphasis
- Community contribution integration
- Industry elevation focus
- Environmental responsibility consideration

This integration transforms scaling from merely more profit to greater purpose fulfillment, creating meaning and motivation beyond financial metrics.

# 2. The Foundation Development Framework

Create structured vehicles for expanded contribution:

**Foundation Structure Establishment** Develop formal impact organizations:

- Legal entity creation and compliance
- Governance and oversight systems
- Mission and focus articulation
- Operational model development
- Integration with business activities

**Program Design and Implementation** Create effective impact initiatives:

- Need assessment and opportunity identification
- Program design and resource allocation
- Impact measurement and evaluation
- Continuous improvement processes
- Scale and sustainability planning

**Partnership and Collaboration Development** Expand impact through relationships:

- Complementary organization identification
- Resource sharing and collaboration
- Collective impact initiatives
- Knowledge and learning exchange
- Amplification through combined efforts

This structured approach transforms generalized giving into systematic impact, creating sustainable change rather than just periodic contribution.

Through the Nehemiah Davis Foundation, we've implemented these approaches to create exponential impact alongside business growth. Our youth programs, community center, and educational initiatives have reached thousands because our business scaling created both the resources and systems to support expanded impact.

When developing your scaling strategy, consider:

- How might increased business capacity enable greater community contribution?
- What systems could create impact alongside profit?
- How could your team's capabilities serve beyond your customer base?
- What structures would create sustainable community benefit at scale?

These considerations transform business scaling from merely more profit to greater purpose fulfillment—creating the foundation for significance beyond success.

## Chapter Summary: Key Takeaways

- Scaling requires fundamental mindset shifts from doer to leader, income to asset building, and scarcity to abundance
- A scalable business model includes leverage optimization, recurring revenue, and systematized delivery

- Team development through strategic role design, talent acquisition, and leadership culture enables sustainable growth
- Growth acceleration through channel diversification, strategic partnerships, and market expansion creates momentum
- Systems and process optimization provides the operational backbone for consistent quality at scale
- Impact integration transforms scaling from merely more profit to greater purpose fulfillment
- Foundation development creates structured vehicles for expanded contribution and legacy

## Action Steps:

1. Assess your current mindset using the three scaling mindset dimensions
2. Identify your highest leverage activities and potential delegation opportunities
3. Evaluate your business model for recurring revenue potential
4. Design your next key team role using the strategic role identification framework
5. Map your current operational systems to identify standardization opportunities
6. Develop a technology needs assessment for your scaling requirements
7. Create an impact integration plan aligned with your growth objectives

If you're passionate about **impact, purpose, and real results,** we want to hear from you. **Partner with Neo**. Visit PartnerWithNeo.com/apply to explore how we can collaborate.

# CHAPTER 17

# FROM SUCCESS TO SIGNIFICANCE

Throughout this book, we've explored the strategies and systems that create business success—from digital product creation and marketing to challenges, presentations, and scaling. Now we arrive at what I consider the most important chapter: how to transform that success into true significance.

Business success alone—no matter how substantial—ultimately feels hollow without deeper meaning and impact. I've met too many entrepreneurs who achieved their financial goals only to ask, "Is this all there is?" They reached the summit only to discover it wasn't the mountain they truly wanted to climb.

In this chapter, I'll share the frameworks and approaches that have helped me transform business success into meaningful impact through the Nehemiah Davis Foundation. These principles can help you build your own bridge from success to significance—creating a legacy that extends far beyond your bank account.

# The Purpose Integration Framework

The journey to significance begins with integrating purpose into your existing business rather than treating impact as a separate activity:

## 1. The Purpose Discovery Process

Before effective integration, clarify your authentic impact mission:

**Personal Significance Exploration** Identify what truly matters to you:

- Causes that create genuine emotional connection
- Communities you feel called to serve
- Injustices that spark your passion
- Transformations you find most meaningful
- Legacies you wish to create

**Impact Vision Development** Create a clear picture of your desired contribution:

- Specific changes you hope to create
- Communities or populations you wish to serve
- Problems you feel called to address
- Transformations you want to facilitate
- Scale and scope of intended impact

**Alignment Assessment** Ensure authentic connection between business and purpose:

- Natural extensions of your expertise and capabilities
- Genuine connection to your personal story
- Resonance with your values and principles

- Sustainability alongside business objectives
- Authenticity that resonates with stakeholders

This discovery process prevents purpose initiatives that feel forced or disconnected, creating instead a natural expression of your deeper values through your business success.

## 2. The Integration Strategy Framework

With clear purpose established, implement these integration approaches:

**Business Model Integration** Weave purpose into your core operations:

- Giving components built into pricing structure
- One-for-one models where appropriate
- Percentage of revenue allocated to impact
- Employment opportunities for underserved populations
- Environmental responsibility in operations

**Product and Service Alignment** Connect offerings to purpose:

- Impact-oriented products or services
- Accessibility options for underserved markets
- Purpose elements in existing offerings
- Special initiatives for target communities
- Skills-based service opportunities

**Marketing and Messaging Integration** Communicate purpose authentically:

- Impact storytelling alongside business messaging
- Transformation documentation beyond financial results

- Community connection throughout communication
- Invitation to participation in purpose
- Transparent impact reporting

This integration transforms purpose from a separate "CSR initiative" to an authentic expression of your business identity, creating alignment that resonates with both customers and team members.

# 3. The Stakeholder Engagement Approach

Involve your entire business ecosystem in your purpose journey:

**Team Involvement Strategies** Engage your team in meaningful participation:

- Purpose discovery and definition inclusion
- Skills-based volunteering opportunities
- Paid community service time
- Team impact initiative development
- Recognition for purpose contributions

**Customer Participation Frameworks** Create ways for customers to join your impact:

- Transparent communication about purpose elements
- Optional contribution opportunities
- Community impact events and activities
- Success celebration connected to purpose
- Shared storytelling and impact documentation

**Community Collaboration Development** Build relationships within your impact focus:

- Listening and learning before action
- Community leadership engagement
- Collaborative program development
- Respectful partnership approaches
- Long-term commitment establishment

This engagement transforms purpose from founder-driven initiative to collective movement, creating significance that extends throughout your business ecosystem.

# The Foundation Development Framework

For many entrepreneurs, formal foundation creation represents a powerful vehicle for impact. Here's how to approach this journey effectively:

## 1. The Foundation Structure Options

Understand the various approaches to formalized impact:

**Private Foundation Model** Traditional dedicated charitable organization:

- Independent 501(c)(3) organization (in US)
- Founder/family governance control
- Endowment-based funding typical
- Formal grant-making processes
- Significant compliance requirements

**Donor-Advised Fund Approach** Simplified giving vehicle through existing foundation:

- Account within established foundation
- Immediate tax benefits with flexible distribution
- Reduced administrative requirements
- Limited control compared to private foundation
- Lower cost and complexity

**Fiscal Sponsorship Framework** Program operation under existing nonprofit:

- Initiative housed within established organization
- Shared administrative and compliance infrastructure
- Maintained program autonomy
- Potential pathway to independent status
- Reduced startup timeline and complexity

**Social Enterprise Integration** Direct impact through business structure:

- Benefit corporation or similar legal structure
- Impact woven into business operations
- Profit and purpose balanced in governance
- Potential certification (B-Corp, etc.)
- Integrated rather than separate approach

This options framework helps you select the approach most aligned with your resources, control preferences, and impact objectives rather than defaulting to the most commonly known structure.

# 2. The Foundation Launch Approach

Create a strong foundation for your formal impact vehicle:

**Purpose and Focus Definition** Establish clear direction and boundaries:

- Specific mission and vision articulation
- Target population or community identification
- Geographic scope determination
- Problem and solution framework
- Impact measurement approach

**Governance Structure Development** Create appropriate oversight and guidance:

- Board composition and recruitment strategy
- Advisory council establishment where appropriate
- Policy and procedure development
- Decision-making framework creation
- Founder role clarification

**Operational Framework Creation** Build the systems for effective functioning:

- Staffing plan and structure
- Volunteer engagement approach
- Program development processes
- Financial management systems
- Reporting and compliance procedures

This launch foundation prevents the common pitfalls of underfocused or operationally challenged impact organizations, creating sustainable structures for long-term contribution.

## 3. The Sustainable Funding Model

Ensure your impact initiatives receive consistent resources:

**Business Integration Funding** Connect business success to foundation support:

- Percentage of profit allocation
- Specific product/service revenue designation
- Team giving and matching programs
- Customer participation opportunities
- Asset and resource sharing

**Development Strategy Implementation** Create diverse funding beyond founder contribution:

- Individual donor cultivation
- Corporate partnership development
- Grant application processes
- Event-based fundraising
- Earned income opportunities where appropriate

**Resource Maximization Approach** Optimize impact per dollar invested:

- Administrative efficiency focus
- Volunteer leverage strategies
- In-kind donation utilization

- Partnership and collaboration for shared costs
- Technology leveraging for scale

This sustainability focus prevents the common pattern of founder-dependent impact organizations that fluctuate with business cycles, creating instead reliable resources for consistent community benefit.

# The Impact Initiative Design System

Beyond structure, the actual programs and initiatives you create determine your ultimate significance:

## 1. The Community Needs Assessment

Begin with understanding rather than assumption:

**Direct Engagement Approach** Learn from those you hope to serve:

- Listening sessions and forums
- Surveys and feedback mechanisms
- Community leadership conversations
- Direct observation and participation
- Existing research and data review

**Asset Mapping Process** Identify existing strengths to leverage:

- Community capabilities and resources
- Complementary organization inventory
- Infrastructure and system assessment
- Leadership and influence identification
- Successful model examination

**Gap Analysis Framework** Determine where impact is most needed:

- Unmet need identification
- Service overlap assessment
- Quality and accessibility evaluation
- Systemic barrier recognition
- Opportunity prioritization

This assessment prevents the common philanthropic mistake of addressing assumed rather than actual needs, creating instead initiatives genuinely valued by those served.

## 2. The Program Design Framework

Create initiatives with meaningful, sustainable impact:

**Theory of Change Development** Establish clear impact logic:

- Ultimate outcome definition
- Precondition and milestone identification
- Intervention strategy determination
- Implementation approach planning
- Assumption and risk acknowledgment

**Implementation Strategy Creation** Design effective delivery approaches:

- Program component development
- Staffing and volunteer requirements
- Timeline and milestone establishment
- Resource needs assessment
- Partnership and collaboration planning

**Participation Design Approach** Create engagement that empowers rather than diminishes:

- Dignity and agency prioritization
- Strength-based rather than deficit-focused methods
- Participant voice and leadership inclusion
- Relationship emphasis alongside service
- Long-term outcome rather than short-term relief focus

This intentional design creates programs that address root causes rather than symptoms, enabling transformation rather than temporary assistance.

## 3. The Impact Measurement System

Track and improve your contribution over time:

**Measurement Framework Development** Create clear evaluation approaches:

- Key outcome indicator identification
- Measurement methodology selection
- Data collection system development
- Analysis and reporting processes
- Learning integration mechanisms

**Continuous Improvement Implementation** Use measurement for enhancement:

- Regular review and reflection cycles
- Participant feedback integration

- Comparative analysis with similar programs
- Innovation and adaptation processes
- Enhanced impact goal setting

**Transparency and Storytelling Approach** Share impact effectively:

- Data visualization and communication
- Individual transformation storytelling
- Challenge and learning transparency
- Stakeholder reporting systems
- Public sharing approaches

This measurement focus prevents the impact ambiguity common in philanthropic efforts, creating instead clear understanding of what works and what needs improvement.

# The Nehemiah Davis Foundation Model

To illustrate these frameworks in action, I'd like to share how we've implemented them through the Nehemiah Davis Foundation:

## 1. Our Foundation Journey

The evolution of our impact approach:

**Foundation Genesis** How we began our formal impact work:

- Initial community events and activities
- Transition to structured programming
- 501(c)(3) establishment process

- Early funding approaches
- Team and leadership development

**Program Evolution** How our initiatives have developed:

- Youth development focus emergence
- Community center establishment
- Educational and mentorship programs
- Family support initiatives
- Entrepreneurship education development

**Integration with Business** How we connect business and foundation:

- Financial support structures
- Team involvement approaches
- Customer participation opportunities
- Marketing and storytelling integration
- Shared resource utilization

This journey illustrates the organic but intentional growth that creates sustainable impact aligned with both community needs and business capabilities.

## 2. Core Initiatives and Approaches

Our primary impact programs:

**Youth Development Programs** Initiatives focused on next generation:

- After-school programming
- Mentorship structures
- Leadership development

- Educational support systems
- Entrepreneurship exposure

**Community Support Initiatives** Programs addressing immediate needs:

- Food security programs
- Family resource provision
- Holiday-focused initiatives
- Emergency assistance approaches
- Health and wellness activities

**Economic Opportunity Creation** Efforts focused on long-term empowerment:

- Job skills development
- Entrepreneurship education
- Financial literacy programming
- Employment pathway creation
- Business incubation support

These initiatives represent our response to community-identified needs while leveraging our specific capabilities, creating authentic impact aligned with both our purpose and community priorities.

## 3. Lessons Learned and Insights

Key discoveries from our impact journey:

**Effective Approaches** What we've found most impactful:

- Long-term relationship emphasis over transactional giving

- Community leadership inclusion in all initiatives
- Consistent presence rather than sporadic engagement
- Strength-based rather than deficit-focused methods
- Integration of entrepreneurial principles in social impact

**Challenges Navigated** Difficulties we've addressed:

- Sustainable funding beyond founder contribution
- Impact measurement complexity
- Capacity constraints and growth management
- Partnership development and maintenance
- Boundary setting and focus maintenance

**Future Direction Development** Where we're heading next:

- Scale expansion while maintaining quality
- Replication and model sharing
- System-level change advocacy
- Enhanced measurement sophistication
- Deeper integration with business evolution

These insights represent our learning journey, offered not as definitive answers but as reflection points for your own impact exploration.

# The Personal Significance Journey

Beyond frameworks and structures, the journey from success to significance creates profound personal transformation:

## 1. The Identity Evolution

How impact work transforms the entrepreneur:

**Purpose Clarity Enhancement** Deepening understanding of personal mission:

- Values clarification and prioritization
- Legacy consideration and definition
- Meaning discovery beyond achievement
- Connection to larger purpose
- Life satisfaction enhancement

**Perspective Transformation** Shift in how success itself is defined:

- Expanded time horizon consideration
- Multi-generational impact awareness
- Balanced scorecard for life evaluation
- Redefined relationship with resources
- Enhanced appreciation and gratitude

**Leadership Expansion** Growth in influence and capability:

- Service-oriented leadership development
- Increased empathy and emotional intelligence
- Enhanced stakeholder engagement ability

- Broader relationship network cultivation
- Deeper community connection and understanding

This personal evolution often represents the most meaningful "return on investment" from the significance journey, transforming not just what the entrepreneur does but who they become.

## 2. The Integration of Success and Significance

Creating harmony rather than division between business and impact:

**Unified Purpose Approach** Connect rather than separate domains:

- Shared mission across endeavors
- Complementary objective setting
- Integrated rather than compartmentalized identity
- Consistent values application
- Aligned decision-making framework

**Resource Flow Optimization** Create positive cycles between success and significance:

- Business success funding impact capability
- Impact work enhancing business meaning
- Shared learning across domains
- Relationship development benefiting both
- Team engagement increasing in both areas

**Holistic Life Design** Build a life incorporating both dimensions:

- Time allocation reflecting priorities
- Energy management across domains

- Relationship cultivation in both worlds
- Skill development serving both purposes
- Legacy creation through integrated approach

This integration prevents the common bifurcation between "making money" and "doing good," creating instead a unified life of purpose-driven success and success-enabled purpose.

## 3. The Ongoing Evolution

Embracing significance as a journey rather than destination:

**Continuous Learning Orientation** Maintain growth mindset throughout:

- Regular reflection and reassessment
- Openness to evolved understanding
- Input seeking from diverse perspectives
- Experimentation and adaptation comfort
- Humility and curiosity cultivation

**Community Connection Deepening** Enhance relationships over time:

- Consistent presence and engagement
- Active listening and learning
- Leadership support and empowerment
- Trust building through reliability
- Mutual transformation acknowledgment

**Expanding Impact Vision** Allow your contribution to evolve:

- Scale consideration as capability grows

- Scope expansion with increased understanding
- System-level change engagement
- Collaborative impact development
- Innovation and adaptation over time

This evolutionary perspective prevents both rigid attachment to initial approaches and constant reinvention without depth, creating instead meaningful impact that grows organically through sustained commitment.

# From Your Success to Your Significance

As we conclude this chapter and this book, I encourage you to consider your own bridge from success to significance:

## Reflection Questions

Contemplate these questions as you begin your journey:

1. What impact would make your business success most meaningful to you personally?
2. Which communities or causes create genuine emotional connection for you?
3. How might your specific expertise and capabilities create unique value beyond your customers?
4. What small steps could you take in the next 30 days to begin your significance journey?
5. How might integrating purpose enhance rather than detract from your business success?
6. What would you want your legacy to be 50 years from now?

7. Who might join you as allies and partners in your impact journey?

## Starting Points

Consider these accessible entry approaches:

**Purpose Integration Initiation** Begin weaving purpose into existing business:

- Impact metric addition alongside business ones
- Team conversation about meaningful contribution
- Customer invitation to purpose participation
- Simple giving component implementation
- Story sharing about your "why" beyond profit

**Hands-On Engagement Commencement** Start with direct involvement before structures:

- Volunteer with aligned organizations
- Meet with community leaders in areas of interest
- Participate in existing impact initiatives
- Offer skills-based support where needed
- Learn directly from those already doing the work

**Resource Allocation Inception** Begin directing resources intentionally:

- Percentage of profit designation for impact
- Team time allocation for community service
- Customer purchase-based contribution program
- Pro bono service offering development

- Scholarship or accessibility program creation

These starting points prevent the common barrier of overwhelm that keeps many entrepreneurs from beginning their significance journey, creating instead momentum through manageable initial steps.

## The Invitation

I close this book with an invitation rather than just information:

Join me in the journey from success to significance. Not because it's expected or because it will benefit your business (though it likely will), but because it's the fulfillment of success itself.

I've experienced the deep satisfaction of seeing business success create community transformation through the Nehemiah Davis Foundation. The programs we've built, the youth we've mentored, the families we've supported—these represent the most meaningful outcomes of my entrepreneurial journey.

My hope is that this book has provided not just the strategies for business success, but the inspiration and framework for translating that success into lasting significance.

Your expertise, your influence, your resources—they aren't just tools for building wealth, but for creating change. The world needs your success to matter beyond the bottom line.

The journey from success to significance begins with a simple decision: that your business will serve a purpose greater than profit. Make that decision today, and let it guide everything that follows.

Your legacy awaits.

## Chapter Summary: Key Takeaways

- True fulfillment requires moving beyond success to significance
- Purpose integration weaves impact into your existing business
- Foundation development creates structured vehicles for contribution
- Impact initiative design determines the effectiveness of your efforts
- The Nehemiah Davis Foundation illustrates these principles in action
- The significance journey transforms not just communities but the entrepreneur
- Integration of success and significance creates harmony rather than division
- Starting points for your journey include purpose integration, hands-on engagement, and resource allocation

## Action Steps:

1. Complete the purpose discovery process to clarify your authentic impact mission
2. Identify one way to integrate purpose into your business model
3. Conduct an informal community needs assessment in an area you care about
4. Allocate a specific percentage of profit for impact initiatives
5. Engage your team in conversation about meaningful contribution

6. Research one foundation structure option that might align with your goals
7. Implement a simple measurement approach for your initial impact efforts
8. Begin building relationships with those already serving your area of interest

If you're passionate about **impact, purpose, and real results,** we want to hear from you. **Partner with Neo**. Visit PartnerWithNeo.com/apply to explore how we can collaborate.

# CHAPTER 18

# YOUR PATH FORWARD

We've come to the end of our journey through this book, but you stand at the beginning of something extraordinary. Throughout these pages, we've explored the strategies, systems, and mindsets that create both business success and meaningful impact. Now it's time to transform this knowledge into your unique path forward.

As I reflect on my own journey from struggling entrepreneur to building multiple seven-figure businesses and the Nehemiah Davis Foundation, I'm reminded that transformation doesn't happen through information alone—it happens through implementation and commitment to a greater purpose.

In this final chapter, I want to help you create your personalized roadmap for applying everything you've learned, while addressing the challenges that may arise and connecting you to the broader community of purpose-driven entrepreneurs.

# Creating Your Personalized Implementation Plan

The difference between knowledge and transformation is implementation. Let's create a structured approach to applying what you've learned:

## 1. The 90-Day Success Sprint

Rather than trying to implement everything at once, focus on a concentrated period of execution:

**Priority Identification** Select your highest-leverage focus areas:

- Review the action steps from each chapter
- Identify the 3-5 most immediately valuable strategies for your situation
- Consider both immediate revenue potential and long-term foundation building
- Focus on implementation rather than additional learning
- Choose areas where you have the most energy and excitement

**Milestone Creation** Establish clear targets and checkpoints:

- 30-day initial implementation milestone
- 60-day momentum checkpoint
- 90-day results measurement
- Weekly progress tracking points
- Daily action commitments

**Resource Allocation** Dedicate specific assets to your implementation:

- Time blocks protected for implementation work
- Financial investment where needed for tools or support
- Team resources aligned with priorities
- Learning resources specific to implementation areas
- Accountability and feedback mechanisms

This focused approach prevents the common pattern of scattered attention across too many strategies, creating instead meaningful momentum in your highest-priority areas.

## 2. The Implementation Environment Design

Create surroundings that support consistent execution:

**Physical Environment Optimization** Design spaces that enhance implementation:

- Dedicated workspace for focused action
- Visual reminders of goals and commitments
- Distraction minimization systems
- Energy management considerations
- Resource accessibility for efficiency

**Digital Environment Structuring** Organize your technology for implementation support:

- Notification management and focus tools
- Project and task tracking systems
- Progress measurement dashboards

- Resource organization for quick access
- Distraction elimination protocols

**Social Environment Creation** Surround yourself with implementation support:

- Accountability partnerships or groups
- Mentorship for implementation guidance
- Peer community for shared learning
- Support system for encouragement
- Celebration relationships for milestones

This environmental design creates external structures that support your internal commitment, reducing the willpower required for consistent implementation.

## 3. The Implementation Rhythm Establishment

Create sustainable patterns for ongoing execution:

**Daily Implementation Practice** Establish consistent daily actions:

- Morning planning and prioritization
- Protected implementation blocks
- Progress tracking and documentation
- Learning integration from the day's work
- Preparation for next day's implementation

**Weekly Review and Adjustment** Create regular reflection and optimization:

- Weekly progress measurement

- Strategy refinement based on results
- Obstacle identification and addressing
- Celebration of wins and milestones
- Following week preparation and planning

**Monthly Expansion Approach** Systematically broaden your implementation:

- Review of 30-day results and learning
- Additional strategy incorporation
- System refinement and optimization
- New goal setting and milestone creation
- Resource reallocation based on results

This rhythm creates the consistency that transforms individual actions into significant results, preventing the start-stop pattern that undermines many implementation efforts.

# Navigating Common Implementation Challenges

As you move forward, anticipate and prepare for the obstacles that typically arise:

## 1. The Consistency Challenge

Address the difficulties of sustained implementation:

**Motivation Fluctuation Management** Prepare for natural energy variations:

- Intrinsic motivation foundations beyond temporary excitement
- Purpose connection for sustained engagement
- Progress tracking for motivation reinforcement
- Environment design for reduced willpower requirements
- Community support for challenging periods

**Distraction Management Systems** Create focus despite competing demands:

- Priority clarity and boundary setting
- Distraction identification and elimination
- Focus time protection strategies
- Energy management for sustained attention
- Recovery protocols for inevitable disruptions

**Overwhelm Prevention Approach** Maintain momentum without burnout:

- Appropriate scope limitation
- Sequential rather than simultaneous implementation
- Progress celebration rather than just gap focus
- Rest and renewal integration
- Sustainable pace establishment

This proactive approach to consistency challenges prevents the discouragement that often accompanies implementation difficulties, creating instead resilience through prepared responses.

## 2. The Results Variation Challenge

Prepare for the reality that results rarely follow a linear path:

**Expectation Management** Create realistic perspectives on results:

- Normal variation understanding
- Timeframe appropriateness for different strategies
- Leading vs. lagging indicator awareness
- Industry and context-specific benchmarking
- Personal circumstances consideration

**Testing and Iteration Framework** Implement structured improvement approaches:

- Rapid testing cycles for new strategies
- Data-based evaluation processes
- Refinement protocols based on results

- Expansion of what works, elimination of what doesn't
- Continuous improvement rather than perfection seeking

**Perseverance Development** Build capacity for continued implementation:

- Temporary setback vs. failure distinction
- Long-term perspective maintenance
- Success evidence collection and review
- Purpose reconnection during challenging periods
- Community support for perspective

This prepared approach to results variation prevents the discouragement that often leads to premature strategy abandonment, creating instead the persistence that ultimately produces breakthrough.

## 3. The Evolution Challenge

Manage the natural progression of your implementation journey:

**Skill Development Integration** Address capability gaps proactively:

- Implementation-specific skill identification
- Focused learning for immediate application
- Practice-based development rather than passive consumption
- Feedback integration for improvement
- Expert modeling and mentorship where available

**Strategy Evolution Management** Adapt your approach based on results and learning:

- Regular strategy review and assessment

- Refinement based on actual results
- New information integration
- Competitive landscape adaptation
- Customer feedback incorporation

**Scale and Complexity Navigation** Manage the progression from simple to sophisticated:

- Foundational system establishment before expansion
- Appropriate complexity introduction timing
- Team development alongside strategy evolution
- Resource scaling aligned with growth
- Simplicity maintenance despite sophistication

This evolutionary approach prevents stagnation through rigid adherence to initial strategies, creating instead ongoing development that matches your growing capabilities and results.

# Building Your Success and Significance Community

Implementation thrives with support from others on similar journeys:

## 1. The Peer Community Development

Create connections with fellow implementation-focused entrepreneurs:

**Aligned Community Identification** Find groups that share your values and focus:

- Implementation-oriented rather than just information-sharing
- Shared commitment to both success and significance
- Appropriate stage and experience alignment
- Value and philosophy resonance
- Positive and supportive rather than cynical or negative

**Meaningful Participation Approach** Engage in ways that create mutual value:

- Consistent and reliable presence
- Value contribution alongside receiving
- Authentic sharing of both victories and challenges
- Support offering to fellow members
- Appropriate vulnerability balanced with confidence

**Relationship Deepening Strategy** Move beyond surface connections:

- One-on-one relationship cultivation
- Specific accountability partnerships

- Collaboration and joint venture exploration
- In-person connection where possible
- Long-term relationship investment

This community foundation provides both practical support for implementation and the emotional encouragement that sustains motivation through challenges.

## 2. The Mentorship and Guidance Connection

Seek wisdom from those further along the journey:

**Mentor Identification Approach** Find guides aligned with your path:

- Demonstrated results in relevant areas
- Values and philosophy alignment
- Teaching and communication capability
- Appropriate accessibility for your needs
- Personal connection and chemistry

**Effective Mentee Practices** Create valuable mentorship relationships:

- Clear goals and expectations
- Prepared and focused interactions
- Implementation of guidance received
- Appropriate respect for mentor's time
- Gratitude and appreciation expression

**Multiple Guidance Integration** Create a comprehensive support network:

- Different mentors for various aspects of development
- Peer mentorship alongside more experienced guidance
- Content and course creator relationships
- Community leadership connections
- Industry-specific and general business mentorship

This guidance network provides the wisdom that prevents common mistakes, creating instead accelerated progress through leveraged experience.

## 3. The Contribution Community Engagement

Connect with those focused on similar impact areas:

**Impact Community Identification** Find groups aligned with your significance goals:

- Shared cause or population focus
- Complementary rather than competitive approaches
- Collaborative orientation toward change
- Evidence-based methodology appreciation
- Long-term commitment to transformation

**Strategic Contribution Development** Create value based on your unique capabilities:

- Specific expertise or skill offering
- Resource sharing where appropriate
- Connection and relationship contribution

- Visibility and voice leveraging
- Learning and humility orientation

**Collaborative Impact Exploration** Develop partnerships for enhanced significance:

- Joint initiative possibilities
- Resource sharing opportunities
- Complementary capability leveraging
- Shared learning and development
- Collective impact approaches

This contribution connection creates both enhanced impact and deeper purpose fulfillment, transforming isolated efforts into collective movement.

# The Nehemiah Davis Community

As you implement what you've learned and build your path forward, I want to invite you to connect with our broader community of purpose-driven entrepreneurs:

## 1. Ongoing Learning and Support

Continue your growth journey through our resources:

**Digital Business Accelerator** Our comprehensive implementation program:

- Structured implementation support for digital business building
- Expert coaching and feedback on your specific situation
- Community of fellow implementation-focused entrepreneurs
- Regular live training and Q&A opportunities
- Resource library for specific strategy execution

**Inner Circle Mastermind** Our high-level entrepreneur community:

- Peer connection with successful purpose-driven entrepreneurs
- Advanced strategy development and refinement
- Accountability and support for ambitious growth
- In-person events and deep relationship building
- Direct access to our team and network

**Foundation Focus Program** Our impact-specific initiative:

- Guidance for creating your significance vehicles

- Connection with fellow impact-focused entrepreneurs
- Resources for effective foundation development
- Implementation support for impact integration
- Networking with potential impact partners

These ongoing resources provide the support that transforms one-time learning into continuous growth and implementation.

## 2. Implementation Events and Experiences

Accelerate your progress through intensive growth opportunities:

**Digital Business Summit** Our annual implementation-focused event:

- Hands-on strategy implementation workshops
- Connection with fellow entrepreneurs
- Expert guidance across business components
- Latest developments in digital business approaches
- Renewed energy and focus for execution

**Impact Acceleration Retreat** Our significance-focused intensive:

- Structured impact strategy development
- Foundation and initiative design workshops
- Connection with purpose-driven entrepreneurs
- Expert guidance from established impact leaders
- Implementation planning for meaningful contribution

**VIP Implementation Days** Our personalized strategy sessions:

- One-on-one guidance for your specific situation
- Custom strategy development and refinement

- Direct feedback on your current approaches
- Personalized implementation planning
- Accelerated progress through focused attention

These experiences provide both the immersive learning and the relationship development that accelerate implementation beyond what's possible through individual effort alone.

## 3. Contribution and Philanthropy Opportunities

Join our impact initiatives directly:

**Nehemiah Davis Foundation Volunteer Program** Contribute your time and expertise:

- Event support opportunities
- Skill-based volunteering aligned with your capabilities
- Mentorship for youth program participants
- Community initiative participation
- Advisory and guidance roles where appropriate

**Sponsorship and Partnership Programs** Support specific initiatives financially:

- Program sponsorship opportunities
- Scholarship funding participation
- Event underwriting options
- In-kind contribution possibilities
- Strategic partnership development

**Joint Impact Initiatives** Create collaborative contribution approaches:

- Aligned program development
- Resource sharing for enhanced impact
- Joint event and activity creation
- Cross-promotion and visibility opportunities
- Collective measurement and reporting

These direct participation opportunities create immediate impact while building your capacity for more significant long-term contribution.

## Your Legacy Begins Now

As we conclude this book, I want to share a perspective that has transformed how I view both success and significance:

Your legacy isn't something you create at the end of your journey—it's something you build with every decision, every day.

Each customer you serve with excellence, each team member you develop with care, each dollar you invest with purpose, each community member you impact with intention—these aren't separate from your legacy, they are your legacy in real-time.

The strategies and systems we've explored throughout this book aren't just about building a successful business or even creating impact initiatives. They're about living a life of purpose and meaning where success and significance aren't sequential but simultaneous.

My hope is that you'll close this book not just with knowledge but with commitment—commitment to building a business that creates both prosperity and purpose, commitment to using your unique gifts to serve others, commitment to leaving every person and community you touch better than you found them.

This isn't about perfection or grandeur. It's about consistent intention and action aligned with a purpose greater than yourself. It's about recognizing that the most successful business is one that creates positive change beyond its balance sheet.

The journey from success to significance isn't a destination—it's a daily choice to let your work matter more than money, to let your impact outlast your income, to let your legacy live beyond your life.

That journey begins now, with your next action after closing this book.

What will you build? Who will you serve? How will you be remembered? What difference will you make?

Your answers to these questions—demonstrated through action rather than intention—will create your unique bridge from success to significance.

I can't wait to see what you build.

Onward with purpose,

*Nehemiah "Neo" Davis*

# Chapter Summary: Key Takeaways

- Transformation requires implementation, not just information

- The 90-Day Success Sprint creates focused momentum in priority areas
- Implementation environment design supports consistent execution
- Common challenges can be navigated with preparation and perspective
- Community support accelerates progress and sustains motivation
- The Nehemiah Davis community offers ongoing resources and opportunities
- Your legacy is built daily through aligned action, not at the end of your journey
- Success and significance are simultaneous rather than sequential
- Purpose-driven business creates both prosperity and positive change

## Action Steps:

1. Select your 3-5 priority strategies for your 90-Day Success Sprint
2. Design your implementation environment for focused execution
3. Establish your daily and weekly implementation rhythm
4. Identify potential challenges and prepare proactive responses
5. Connect with at least one accountability partner for your journey
6. Explore one additional resource or community for ongoing support
7. Schedule your first 30-day review to assess progress and adjust

8. Write your personal purpose statement connecting success and significance

If you're passionate about **impact, purpose, and real results,** we want to hear from you. **Partner with Neo.** Visit PartnerWithNeo.com/apply to explore how we can collaborate.

## A PERSONAL NOTE FROM NEHEMIAH

When I began my entrepreneurial journey in the streets of West Philadelphia, I never imagined where it would lead. The moving company that started with a rented truck, the digital businesses that grew from late nights of learning, the foundation that began with a simple community event—all of these were beyond my vision at the start.

What I did have was a simple but powerful commitment: "It has to work, or it has to work." There was no Plan B, no fallback option. Just determination that whatever obstacles arose, I would find a way forward.

That same commitment is what I hope you'll take from this book. Not just strategies and systems, but the unshakable conviction that your success matters—not just for you, but for all those your life and work can impact.

I've seen firsthand how business success can transform communities. The basketball courts we've built, the food programs we've established, the youth we've mentored, the families we've supported—none of this would have been possible without building successful businesses first.

Your journey may look different than mine. Your businesses may serve different customers, your impact may focus on different communities or causes. But the fundamental truth remains: when purpose drives profit, both expand beyond what either could achieve alone.

I believe you're reading this book for a reason. Something in you resonates with this integration of success and significance. Something in you knows that you're meant for more than just making money—you're meant to make a difference.

Trust that instinct. Follow that calling. Build with that purpose.

The world needs your success to matter.

With gratitude and belief in your journey,

*Nehemiah*